Unless Recalled Earlier

DATE DUE

DEMCO, INC. 38-2931

American Sports History Series
edited by
David B. Biesel

A related title by the series editor:

Can You Name That Team? A Guide to Professional Baseball, Football, Soccer, Hockey, and Basketball Teams and Leagues by David B. Biesel, 1991.

For Pride, Profit, and Patriarchy

Football and the Incorporation of American Cultural Values

Gerald R. Gems

American Sports History Series, No. 16

The Scarecrow Press, Inc.
Lanham, Maryland, and London
2000

SCARECROW PRESS, INC.

Published in the United States of America
by Scarecrow Press, Inc.
4720 Boston Way, Lanham, Maryland 20706
http://www.scarecrowpress.com

4 Pleydell Gardens, Folkestone
Kent CT20 2DN, England

British Library Cataloguing in Publication Information Available

Library of Congress Cataloging-in-Publication Data
Gems, Gerald R.
    For pride, profit, and patriarchy : football and the incorporation of
American cultural values / Gerald R. Gems.
        p. cm. — (American sports history series ; no. 16)
    Includes bibliographical references and index.
    ISBN 0-8108-3685-8 (alk. paper)
        1. Football—Social aspects—United States—History. I. Title: Football
and the incorporation of American cultural values. II. Title. III. Series.
GV950 .G46 2000
    796.332'0973—dc21   00-023773

⊖™ The paper used in this publication meets the minimum requirements of
American National Standard for Information Sciences—Permanence of
Paper for Printed Library Materials, ANSI/NISO Z39.48-1992.
Manufactured in the United States of America.

To the guys: my father, who coached me; my brother, who served as my teammate; and my son, who still plays the game, but for the right reason—fun.

Contents

Acknowledgments

In the course of research and writing one inevitably incurs many debts to collaborators, who, in varying degrees, help to bring the concept to fruition. The following have been particularly helpful: the university librarians and archivists of Harvard, Yale, Chicago, Notre Dame, Illinois, Michigan, and Martin Hackett at Penn, Elizabeth Nielsen at Oregon State, William E. King at Duke, David J. Rosenblatt at Auburn, Ellen Kuniyuki Brown at Baylor, William H. Richter and others at Texas, Michael G. Martin at North Carolina, Lori Olson at Wyoming, Kent Stephens at the College Football Hall of Fame in South Bend, Indiana, the archivists at the Woman's Christian Temperance Union in Evanston, Illinois, and at the Butte-Silver Bow Archives in Butte, Montana.

North Central College generously provided grant money and a sabbatical in which to conduct the research. Becky Botos, Sandy Kulawiak, Yolanda Jamnik, and Sean Gems contributed their word processing skills, while Steve Riess and Ray Schmidt gave valuable input as reviewers, and Dave Biesel, as editor, brought the project to culmination.

The American Dilemma

Sport history, cultural studies, and social history have emerged as important subdisciplines over the past quarter century, and scholars in these areas have provided a wealth of information and analysis relative to popular culture. Sport studies, however, have focused largely on baseball and its role in American culture; thus neglecting the importance of football and its links with cultural values. The relative dearth of research on football leaves many questions unanswered. A number of narratives have traced the evolution of both collegiate and professional football; but without assessing its rise as a commercial spectacle within the larger capitalist economic system, nor its cultural meanings.[1]

Sport sociologists have begun to examine the relationship of football to masculinity; but we still know too little of its correlation with feminism or militarism.[2] Did the game serve or even promote imperial ambitions or a martial character in the United States, or foster particular group interests? Did it contribute to or retard the inclusion of disparate ethnic, racial, and social groups in the assimilation process? How and why did the various regions of the country adopt an eastern game and become incorporated in a national sporting culture that surpassed the "national game" of baseball? What role did it play in the formation of national character?

A few recent books have begun to address some of these questions as case studies of particular institutions. Murray Sperber's *Shake Down the Thunder: The Creation of Notre Dame Football*; Ron Smith's *Big Time Football at Harvard, 1905*; Robin Lester's *Stagg's University: The Rise, Decline, and Fall of Big-Time Football at Chicago*; and H. G. Bissinger's *Friday Night Lights* are important beginnings. Wiley Lee

Umphlett's, *Creating the Big Game: John W. Heisman and the Invention of American Football*, provides insight into the role of coaches in the evolution of the game; while Michael Oriard, in *Reading Football: How the Popular Press Created an American Spectacle*, examines the function of the eastern media in the popularization of the sport. John Carroll's *Fritz Pollard: Pioneer in Racial Advancement* and Jack Newcombe's *The Best of the Athletic Boys: The White Man's Impact on Jim Thorpe* remain the lone scholarly biographies to treat football and race in a comprehensive fashion.[3]

This study assumes a broad scope in trying to analyze the ways in which football addressed a number of cultural and ideological tensions within American society during its period of development and consolidation after the Civil War. The rise of the United States as a world power and football as a national spectacle with rituals, symbols, and meanings occurred simultaneously. Such evolution seems more than coincidental. Before the United States could gain ascendancy on the world stage it had to define itself as a nation. In doing so it wrestled with cultural dilemmas and apparent ideological conflicts in the various class, race, gender, religious, and regional factions that hampered unity.

The transition from a rural, agrarian society to an urban, industrial one reached a denouement in the twentieth century. Debates over elitism versus egalitarianism, nativism versus pluralism, labor versus capital, minorities' status in the society, and women's rights challenged the extent of democracy. During the nineteenth century the United States still served as an experiment in a world of monarchies. After a century of independence the United States sought recognition of its differences, a departure from its British influences, the definition of its national character, and the introduction of its perceived virtues to a wider audience, both at home and abroad. To do so required an amalgamation of sectional, exuberant, antimodern, communal impulses with the rational, corporate, disciplined, aggressive values favored by the commercial leadership. Football helped to bridge the gap between such conflicting perspectives as it assumed national proportions. Sporting enterprises during the Progressive Era (1880–1920) aligned with urban, commercial, and patriotic impulses to forge the American national character; but the homogenization process proved long and unstable as exemplified by continuing debates about the exploitation of athletes, the commodification of sport, and its role in higher education.

The period between the Civil War and World War I presented particularly troublesome dilemmas for the United States as it wrestled with its national identity. The culmination of the Civil War had answered the most fundamental questions regarding slavery and the powers of a more urban, industrial society; but the succeeding years raised other questions that provoked cultural tensions.

An immediate concern revolved around reunification of the South and the status of its freed slaves in the society. Emancipation unleashed millions, whose economic, political and civil rights posed a challenge for the government and their former masters. Their plight remained largely a regional issue, until blacks began migrating northward in large numbers during World War I.[4]

Before that exodus even commenced floods of foreign immigrants, mostly southern and eastern Europeans, reached American shores. The Irish potato famine and German revolution brought many to the United States as early as the 1840s. Those that arrived after 1880, however, were largely peasants lacking technical skills or a fluency in English. The Catholics and Jews among them held different customs, priorities and beliefs, causing nativists to fear the loss of their culture and power. Assimilation would prove more difficult for the latecomers, of whom there were more than 20 million by 1914.[5]

Some European workers, already familiar with wage labor and the industrialization process, brought a socialist philosophy that confronted the capitalist state. A series of conflicts between capital and labor questioned the extent of American democracy, liberty, and opportunity. When a national strike and rioting followed wage reductions on eastern rail lines in July 1877, it signaled decades of future discontent and militant upheaval. Chicago became the center of an anarchist movement, which reached its zenith in the so-called Haymarket Massacre on May 4, 1886. Another 528 strikes at a cost of almost $9 million ensued in Chicago alone over the next eight years.[6]

In 1892 the Homestead strike against the Carnegie steel plant in that Pennsylvania town resulted in several deaths and numerous injuries, and required 8,000 militiamen to curtail. Two years later Coxey's Army of unemployed workers marched on Washington. That same year Chicago erupted once again in the Pullman strike that brought federal intervention. Similar occurrences rocked other municipalities and the Industrial Workers of the World posed a radical threat thereafter.[7]

Not only urbanites but agrarians as well questioned the cultural transition of the period. Between the 1870s and 1890s the price of cotton, wheat, and corn fell by about half and revenues often failed to meet production costs. Farmers lost their lands to banks or labored for landlords and blamed the railroads, bankers, and economic cartels that controlled the markets. Throughout the 1890s populist movements in the Midwest, South, and West mounted a third political party in an attempt to reform the monetary system and counteract corporate interests. The vindictive debate over the coinage of silver versus adherence to the gold standard characterized an ongoing rural-urban conflict. Mary E. Lease, a populist activist from Kansas, urged farmers "to raise less corn and more hell."[8] The economic depression of 1893 only worsened conditions, forcing bankruptcies, unemployment, and lack of faith in the system.

Yet another group desirous of change, the feminists, also began to challenge the power structure of entrenched male dominance. A nascent move toward women's rights had begun after the American Revolution and by the 1830s some women took a more active role in public life. Emma Willard, Mary Lyon, and Catherine Beecher founded educational institutions for females; while other participants in the abolitionist movement questioned their own servitude, leading to a Women's Convention at Seneca Falls, New York, in 1848. In the post-Civil War years women agitated for suffrage, with seventeen referenda to deliver the vote between 1870 and 1910. By 1917 the National American Woman Suffrage Association counted 2 million members.[9]

Women's rights included more than the vote. Even as the industrial process displaced men from the workplace, women wanted jobs. Before 1860, 90 percent of men enjoyed self-employment. That number dwindled to less than 33 percent by 1910. Each year brought more women into the workforce, thus questioning the traditional gender and power relations. Men who could no longer sustain themselves or needed a woman's support lost a good measure of their freedom and their masculinity.[10]

Both working and nonworking women sought greater freedom in their leisure lives as well. Sport proved a very visible symbol of change in that process, as women moved from passive to more active roles. Women engaged in more sedate activities such as croquet or archery in the postwar years. In the 1880s tennis required greater mobility; succeeded by the cycling craze of the 1890s. Power sports, like cycling, necessitated dress reform, including pants or bloomers, attire previously reserved for men. Such "new women" represented an independence and physical vitality previously shunned in Victorian culture. In the twentieth century women moved rapidly into the mass, popular leisure culture that included amusement parks, vaudeville, dance halls, movies, and nightclubs.[11]

Such cultural displays, as well as American language, literature, and art had long been influenced by Great Britain. By the mid-nineteenth century writers such as James Fenimore Cooper, Edgar Allan Poe, Nathaniel Hawthorne, Herman Melville, and Harriet Beecher Stowe had published works that emphasized American themes, and in the latter half of the century Mark Twain (Samuel Clemens) gained international stature with his frontier prose. Artists, too, gradually broke away from their European influences to paint American landscapes, pastorals, and urban blight. Americans took notice of and reveled in their differences. The founding of the American Historical Association in 1884, however, indicated that, after a century of independence, Americans perceived themselves to be a new and separate culture, no longer needful of Anglo guidance. The United States was beginning to emerge as a world power, one desirous of spreading the perceived benefits of a democracy to less enlightened regions of the world. That mission began in earnest with the Spanish-American War, and despite brief periods of isolationism, continued throughout the twentieth century.[12]

Such proselytism required a clear definition of American values, but in the wake of the Civil War, the United States had yet to establish its own cohesive identity. At that time it consisted of several distinct regional cultures often at odds with one another. Easterners assumed cultural, commercial, and religious leadership as an historical given, while others resented such presumptions as elitist. The South disdained political mandates from the North, which appeared as a colonizer during the postwar Reconstruction. The isolated, regional markets of the South provided its inhabitants with only half the per capita income of the more affluent North and Midwest, thereby reinforcing a sense of economic inferiority.[13]

In the Midwest, rapidly growing commercial centers, such as Chicago, St. Louis, Cincinnati, and Milwaukee vied with each other and New York for western markets, as national production surpassed that of Great Britain, Germany, and France. The northern supremacy attained in the Civil War and eastern commercial domination faced continued competition in succeeding years. Chicago, fully expecting to surpass New York in population and influence, showcased its own version of American society at the 1893 World's Fair, and its Chicago School of Architecture soon extended a more radical vision with its skyscrapers and urban planning.[14] The West, too, professed a frontier egalitarianism at odds with the urban East. Frederick Jackson Turner had defined American democracy and individualism as a product of westward expansion, a process that no longer included the presumably elitist and effete Easterners.

Such internecine quarrels between regional residents, coupled with the perceived threats of immigrants, labor, and feminism produced a crisis for bourgeois males, whose status, leadership, and future seemed imperiled. One way in which young men sought to regain distinction and honor while restoring a sense of order and hierarchy was through their sporting pastimes. The "American" games of baseball, football, and basketball exemplified clear differences with the Anglo interests of the past. In the colleges football had superseded other forms of sport by 1880. Football, in particular, addressed masculinity issues directly and in a most primitive fashion in accordance with the "survival of the fittest" principles of Social Darwinists. More symbolically, the game also helped to settle cultural tensions that revolved around regionalism, honor, and issues of gender, ethnicity, race, and social class. More than mere athletic competitions, such cultural contests took place on and off the playing fields. In the century after the Civil War the process of struggle and negotiation contributed to a fusion of pluralistic differences in a national sporting culture that merged the Victorian values of discipline, order, control, and self-reliance with modern American society. The symbols, rituals, and meanings inherent in the game resulted in a clear definition of the United States as an aggressive, commercial, patriarchal culture ready to promote its ideals on the world stage.[15]

Notes

1. John Nauright, "Writing and Reading American Football: Culture, Identities and Sport Studies," *Sporting Traditions*, 13:1 (Nov. 1996), 109–127, laments the limited research on football, citing only a handful of sources. Popular narratives include: Parke H. Davis, *Football: The American Intercollegiate Game* (New York: Scribner's, 1911); Alexander M. Weyand, *The Saga of American Football* (New York: Macmillan, 1955); and Allison Danzig, *The History of American Football* (Englewood Cliffs, NJ: Prentice-Hall, 1956). A more analytical study is offered by Guy M. Lewis, "The American Intercollegiate Football Spectacle, 1869–1917," Ph.D. diss., University of Maryland, 1965.

A recent, but flawed history of professional football is Robert W. Peterson, *Pigskin: The Early Years of Pro Football* (New York: Oxford University Press, 1997). Ronald A. Smith, *Sports and Freedom: The Rise of Big-Time College Athletics* (New York: Oxford University Press, 1988) provides an excellent account of the development of several intercollegiate sports, including football, in eastern schools.

2. Donald J. Mrozek, *Sport and American Mentality, 1880–1910* (Knoxville: University of Tennessee Press, 1983), 28–66, offers an important exposition of sport and military values. Sociological studies include David Riesmen and Reuel Denney, "Football in America: A Study in Cultural Diffusion," *American Quarterly*, 3 (1951), 309–325; Allen Guttmann, *From Ritual to Record: The Nature of Modern*

Sports (New York: Columbia University Press, 1978), 117–136; Lois Bryson, "Sport and the Maintenance of Masculine Hegemony," *Women's Studies International Forum*, 10:4 (1987), 349–360; and Michael A. Messner, "When Bodies Are Weapons: Masculinity and Violence in Sport," *International Review of the Sociology of Sport*, 25:3 (1990), 203–218. Steven A. Riess, "Sport and the Redefinition of American Middle-Class Masculinity," *International Journal of the History of Sport*, 8:1 (1991), 5–27, provides an historical analysis; as does Kim Townsend, *Manhood at Harvard: William James and Others* (New York: W. W. Norton, 1996).

3. Murray Sperber, *Shake Down the Thunder: The Creation of Notre Dame Football* (New York: Henry Holt, 1993); Ronald A. Smith, ed., *Big-Time Football at Harvard, 1905: The Diary of Coach Bill Reid* (Urbana: University of Illinois Press, 1994); Robin Lester, *Stagg's University: The Rise, Decline, and Fall of Big-Time Football at Chicago* (Urbana: University of Illinois Press, 1995); H. G. Bissinger, *Friday Night Lights: A Town, A Team, and a Dream* (New York: HarperCollins, 1991); Wiley Lee Umphlett, *Creating the Big Game: John W. Heisman and the Invention of American Football* (Westport, CT: Greenwood Press, 1992); Michael Oriard, *Reading Football: How the Popular Press Created an American Spectacle* (Chapel Hill: University of North Carolina Press, 1993); John M. Carroll, *Fritz Pollard: Pioneer in Racial Advancement* (Urbana: University of Illinois Press, 1992); Jack Newcombe, *The Best of the Athletic Boys: The White Man's Impact on Jim Thorpe* (Garden City, NY: Doubleday, 1975).

4. Gaines M. Foster, *Ghosts of the Confederacy: Defeat, The Lost Cause, and The Emergence of the New South* (New York: Oxford University Press, 1987); Eric Foner, *Nothing But Freedom: Emancipation and Its Legacy* (Baton Rouge: Louisiana State University Press, 1983); Dewey W. Grantham, *The South in Modern America: A Region at Odds* (New York: Harper Collins, 1994), 1–22; Thomas C. Cox, *Blacks in Topeka Kansas, 1865–1915* (Baton Rouge: Louisiana State University Press, 1982); James R. Grossman, *Land of Hope: Chicago, Black Southerners, and the Great Migration* (Chicago: University of Chicago Press, 1989).

5. Stephen Steinberg, *The Ethnic Myth: Race, Ethnicity, and Class in America* (Boston: Beacon Press, 1989), 174, estimates 24 million immigrants between 1865–1914. Oscar Handlin, *The Uprooted* (New York: Grosset & Dunlop, 1951), 36, places the total number at 35 million.

6. Hartmut Keil and John B. Jentz, eds., *German Workers in Industrial Chicago, 1850–1910: A Comparative Perspective* (DeKalb, IL: Northern Illinois University Press, 1983); Bruce Nelson, *Beyond the Martyrs: A Social History of Chicago's Anarchists, 1870–1900* (New Brunswick, NJ: Rutgers University Press, 1988); Bessie Louise Pierce, *A History of Chicago* (New York: Alfred A. Knopf, 1957), 3:275–281, 289–292, 298.

7. Franklin Folsom, *Impatient Armies of the Poor: The Story of Collective Action of the Unemployed, 1808–1942* (Niwot, CO: University Press of Colorado, 1991), 180–186; Stanley Buder, *Pullman: An Experiment in Industrial Order and Community Planning, 1880–1930* (New York: Oxford University Press, 1968); Nick Salvatore, *Eugene V. Debs* (Urbana: University of Illinois Press, 1982).

8. Norman Pollack, *The Populist Response in Industrial America: Midwestern Populist Thought* (Cambridge, MA: Harvard University Press, 1962); Lawrence Goodwyn, *Democratic Promise: The Populist Movement in America* (New York: Oxford University Press, 1976); John M. Blum, et al., *The National Experience: A History of the United States* (New York: Harcourt, Brace, Jovanovich, 1981), 509–520 (quote, 512).

9. Eric Foner and John A. Garraty, eds., *The Reader's Companion to American History* (Boston: Houghton Mifflin, 1991), 391–393; Stanley Coben, *Rebellion Against Victorianism: The Impetus for Cultural Change in 1920s America* (New York: Oxford University Press, 1990), 94.

10. Michael S. Kimmel, "Men's Response to Feminism at the Turn of the Century," *Gender and Society*, 1:3 (Sept. 1987), 261–283; Susan Estabrook Kennedy, *If All We Did Was to Weep at Home: A History of White Working Class Women in America* (Bloomington: Indiana University Press, 1979).

11. Joanne J. Meyerowitz, *Women Adrift: Independent Wage Earners in Chicago, 1880–1930* (Chicago: University of Chicago Press, 1988); Lewis A. Erenberg, *Steppin' Out: New York Nightlife and the Transformation of American Culture* (Chicago: University of Chicago: 1984); David Nasaw, *Going Out: The Rise and Fall of Public Amusements* (New York: Basic Books, 1993).

12. Lawrence W. Levine, *Highbrow / Lowbrow: The Emergence of Cultural Hierarchy in America* (Cambridge, MA: Harvard University Press, 1988); Arthur Mann, *The One and the Many: Reflections on the American Identity* (Chicago: University of Chicago Press, 1979);

Richard Slotkin, "Nationalizing Memory: Myth, Fiction, and the Creation of the American Past," Organization of American Historians Convention, Chicago, March 23, 1996; Edward Countryman, *Americans: A Collision of Histories* (New York: Hill and Wang, 1996) 238; Eric A. Foner and John A. Garraty, eds., *The Reader's Companion to American History*, 670–674, 815–818.

13. Dewey W. Grantham, *The South in Modern America*, 4–6, 16–18.

14. H. W. Brands, *The Reckless Decade: America in the 1890s* (New York: St. Martin's Press, 1995), 39; R. Reid Badger, *The Great American Fair: The World's Columbian Exposition and American Culture* (Chicago: Nelson Hall, 1979); Carl S. Smith, *Chicago and the American Literary Imagination, 1880–1920* (Chicago: University of Chicago Press, 1984); Sarah J. Moore, "On the Frontier of Culture," *Chicago History* 16:2 (Summer 1987), 4–13; David Lowe, *Lost Chicago* (New York: Wings Books, 1975), 125.

15. Among numerous studies that analyze the bourgeois crisis and the change in values, see T. J. Jackson Lears, *No Place of Grace: Antimodernism and the Transformation of American Culture, 1880–1920* (New York: Pantheon Books, 1981); Brands, *The Reckless Decade*; Larzer Ziff, *The American 1890's: Life and Times of a Lost Generation* (New York: Viking Press, 1973); Alan Trachtenberg, *The Incorporation of America: Culture and Society in the Gilded Age* (New York: Hill and Wang, 1982); Robert H. Wiebe, *The Search for Order, 1877–1920* (New York: Hill and Wang, 1967); John Higham, "The Reorientation of American Culture in the 1890s," in Higham, ed., *Writing American History: Essays on Modern Scholarship* (Bloomington: Indiana University Press, 1972), 73–102.

The role of sport and its cultural meanings is explored by Michael Oriard, *Sporting with the Gods: The Rhetoric of Play and Games in American Culture* (New York: Cambridge University Press, 1991) 7–8, 12–13, 27; and Elliot J. Gorn and Warren Goldstein, *A Brief History of American Sports* (New York: Hill and Wang, 1993), 28, 35, 94, 145, 168–169, 184–188.

Chapter 1

For Victory and Profit:
The Rise of Football

Football emerged as an American intercollegiate spectacle in the late nineteenth century, merging the values of winning and commercialization within the culture of higher education, and instilling such convictions in future generations of Americans. But, ironically, the game had its roots in the physicality of the English peasantry. Traditionally played on Sundays and Shrove Tuesday, young men of competing villages tried to kick a ball (often a bull's head or animal bladder) to their opponents' hamlet with little regard for any rules or decorum. As early as 1531 Sir Thomas Elyot, an English statesman, declared football to be "*nothynge but beastlye furie and exstreme violence, whereof proceedeth hurte; and consequently malice and rancour do remain with they that be wounded....*"[1] Serious injuries and death occurred all too often and both Oxford and Cambridge banned the game as too unseemly and vulgar for scholars. It persisted among schoolboys and peasants, however, gradually assuming the modern form of soccer.[2]

Soccer players advanced the ball by propelling it forward without using their hands or arms, usually by kicking it. A ball propelled across the opponents' goal line, located at the end of the field, won the contest. Early games had no time limits or restrictions on the number of players; but as the game became codified in the latter half of the nineteenth century, the number of players decreased to fifteen, and eventually eleven per side, and goalposts were added.[3]

A deviant form of the game ensued in 1823 when William Webb Ellis, a student at the Rugby School in England, allegedly picked up the ball and ran with it. Rugby rules allowed players to carry the ball toward the opponents' goal line, or to toss it backward to a teammate to avoid being tackled; but blocking, or "interference" with a tackler was prohibited. Americans adhered to the soccer version, and by 1827 Harvard students used it as an excuse to throttle each other in intramural contests on "Bloody Monday" at the start of each school year. Yale followed by 1840 until school authorities banned the ritual in 1860; but it continued among Boston schoolboys. Such perseverance and resistance to control marked interscholastic athletics throughout the nineteenth century.[4]

In 1868 William S. Gunmere, a Princeton student, who later became Chief Justice of the New Jersey Supreme Court, adapted the London Football Association Rules for his institution. On November 6, 1869, Princeton traveled to Rutgers, where it lost 6–4 in what is considered to be the first intercollegiate football game in the United States. Princeton salvaged a measure of pride in a return match a week later with an 8–0 win. Both teams used twenty-five players per side; but other rules differed and had to be negotiated, a condition that endured for more than a quarter century.[5]

The rivalry continued the following year, interrupted by a game between Columbia and Rutgers on November 12, 1870. In 1871 Princeton codified ten new rules, deviating from its previous acceptance of the use of hands to catch the ball before a free kick, in favor of soccer. The following year Harvard adopted rugby rules and ten to fifteen players per team, while Yale allowed catching and used twenty players and referees. Students from each school served the latter role in a game with Columbia. Princeton took the lead in attempting to alleviate the confusion by calling a rules convention in New York in 1873. Harvard declined participation with an ominous note, stating that

> it is manifestly impossible for us to take part in any such (rules) convention as you propose...Harvard stands entirely distinct by herself in the game of foot ball, and has...hardly any rules in common with others...we consider the game played here to admit of much science, according to our rules. We cannot but recognize in your game much brute force, weight, and especially the "shin" element.[6]

Such condescension and elitist independence marred such negotiations for years. The rules convention marked the first step in the American departure from British soccer. Despite agreement on eleven players per side the Yale representative admitted to dissension over batting of the ball; "but we want our game to be distinctive and that batting will make it so... we far prefer the game now played in America...(rather than the English version) it admits of more real science in the position of playing."[7]

The comparison with English might was timely. Yale had competed with Eton earlier that year as the United States began testing itself in the international athletic arena. In a test of regional importance, the Cornell-Michigan challenge match to be played at Cleveland fell asunder when Cornell president, Andrew White, declared that "I will not permit 30 men to travel 400 miles merely to agitate a bag of wind."[8]

Another match of international consequence did transpire in 1874 when McGill University of Montreal offered to play Harvard in a series of games. The *Harvard Advocate* urged immediate and regular practice to pick "as strong a Ten as possible in the American quest for victory."[9] Playing two games, one by each team's rules, Harvard admitted that "the Rugby game is in much better favor than the somewhat sleepy game now played by our men."[10] Spectators, including women, who paid 50¢ for the privilege of watching, were moved to shouting as individual heroics excited them beyond Victorian strictures of decorum. Harvard's preparation paid off when it prevailed again in a fall trip to Montreal. The McGill series proved notable in the Americans' commercialization of the event and in the value they placed on winning. Proper British gentlemen extolled athletic efforts, but deemed an overemphasis on bettering one's peers as ill mannered.[11]

Harvard lamented a loss to Tufts, who displayed better teamwork in 1875. Nevertheless, about 140 Harvard fans accompanied the team for its game against Yale at New Haven that year, and were rewarded with a Harvard victory. The defeat was somewhat softened for Yale by the approximately 1,200 patrons who paid 50¢ to see the contest. The Princetonians who witnessed the rugby game judged it to be "less fair, more rowdyish and ungentlemanly" than their soccer version.[12] They further added that "We fail to see the sport in being disgracefully mauled in such unmanly scrimmages...."[13]

Princeton initiated another rules meeting on November 23, 1876, with Harvard, Yale, and Columbia in Springfield, Massachusetts. The student delegates agreed on sixty-one rules that followed the English Rugby Union Code, allowing for touchdowns to count as scores, somewhat diminishing the influence of the kicking game. The representatives of the elite institutions voted not to accept any new members to the Intercollegiate Football Association without unanimous consent. Yale still chose to maintain its independence until 1879, although it agreed to abide by the rules.[14]

Harvard still feared that "the game is much too violent a one to be played by only eleven men."[15] The game at Yale did not disappoint in that regard. The *Harvard Advocate* reported that "Disputes began immediately, and were faithfully kept up during the game."[16] Harvard led at the half; but with a Yale goal the

> ...wildest enthusiasm ensued. The nearly three thousand spectators rushed into the field, shouldered the players, and cheered till (sic) they were hoarse; while only here and there along the edges of the field could a man with a very, very small piece of crimson ribbon in his buttonhole be seen hopeful, and willing to bet.[17]

It took fifteen minutes to restore order and Yale later went on to win the first official intercollegiate championship against Princeton, a claim later disputed by Harvard.[18]

Harvard chafed at the loss and looked forward to new rules for 1877, "because of our late defeat, and the universal desire to see another game with Yale; (and) to give the Senior members a final opportunity to wipe out that defeat."[19] More than half of Harvard's team would be seniors, and athletic contests, particularly football games, took on added importance as the nouveau-riche of Yale challenged the Boston Brahmins for societal and institutional pride. Such implications extending beyond college campuses began to exert undue pressure on the young athletes during the final decades of the nineteenth century as alumni, trustees, and benefactors expected and relished the honors and public recognition wrought by athletic success.

The new rule for 1877 allowed for fifteen players on a side and the Polo Club offered a championship trophy for a game to be played at its New York grounds, undoubtedly expecting a commercial bonanza. Both the trophy, symbolic of national supremacy, and the game's location, in the media capital of the country, heightened expectations. By November Harvard had defeated McGill and Tufts and looked forward to the Yale match; but the Yale-Tufts game brought further disrepute. The Tufts *Collegian* charged that

> ...the gentlemen who compose the Yale team have cultivated a habit of losing their tempers, and mauling their antagonists with doubled fists; and though this imparted an increased interest in the game, and seemed to offer exquisite gratification to the cultured spectators, it is not without its drawbacks. The bitterness of our defeat was lessened by the kind attention of the lookers-on, mostly students, who showed their magnanimity by facetiously pelting our men with pebbles and second-hand tobacco quids.[20]

Yale denied Harvard the opportunity for such largesse when it refused to play by the 15-player rule; then claimed the championship of 11-man football. Yale agreed to use fifteen players in the 1878 game; but wanted a $100 guarantee for the Thanksgiving date when it realized it had a product to sell. Yale won; but then lost the championship game to Princeton before 2,000 fans in the mud at Hoboken, New Jersey. Princeton had prepared itself with four practice games before facing Harvard and Yale. Woodrow Wilson, the future president, served as secretary of the Princeton board of coaches; while Walter Camp captained the Yale team. Most importantly, Camp became secretary of the rules committee, which he headed until his death in 1925, by which time sportswriters acclaimed him as "the father of American football."[21]

Equipment innovations had begun in 1877, when both Harvard and Princeton adopted canvas jackets. Yale added canvas pants instead of tights the following year. Not only were the uniforms more durable; but the canvas could be greased to thwart would-be tacklers and provide a winning advantage.[22]

Under Wilson's guidance in 1879, Princeton introduced strategic innovations as well, running interference to protect the runner and an onsides kick against Harvard. The exciting new style and burgeoning rivalry drew 7,000 to Hoboken for the game with Yale. The choice of urban sites for such battles helped to fill the football clubs' coffers. A similar clash in the Midwest between the University of Michigan and Racine, Wisconsin club team used the White Stockings' baseball park in Chicago for the same purpose in the spring of 1879.[23]

Yale's "win at all costs attitude," allegedly instilled by team captain Eugene Von Voy Baker in 1876, won it no friends in 1879. Princeton charged that "Yale sustained her reputation for ungentlemanliness on the field by throttling, foul tackling and loud talking."[24] Harvard concurred that Yale "deliberately set to work to win a game by disabling the opposing players; while Yale rebutted that it was the Harvard fans that swore and rushed the field and Harvard players who throttled and slugged opponents, and twice kicked the shins of its captain, Walter Camp."[25] Despite the recriminations the Harvard-Yale game ended in a tie.

Camp introduced a major change at the rules convention on October 12, 1880, in the concept of a scrimmage line, which would allow one team to retain possession of the ball, rather than the previous rugby scrummage that allowed for a mass scramble after every tackle. Another noteworthy occurrence of the 1880 season happened in Kentucky, where Centre College challenged cross-town rival, Transylvania, to a soccer-style game, the first in the South. An Australian student had introduced the game to Transylvania in the spring of 1879, where it was played on an intramural basis.[26]

The introduction of the scrimmage line clearly distinguished American football from English soccer or rugby at a time when the origins of baseball were still debated. Not until 1907 did the Mills Commission erroneously fabricate the Doubleday myth as the birth of the "national pastime." The scrimmage line also required strategic maneuvers to put the ball in play by a snap back and to retain possession, making the contest analogous to war.

In the most important game of 1881, the Thanksgiving championship at New York's Polo Grounds between Yale and Princeton, the simplest strategy proved effective, but boring. Each team played defensively, hoping not to lose. Princeton gave way throughout the first half but protected the ball, and Yale followed suit in its half, producing an uninspired scoreless tie. At the 1882 rules convention, Camp promptly rectified that mishap by introducing a system requiring the offense to gain five yards within three tries. Adoption of the rule required a lined field and further removed the American game from rugby. Furthermore, after 1882 the American schools no longer engaged the Canadians in competition, as football literally became an "American" game.[27]

In 1882 the rules committee tried to bring greater regulation to the game by limiting player eligibility to five years. Walter Camp, however, played his sixth consecutive season that year, introducing a system of coded verbal signals to designate plays. Over the next two years the rules committee altered the scoring system, but the emphasis remained on the kicking game, with field goals counting for five points, and kicks after a touchdown amounting to four points.[28]

Newspaper accounts and university graduates spread the word as football moved beyond its eastern origins. In 1881 the University of Michigan team made an eastern tour, and schools in Virginia began play. By 1882, the game was being played in Minnesota, Illinois, Wisconsin, and as far west as Colorado. It took only four more years to reach California.[29]

In its expansion, football assumed even greater characteristics of industrial capitalism. In addition to the commercialization of the game, already evident in the 1870s, the next decade witnessed greater specialization as well. Before 1882, all linemen except the ends were called forwards; but by mid-decade the tackles, guards, and center had acquired their distinctive positions. By 1887 Walter Camp declared that the "Division of labor has been so thoroughly and successfully carried out on the football field that a player nowadays must train for a particular position."[30]

The Yale-Princeton game of 1884, again played before a New York crowd, nearly derailed that sense of progress, resulting in a public outcry and calls for cessation of football.

An observer described the "elevens...hurl themselves together...in kicking and writhing heaps...throttling, wrestling,
and the pitching of individuals headlong to the earth...savage
blows that drew blood, and falls that...crack the bones....”[31]
Yale's captain required the services of a surgeon, while a
Princeton player, who was carried from the field unconscious,
returned only to have his shoulder dislocated. Two others left
the field, disqualified for slugging. A 40-minute dispute with
the umpire resulted before darkness ensued and the game was
declared a draw.[32]

Such games raised the blood lust of spectators, who encouraged wanton violence, acceptable under the 1883 rules, "which
allowed a player to hack, throttle, butt, trip up, tackle below
the hips, or strike an opponent with closed fist three times
before he was sent from the field.”[33]

Both Harvard and Yale faculties tried to regulate such
extracurricular student activities, resulting in rule revisions
to decrease the brutality for 1884. Additionally, Harvard faculty formed a watchdog committee to study implementation
of the new rules. After observing four games the committee
concluded that

> In every one of these games there was brutal fighting with
> the fists....In addition there were numerous incidents where
> a single blow was struck. In the Wesleyan-Pennsylvania
> game, a man was thrown unfairly, out of bounds, by an
> opposing player. Then, as he was rising, but before he was
> on his feet, his antagonist turned, struck him in the face and
> knocked him down, and returned in triumph with the ball.[34]
>
> Unfair play, often premeditated and sometimes con-
> certed was a permanent feature in all of the games....We
> often heard cries of "kill him," "break his neck," "slug him,"
> "hit him," and "knock him down"....
>
> After deliberate investigation we have become convinced
> that the game of football, as presently played by college
> teams, is brutalizing, demoralizing to teams and spectators,
> and extremely dangerous....”[35]

The committee recommended a ban on football, and Harvard resigned from the football association, albeit temporarily.

Reinstatement, and further observance of the new rules ensued; but the brutality remained a central issue to the game.[36]

The Princeton-Yale game of 1886 reemphasized the problem when the Princeton crowd rushed the field late in the game with Yale leading 4–0. The inability to continue resulted in a declaration of no contest. Despite such conflicts the sport continued to grow among colleges and prep schools, particularly in the East and Midwest. In Chicago, annual Thanksgiving Day games began to parallel those of the East, as an all-star team opposed the University of Michigan, standard bearers of regional play.[37]

By 1887 football had surpassed baseball on college campuses in the level of interest and its accompanying festivity. One writer described "an enormous crowd, coaches filled with men and horns, the masses and shades of color among the spectators, the perpetual roar of cheers, including the peculiar slogans of almost all the Eastern colleges, combine to make up a spectacle such as no other intercollegiate game can offer."[38]

Although retaining an emphasis on kicking, and still exhibiting its similarities to rugby, new rules and player responsibilities throughout the decade further distinguished American football from its British counterparts. Field goals counted for five points; but touchdowns earned four points, with safeties and points after touchdown each accounting for two. Both officials' and players' roles became more clearly defined, with alumni judges replacing team captains as on field rule arbitrators. The alums were replaced by a single referee in 1885, who was joined by an umpire in 1888, with the intention of limiting the more brutal aspects of play. Like the linemen, backs assumed distinctive names and responsibilities, with the quarterback emerging as signal caller and eventually team leader.[39]

Other important characteristics of the game appeared as well. During 1888–1889 American baseball teams set out on a worldwide tour to promote the "national" game. The excursion failed to impress the Anglo world, and the British declared baseball no more than its juvenile game of rounders. As the United States began to emerge as a world power football provided significant messages to both American and foreign onlookers. The game elicited comparisons with the battlefield where "two armies are managed on military principles...," and the "American" competition was judged "one of the most scientific of outdoor games...where players worked with 'clock-work precision'."[40] In the aggressive, competitive, industrial modern world football served as a training ground.

The American emphasis on winning further diverged from the British ideal of sportsmanship. Americans adhered only to the letter of the law rather than the spirit, often circumventing both in their zeal for victory. Yale opponents greased their jackets with lard, forcing Yale tacklers to use handfuls of sand to gain a hold. Other tacklers used turpentine on their hands to better their grasp, while runners placed it on the ball to avoid fumbling. Winning became all important not only for masculine pride, school spirit, and the large wagers placed on games, but in defining American distinction, power, and nationalism.[41]

Walter Camp stated that "our players have strayed away from the original Rugby rules, but in so doing they have built up a game and rules of their own more suited to American needs."[42] James Knox of Harvard later explained that "football...embodies so many factors that are typically American... virile, intensive, aggressive energy that makes for progress is the root which upholds and feeds American supremacy and American football."[43] The delivery of such messages occurred on a weekly basis to ever-increasing numbers.

Winning, however, required a stronger work ethic than one's opponents, especially if played within the rules. In March of 1889 Harvard's captain, Arthur Cumnock, began spring football practices to sharpen his team. Others simply employed ineligible players, often marginal, part-time, or graduate students or some who enrolled just during football season. Tramp athletes traveled from school to school amidst charges of professionalism that have endured over the succeeding century.[44]

Despite the abuses inherent in the overemphasis on winning the most prestigious schools measured their masculinity by football triumphs and rewarded players accordingly. When Harvard beat Yale 12–6 in 1890 the football victory was celebrated by a procession of some 2000 men, headed by a band and a drum corps. The team was borne on a tally-ho, and followed by a cart displaying fireworks. There was an almost universal illumination of the route...both by townspeople and students, and a great display of fireworks and red bunting, the John Harvard statue being draped in red, and three Harvard banners flown from the flag pole on the Common....The procession ended at Jarvis Field, where a large bonfire had been built, after having twice halted to listen to speeches from Pres. (sic) Eliot and Prof. (sic) A.B. Hart.

The college defrayed the expenses for such an extravaganza and a week later the players were honored with a dinner at the Revere House, followed by private dinners in local homes and a commemorative book. Similar fetes accompanied other champions in other parts of the country as teams strove for regional prestige, national recognition, and a definition of success unattainable in their academic ventures.[45]

The cult of the athletic hero had been assured the year before, when Walter Camp and Caspar Whitney, one of the foremost sportswriters of the era, inaugurated the first of the annual All-America teams to signify individual excellence. The "All-American" designation symbolized a nationalistic ideal of manhood, and pointed to a further separation from British roots. Selection also honored college players who exemplified institutional loyalty, in contrast to the professional baseball players, who revolted to form the Players' League based on socialist principles in 1889. In so doing, Camp and Whitney, both entrenched in the bourgeoisie, highlighted football as sustainer of the capitalist status quo. Camp, an executive for a watch manufacturer, and Whitney, the foremost apologist of the amateur ideal, honored players representative of their own value systems and ignored others. Their selections, all members of Harvard, Princeton, and Yale, further reinforced the perception of elite eastern leadership.[46]

That leadership would be challenged in the 1890s, starting with the founding of the Intercollegiate Athletic Association of the Northwest in 1892, precursor to the Western, and later, Big Ten conference. Eastern might still prevailed, however, as witnessed by the Harvard-Yale game of 1892. Mass plays had been prevalent since the mid-1880s; but under the guidance of Coach Loren F. Deland, a chess master and military strategist, Harvard devised the flying wedge. The V-shaped, mass momentum phalanx unveiled in the second half provided a concentration of mobile force at one point, which devastated opponents' defenses and personnel. The havoc wreaked soon forced a ban on the play; but coaches devised variations to exploit winning possibilities. Media coverage sensationalized the rising brutality, and Walter Camp admitted that "The captain usually desires to win...no matter at what expense."[47] As the game spread westward and southward students imported former eastern players as coaches to teach such techniques.

More than fifty eastern colleges fielded football teams by 1889, and at least forty midwestern schools adopted the game between 1890 and 1892. In the latter year Biddle University of Charlotte, North Carolina (now Johnson C. Smith University), defeated Livingstone College (Salisbury, North Carolina) 5–0 in the first football game between African-American institutions of higher learning. Also, Stanford and the University of California began their long rivalry on the West Coast. Former players served as missionaries for the cause of football, extolling its virtues, and creating a market for their expertise. By 1901 well over 100 Yale and Princeton players held lucrative positions as coaches, further promoting commercial values and the win-at-all-costs attitude of their mentors.[48]

One of the most influential of such agents arrived on the campus of the new University of Chicago in 1892. William Rainey Harper, the school's young president, convinced Amos Alonzo Stagg, a Yale All-American and his former student, to accept the position as a tenured faculty member with associate professor rank and a substantial salary. Such an appointment gave immediate accreditation to the professional trainers that teams had been hiring for the past decade to improve their chances. Stagg's role included more than just physical training, however. He served as physical culture director, teacher, residence hall supervisor, and publicist. The latter, perhaps, of greatest importance, as Dr. Harper fully intended to increase public interest in the school built largely with John D. Rockefeller's dollars, by producing a winning athletic program. Stagg did not disappoint. Within two years the football team traveled as far as California for post-season games.[49]

Promoters, businessmen, civic boosters, and the student managers of the football teams allied in staging commercial spectacles throughout the country. The Manhattan Athletic Club promoted the 1891 Yale-Princeton game in New York and earned an equal share (one-third) of the $50,000 in receipts. Football games enhanced the regional Rose Parade celebration in California. Begun in 1890, the floral extravaganza gained national attention with the addition of a football game in 1902. In Dallas, local businessmen and the railroad organized the "championship of Texas" between the university team and the local athletic club in 1893. C. B. Culbertson, the Wisconsin manager, falsely claimed that eastern stars would appear for each team in its 1893 game against Minnesota. The rivals used only their own players; but the ruse worked. The capacity crowd witnessed a 40–0 rout by Minnesota; yet saved Wisconsin by balancing the team budget, which had been operating at a loss.[50]

Other occurrences took place throughout the South; but New York featured the grandest spectacle amidst the nation's worst economic depression. The contests of the cultural elites of the Northeast assumed the title of "national championships," and the 1893 affair between Princeton and Yale attracted 40,000. The four-hour parade that preceded the game served as a pageant of ostentatious display and a reaffirmation of bourgeois vitality.[51]

Richard Harding Davis reported on the scene for *Harper's Weekly*. Three days before the event vendors "swarm up town like an invading army...with banners and flags....Photographs of players show in every shop window; and their pictures appear and reappear with every edition of the daily papers." The Stock Exchange postponed its "legitimate gambling," as lesser folk termed its entrepreneurial ventures, in order to wager on the game. Seats sold for $15 and boxes for $150. Private transport coaches had to be reserved a year in advance at $20 apiece. Alumni came from as far away as Texas and Oregon to stake $2,000 to $3,000 on their favorites. An ex-prizefighter who served as bartender at the Hoffman House Hotel, headquarters for the Yale team, was entrusted with $50,000 in bets from complete strangers.[52]

The parade began at 10 a.m. "like a circus procession many miles long," accompanied by "the sounds of the bugle calls and the coach horns and the rifle-like cheer of Yale and the sky-rocket yell of Princeton...like the advance of any army going forth triumphantly to war." At the game fans sang songs that immortalized star players, like "the ancient Goths in their war-songs." The *Evening Sun* alone sent seventeen reporters to chronicle the affair. Davis recorded that the victorious Princeton players stood naked in their post-game dressing room, caked in "muck, blood, and perspiration," and sang the doxology as a crowd of a thousand clamored for them outside. Davis further remarked on "how great and how serious is the joy of victory to the men who conquer," and suggested that all foreigners be taken to witness the grand spectacle.[53]

Francis A. Walker, president of the Massachusetts Institute of Technology and a Harvard alum, acknowledged that "the rising passion for athletics has carried all before it...it is welcomed as a relief to the monotony of life, and as giving to the community, not merely two hours...of intense excitement, but something to look forward to and back upon, for weeks and for months, with pleasure.[54] Football served as much more than diversion though. Within twenty-five years football had become a tradition, a weekly anthropological play that celebrated American might and vitality, as it signaled the transition in power relations, both internally and abroad.

Yale, the preferred institution of the noveau riche and social aspirants, established its domination over Harvard's Boston Brahmins by winning sixteen of the eighteen contests between 1875 and 1898. Yale's efficient, business-like system, perfected under Walter Camp, had produced a record of 124-3-3 between 1886 and 1895, still the best 10-year winning percentage. The fabulous 1888 contingent outscored its opponents 698–0. Throughout the 1880s team play, important in a democracy, proved more effective than individualism. By the 1890s football, and Yale in particular, represented the transition to an urban, commercial, efficient, and systematic modern society, spearheaded by a progressive middle class.[55]

The game still retained frontier aspects, however, and the brutality issue continued to linger. The Harvard-Yale game of 1894 caused such animosity that Harvard suspended all sports with Yale for two years. A standing-room-only crowd saw three players from each team carried from the field as the ferocity only increased after Yale's captain, Frank Hinkey, "dropped with his knees on Wrightington, breaking his collarbone, when the latter was already down."[56] Such intensity earned Hinkey All-American honors for four straight years. The Penn-Princeton contest of 1894 ended in a post-game riot and another severance of athletic relations.

Nor was such aggressiveness unusual. Downed ballcarriers might crawl forward until verbally admitting that they were "down," which resulted in tacklers piling on or delivering an effective knee to the back. After crossing the goal line a runner had to place the ball on the ground and declare a "touchdown." A defender who reached him before doing so might try to wrest the ball away, resulting in the embattled "maul in goal." The rules committee eliminated the maul in goal and allowed tackling below the waist to lessen the injuries caused by the typical maneuver of delivering a knee to the chest or head. Despite the new rulings mass plays remained popular, and players began growing their hair long and adopting even more protective headgear and nosepieces in the 1890s.[57]

Despite the introduction of protective equipment, new momentum plays, such as the flying wedge, increased the injury rate. As early as 1889 Yale began using the "pulling guard" technique, with big, fast "Pudge" Heffelfinger leading the way. Perhaps the greatest and most famous player of the era, Heffelfinger proved devastating in the role. Other Yale players who became coaches also proved master tacticians in the use of momentum plays. George Woodruff devised the guards back formation to gain a blocking advantage and lead Penn to a 26-game winning streak. When momentum plays were banned, Amos Alonzo Stagg at Chicago, and Henry Williams at Minnesota led the Midwest to national prominence with shifts that accomplished the same objectives.[58]

The resultant bloodshed and deaths brought a shrill outcry of protest, especially by religious leaders. As early as 1885 opponents had characterized the sport as "The playful gamboling of twenty-two prizefighters."[59] Clergy, doctors, and college faculty members led the movement to ban the game in all regions of the land. Apologists, led by Walter Camp, countered with a media barrage extolling the benefits of football and a rationale for its necessity. Camp surveyed school administrators and former players and published their positive responses in an 1894 book, *Football Facts and Figures,* to support his cause. The prominence of Social Darwinism lent additional support for football as training for the survival of the fittest. Senator Henry Cabot Lodge stated that "...the injuries incurred on the playing field are part of the price which the English-speaking race has paid for being world conquerors...victories...are the manifestation and evidence of a spirit which is all important...this great Democracy is moving onward to its great destiny. Woe to the men or nations that bar its imperial march...."[60] Football thus served American nationalism and its Manifest Destiny, soon to be pursued in the Spanish-American War.

Ongoing disputes over violence, the rules, and regionalism fractured intercollegiate football in 1895. Successful teams did not hasten to change the status quo; but as colleges throughout the country began to organize into athletic leagues they began to question the conservative policies and rules of the eastern elites. By 1894 three different sets of rules ensued, with easterners favoring the old guidelines under which they could retain their supremacy. The University Athletic Club of New York tried to bring some stability to the situation by calling together the eastern powers in February of that year for the purpose of reforming the rules committee. Although Harvard, Princeton, Yale, and Penn reached consensus, smaller schools, and those outside the East followed their own course. Faculty members assumed greater control over students' extracurricular activities, and in the Midwest, President James Smart of Purdue requested a meeting of the football titans of that area. A year later, on February 8, 1896, they formed the Intercollegiate Conference of Faculty Representatives, later known as the Western Conference and Big Ten. Their union challenged the East, and negotiation of the rules and regulations continued for two decades.[61]

If coaches and players could not agree on the rules they did agree on the importance of winning. Thirteen years after their initial meeting with Harvard in 1876, Yale admitted that it had wanted a three-game series, hoping to learn the new rules in the first encounter and salvage victory in the next two games. When it unexpectedly won the first game, it denied the same proposal from Harvard. The American perception of fair play consistently diverged from the British concept thereafter. A tie game became as dishonorable as a defeat. When Wisconsin led Chicago at the half of their 1895 game, President Harper entered the locker room to inform the players that John D. Rockefeller, the school's benefactor, had offered another $3,000,000 for a win. The Chicagoans obliged with a 22–12 come from behind victory. When Penn suffered its only defeat between 1894 and 1897 in a 6–4 loss to Lafayette, it offered a $7,500 guarantee for a rematch.[62]

Within such an environment coaches and players faced intense pressure to succeed. Extensive, national recruiting networks fueled by zealous alumni offered inducements to star players ranging from jobs, tutoring, clothes, room and board, to money and more. By the 1890s spying on opponents became commonplace. Supposedly neutral referees informed their alma maters about future opponents whose games they had already officiated. One informant wrote to Michigan to let them know that Stagg's Chicago team hurriedly kicked their points after touchdowns before opponents got to the scrimmage line, so that they could claim an offsides infraction if they missed. Stagg devised numerous other trick plays to gain an advantage, as did John Heisman, "Pop" Warner, and later, Knute Rockne. Adherents to the British code of sportsmanship might consider them cheaters, while Americans came to recognize such coaches as great innovators.[63]

Bill Reid, who became the Harvard coach in 1905, acknowledged that "...it has been considered always perfectly legitimate and justifiable for a coach to take advantage of any loopholes offered...."[64] Not only participants transgressed the rules in order to win. In an 1897 game with Colgate, the Syracuse captain, Haden Patten, was tackled by a spectator and a local reporter. Harvard suspended play with Penn for

seventeen years after the latter watered down the field to win
the 1905 game.[65]

By that time Americans had more clearly defined their
differences with Great Britain in literature, art, and history.
The differences in sporting philosophy accentuated the con-
trasts in national character. In comparing the two cultures in
a national publication, Ralph Paine suggested that "English
boys play for health and fun, Americans play to win." He
explained American economic production similarly, in that
Americans were far more serious in business and sport and
had surpassed England in both areas.[66] Sport and work had
seemingly merged in the United States, where athletics assumed organized, specialized, and disciplined approaches in
a quest for victory rather than a leisurely pursuit of fun and
diversion.

Despite whatever benefits might be derived from such a
union, its violence continued to bring opposition. At least 18
deaths and 159 serious injuries occurred during the 1905
season, and a particularly brutal play in the Yale-Harvard
game nearly brought a permanent ban to the game. Harvard's
president, Charles W. Eliot, had already stated his opposition
to a sport that caused

> absorption of the minds of students for months, dispropor-
> tionate exaltation of the football hero...distraction from
> proper studies...distrust and hostility between colleges...
> unnecessary roughness and rules violations in order to win
> ...and a strategy and ethics compared to war.[67]

Several Yale faculty concurred in Eliot's assessment, and
coaches were hard-pressed to make amends. They found a
most formidable ally in the White House. Though his own son
suffered a broken nose in Harvard's freshmen game against
Yale, Teddy Roosevelt had always extolled the benefits of sport
in building character and manhood. Concerned that injurious
and unethical play endangered the game, Roosevelt inter-
vened by calling the coaches of Harvard, Princeton, and Yale
to Washington. With reforms promised he assumed that other
schools would follow the lead of the Big Three.[68]

In 1905 H. M. McCracken, Chancellor of New York University, convened a series of meetings with sixty-eight schools to elicit reforms; but the Big Three failed to attend. By the end of the year McCracken's group had organized the Intercollegiate Athletic Association of the United States, which later became the National Collegiate Athletic Association, still the governing body for intercollegiate sport. Columbia, Northwestern, Stanford, and California chose to ban the sport; the latter two opting for rugby. Harvard, too, joined the ban, but only briefly; for football was big business. Harvard had built a 40,000-seat, concrete stadium in 1903.[69]

The reorganization maintained eastern power on the rules committee; but allowed for more representation from the West and South. More than thirty rule changes ensued, which eventually brought greater modernization by decreasing massed play and allowing for the more open game of speed, passing, and end runs favored by the West and South. The reforms included allowance for forward passes, although an incompletion caused a turnover; requiring ten yards on three downs to retain possession; greater penalties for unnecessary roughness, including disqualification; and allowing all four officials to call fouls; providing a neutral zone with six players on the line; and two 30-minute halves.[70]

The new rules opened up the game but did not immediately curtail injuries. Eastern schools in particular proved reluctant to change winning strategies. Eighteen deaths and 159 serious injuries occurred in 1905; and the death toll rose to thirty-three by 1909. Passing, in fact, caused many of the injuries as defenses attacked the receiver as he waited for the ball. Walter Camp claimed that a team needed six to eight ends due to such punishment. Football underwent another crisis of violence, and high schools in New York and Washington, D.C., forbade play. Caspar Whitney asked "Is Football Worthwhile?," and polled college presidents for an answer. Most favored the game, but additional reforms followed in 1910. Pushing or pulling the ball carrier was disallowed; seven men had to be on the line of scrimmage; assessment of penalties for an incomplete pass ceased in favor of a loss of down; and a sixty-minute game of four equal quarters appeared. A fourth down to gain ten yards, a shorter field, and the six-point touchdown ensued in 1912.[71]

As the United States approached World War I Americans had a clearer image of themselves. Sports, in general, and football, in particular, eased the transition from a rural, agrarian, frontier society to an urban, industrial, commercial and modern world by combining elements of both cultures. Nineteenth-century Victorian values of the work ethic, self-sacrifice, order, and community still abounded in sport, even as technology, innovation, productivity, and profit assumed greater importance. Conflicting, and sometimes contradictory value systems merged in sporting practices.[72]

Americans saw themselves as exceptional in the vanguard of such transition and trumpeted their uniqueness in the process. In 1891 Walter Camp maintained that the lack of conservatism allowed for rapid progress and he urged both Canadians and Englishmen to take note of American football. At the 1893 World's Fair, Professor Frederick Jackson Turner proclaimed an end to the American frontier. He theorized that the frontier experience created a distinct American character, a point still debated by historians. Frederick Paxson claimed that sport replaced the frontier as the social safety valve by World War I. The early evolution of football provided some support for such contentions, at least in Americans' self-perceptions.[73]

Although clearly derived from soccer and rugby, Americans recognized and promoted football as a unique game as early as 1873. Moreover, the American emphasis on winning and its consequent professionalization conflicted with the British amateur ideal. Similar to Jackson's contention that the frontier experience required adaptation and innovation, so did football in its desire for victory. From the 1870s onward, the introduction of new equipment, in the form of smocks, canvas and leather jackets, cleated shoes, and protective gear sought an advantage. Also, new skills and strategies marked innovative changes in the game, often meant to deceive opponents or to gain a tactical benefit. The snap-back from center, and the introduction of the quarterback, peculiarly American, required defenses to spread out to guard against fixed plays and end runs. Prearranged blocking, in the form of interference preceding the ballcarrier, appeared by 1879 in a further departure from rugby. Signals, spiral punts, mass plays, and pulling guards came about in the 1880s; while the 1890s featured the flying wedge, new formations, trick plays, direct snaps to the punter, and place kicks. Shifts, unbalanced lines, and the forward pass continued to change the game dramatically thereafter.[74]

The commercialization of football packaged the sport as a commodity that could be sold as entertainment. As early as 1874 Harvard began charging admission to its games, and Yale garnered more than a thousand paying customers for the Harvard game only a year later. Teams soon negotiated for the largest markets and guarantees of profit, and coaches sold their knowledge for a price.[75]

Football became a business, and the University of Chicago turned a profit in its first year. By 1896 Chicago and Michigan paid a local advertising company at least $500 to ensure a large crowd, and Chicago's opponents soon clamored for an equal share of the gate. By 1904 Harvard enjoyed a $50,000 surplus in its football budget, the most profitable program on its campus. Yale earned even more, allegedly $100,000 by the 1890s. Only tuition accounted for greater revenue. Chicago's receipts, in excess of $42,000, funded all other sports by 1906.[76]

Athletic contests, with their inherent drama, easily lent themselves to public displays of commercialized entertainment. Coaches and promoters, similar to directors, orchestrated the images and meanings delivered to paying customers. Amos Alonzo Stagg declared that "when playing against a team we can beat it yields a better result from the spectators (sic) stand point to have the game end up in brilliancy; so that where substitutes are used they better go in at first & (sic) then taken out for the regular men to finish the game in a rush."[77] James R. H. Wagner, president of the 1902 Rose Bowl, stated that as "President of this Tournament ...it is up to me to give them a carnival far superior to anything they have ever seen..."; and, in trying to obtain Michigan as a featured team, he promised that "...you would not be put to one penny of expense from the time you left your University until you returned, including entertainment while here..."[78]

Such solicitations encouraged team managers or coaches to negotiate financial windfalls. When Michigan won a $3,500 guarantee for the game against Stanford, Wagner admitted that "...the expense of the whole thing is staggering some of these primitive westerners."[79]

Such public spectacles brought hordes of spectators who served as witnesses to not only the contest, but its inherent values and meanings. As early as 1885 the Princeton faculty suspended classes, so that 350 students could join 800 alumni to behold Princeton's 6–5 victory over Yale. At the Thanksgiving games the media lionized players as heroes, who were feted at the best hotels, and carried to the contest on decorated tallyhos amidst cheering fans. The procession and game served as cultural performances that taught civic lessons. Following the labor upheavals of 1886, the Yale-Harvard game drew 25,000 to New York, where "the crowd swarmed all over the field in the wildest excitement, sweeping fences and ropes before them...victorious players borne off the field by fellow wearers of the blue."[80] The raucous Yale win symbolized a transition to bourgeois power; but, unlike the unruly laborers at Haymarket, the magnanimous victors restored order and a sense of inclusion by adopting Harvard colors, draping the city in crimson for the night-time festivities.

In 1891, 35,000 braved a cold rain in New York as Princeton faced Yale in a battle of bourgeois powers, both of whom had held opponents scoreless throughout the season. Although not a local game, the *Chicago Tribune* reflected the national importance of the spectacle with front page coverage.

> There was a sudden wild deluge of shouting and blowing of hoarse horns and waving of flags when the two teams were seen to crystallize out of the scattered lot of players and line up in the middle of the gridiron...the noise was suddenly stopped and every one of those wild men and women were as still as a statue and every one of those eyes was focused on one little spot where the ball was. The great struggle that had been written about and talked about and dreamed about and bet about for just one year was about to begin...[81]

Team managers provided complimentary tickets for the media to assure such florid coverage for the games which took place in all regions of the country by the turn of the century. They also provided expensive mementos of such occasions to commemorate their historical importance. The 1897 Chicago booklet for its Thanksgiving game with Michigan provided each ticket holder with photos of the school presidents and players, rules, team and school histories. Horace Butterworth, Stagg's managerial assistant, stated that "This will cost a lot of money, but it would be nice and worth keeping..."[82] The programs' printing cost was covered by solicited advertisements from business, further commercializing the event. By 1906 James Angell, president of the University of Michigan, complained that such ventures had become too expensive, and that the schools were viewed as training grounds for public spectacles rather than public service.[83]

Through such commemorative weekly spectacles, promoters created rituals that became annual traditions at special times and places for the young nation in quest of its identity and character. During a tense period of transitional turmoil football both rejected the modern world in its emphasis on physicality, and embraced modernity in its claims to science, technology, and innovation. By 1898 Amos Alonzo Stagg was charting the distances achieved by his punter with balls of various weights, using the scientific method to gain a competitive advantage.[84]

The evolution of the game accommodated the new industrial order as well. Rugby play allowed for chaotic runs by anyone who obtained the ball. New American rules and signals engendered prearranged plays, positional roles, and responsibilities requiring teamwork. As in the factory, division of labor, cooperation, and an acceptance of hierarchy that produced greater efficiency elicited the greatest profit. Walter Camp proclaimed that "If ever a sport offered inducements to the man of executive ability, to the man who can plan, foresee, and manage, it is certainly the modern American football."[85] As the most dominant team of the nineteenth century, Yale's players found ready employment as coaches for teams eager to adopt its "system." By 1890 teamwork proved readily noticeable to an observer, who noted that each man was "a part of the machine; the failure of one part to perform its function, causing a collapse in its entire working....The idea of individuality was lost and swallowed up in the more important element of combined effort."[86] Yet the game still allowed for the cherished American individualism, and such brilliance was honored in the All-American "team" selections.

The celebration of shared experiences by players, spectators, and the public who had such events interpreted for them by the newspapers each year provided some continuity with the past, and a sense of stability for the embattled capitalists as displaced farmers and workers questioned the system in the late nineteenth century. The tradition continues in the annual hype and festive celebration of the bowl games, fueled by corporate money and influences. As Americans entered the twentieth century the merger of bourgeois values and sport emanated from college campuses across the nation, inculcating particular beliefs in the young men who would assume the roles of leadership. However, the majority of the population, women, remained unsure of their status in the society and began to challenge the traditional roles that had been assigned to them.[87]

Notes

1. Emmett A. Rice, John L. Hutchinson, and Mabel Lee, *A Brief History of Physical Education* (New York: Ronald Press, 1958), 126.

2. Louis B. Wright and Virginia A. LaMar, *Life and Letters in Tudor and Stuart England* (Ithaca, NY: Cornell University Press, 1962), 364–365; Philip Stubbs, *Anatomy of the Abuses of England* (London: N. Trubner & Co., 1877), 186.

3. Sam Foulds, "The American Soccer Tradition" (United States Soccer Federation, n.d.), provides an early history of the game; and George B. Kirsch, *Sport in North America: A Documentary History* (Gulf Breeze, FL: Academic International Press, 1992), vol. 3, 238–246, offers primary accounts of American intercollegiate games at midcentury.

4. A number of historians have discounted the Ellis affair as the origin of rugby, among them, see K. G. Sheard, "The Webb Ellis Myth," in David Levinson and Karen Christensen, eds., *Encyclopedia of World Sport: From Ancient Times to the Present* (Santa Barbara, CA: ABC-Clio, 1996), vol. 2, 842. Benjamin G. Rader, *American Sports: From the Age of Folk Games to the Age of Spectators* (Englewood Cliffs, NJ: Prentice-Hall, 1983), 80–81. Weyand, *The Saga of*

American Football, 5, 10–11, provides evidence of football at Yale in 1806; and Danzig, *The History of American Football*, 7, indicates soccer games at Princeton in 1820.

See Ronald A. Smith, *Sports and Freedom: The Rise of Big-Time College Athletics* (New York: Oxford University Press, 1988), on the struggle for athletic control.

5. David M. Nelson, *Anatomy of a Game: Football, The Rules, and the Men Who Made the Game* (Newark: University of Delaware Press, 1994), 25; Frank Presbrey and James H. Moffatt, eds., *Athletics at Princeton: A History* (New York: Frank Presbrey Co., 1901), 27; Davis, *Football*, 43–50.

6. Davis, *Football*, 40, 51; Nelson, *Anatomy of a Game*, 26, 28–30; Presbrey and Moffatt, *Athletics at Princeton*, 27, 29, 274; *Yale Record*, October 29, 1873, 96 (quote), in Yale Archives.

See *Harvard Advocate*, 16:4 (October 31, 1873), 52–53 for Harvard's rules, in the Harvard Archives.

7. *Yale Record*, December 17, 1873, 184.

8. Nelson, *Anatomy of a Game*, 32.

9. *Harvard Advocate*, 17:4 (April 3, 1874), 58–9.

10. *Harvard Advocate*, 17:8 (May 29, 1874), 113.

11. *Yale Record*, May 27, 1874, 419–420; *Harvard Advocate*, 18:3 (October 30, 1874), 35–36; Weyand, *The Saga of American Football*, 11.

12. *Harvard Advocate*, 19:9 (June 11, 1875), 107; 20:5 (Nov. 19, 1875), 56–58, Weyand, *The Saga of American Football*, 13; Presbrey, *Athletics at Princeton*, 30 (quote).

13. Presbrey, *Athletics at Princeton*, 278.

14. *Harvard Advocate*, 22:4 (November 10, 1876), 47; Nelson, *Anatomy of a Game*, 33–34; Rader, *American Sports*, 82.

15. *Harvard Advocate*, 22:4 (November 10, 1876), 39

16. *Harvard Advocate*, 22:5 (November 24, 1876), 52–54.

17. Ibid.

18. *Harvard Advocate*, 24:5 (November 16, 1877), 49.

19. *Harvard Advocate*, 23:2 (March 2, 1877), 17. See Allen Sack, "Yale 29–Harvard 4: The Professionalization of College Football," *Quest*, 19 (January 1973), 24–34, on the rivalry; and David Westby and Allen Sack, "The Commercialization and Functional Rationali-

zation of College Football," *Journal of Higher Education*, 47 (November/December 1976), 625–647, on transition from the Old Guard.

20. *Harvard Advocate*, 24:1 (September 26, 1877), 10; 24:4 (November 2, 1877), 44–45; 24:5 (November 16, 1877), 49 (quote).

21. *Harvard Advocate*, 24:6 (November 28, 1877), 70; 26:3 (October 18, 1878), 25; 26:6 (December 2, 1878), 61–62, 68–69; Presbrey, *Athletics at Princeton*, 33; Weyand, *The Saga of American Football*, 18; Nelson, *Anatomy of a Game*, 42.

22. *Harvard Advocate*, 24:5 (November 16, 1877), 58; Weyand, *The Saga of American Football*, 17–18.

23. Weyand, *The Saga of American Football*, 19; Howard Roberts, *The Big Nine: the Story of Football in the Western Conference* (New York: G. P. Putnam's Sons, 1948), 38, asserts a 7–2 Michigan victory. *Chicago Times Herald*, November 14, 1897, clipping in Amos Alonzo Stagg Papers, Box 24, folder 2, at University of Chicago, Special Collections. Davis, *Football*, 72, states 4,000 fans at the 1878 Princeton-Yale game and a $300 bill for rental of the field.

24. Weyand, *The Saga of American Football*, 15; Presbrey, *Athletics at Princeton*, 296.

25. *Harvard Advocate*, 28:5 (November 28, 1879), 49 (quote), 55; 28:6 (November 25, 1879), 66–67. Camp states that "To throttle a man it is necessary either to close the fingers around his windpipe or get the forearm or wrist in a particular fashion under his chin and across his throat...for a man who is being throttled cannot breathe," in "Football—Detail of a Defensive Play," *Outing* (December 1892), 210.

26. Weyand, *The Saga of American Football*, 21; Gregory Kent Stanley, *Before Big Blue: Sports at the University of Kentucky, 1880–1940* (Lexington: University of Kentucky Press, 1996), 7–8.

27. Walter Camp "The American Game of Football," *Harper's Weekly* (November 10, 1888), 858; Rader, *American Sports*, 84; John A. Blanchard, ed., *The H Book of Harvard Athletics, 1852–1922* (Harvard Varsity Club, 1923), 378. The last sentence reflects the ethnocentric assumption of U.S. citizens that they are the "Americans" while Canadians and Mexicans represent "others." American teams resumed play with Canadian schools after the turn of the century; see Norman E. Brown, "International Football Games May Follow Intersectional Ones," *Joliet Herald*, 1922, in *College Football Historical Society*, (November 1997), 17, for a resumption of a Syracuse–McGill series in 1921–1922.

28. Nelson, *Anatomy of a Game*, 50–53.

29. Richard Dott Papers, University of Michigan Archives; *NCAA News*, September 16, 1991, 8.

30. *Harvard College Report Upon Athletics* (Cambridge, MA: John Wilson & Son, 1888), 10, indicates that Harvard tried to ban commercialization to discourage professionalism as early as 1873. F. R. Vernon to Parke Davis, July 22, 1911; and Davis to Vernon, August 3, 1911, Reel 7 of Walter Camp Papers, Yale Archives. Walter Camp, "The Game and Laws of American Football," *Outing* (October 1887), 68 (quote).

31. Presbrey, *Athletics at Princeton*, 317.

32. Ibid, 317–318.

33. Athletic Committee Minutes, December 2, 1884, in Harvard Archives.

34. Ibid, November 22, 1883; December 10, 1883.

35. Morris A. Beale, *The History of Football at Harvard, 1874–1948* (Washington, DC: Columbia Pub. Co., 1948), 58–60.

36. Athletic Committee Minutes, December 2, 1884; January 6, 1885; January 4, 1886 in Harvard Archives; *Chicago Tribune*, November 27, 1884, 1.

37. "The Football Season of 1886," *Outing* (January 1887), 391–392; *The Graphic*, December 3, 1892, 409, in Stagg Papers, University of Chicago, Box 24, folder 2. For high school play in the 1880s, see *High School Journal*, 2:1 (October 1884), 2; Jeffrey Mirel, "From State Control to Institutional Control of High School Athletics: Three Michigan Cities, 1883–1905," *Journal of Social History*, 16 (1982), 82–99; 136; and Stephen Hardy, *How Boston Played: Sport, Recreation and Community, 1865–1915* (Boston: Northeastern University Press, 1982).

38. Alexander Johnston, "The American Game of Football," *Century*, 12 (1887), 898.

39. Ibid, 888–898; Walter Camp, "The Game and Laws of American Football," 68–76; "Football," *Outing* (January 1888), 376–381; Oriard, *Reading Football*, 28.

40. Johnston, "The American Game of Football," 891, 888, 893.

41. Camp, "The Game and Laws of American Football," 75–76; Oriard, *Reading Football*, 30, 31, draws the distinction between

American gamesmenship and British sportsmanship. See John Dizikes, *Sportsmen and Gamesmen* (Boston: Houghton Mifflin, 1981).

42. Walter Camp, "The American Game of Football," *Harper's
Weekly* (November 10, 1888), 858–859.

43. Knox cited in Blanchard, *The H Book of Harvard Athletics*,
389–390.

44. Ibid, 386; George H. Ade to Walter Camp, December 4, 1889,
in Camp Papers, Reel 1; *Boston Post*, November 25, 1889, clipping in
Harvard Archives, HVD 10889.2; Rader, *American Sports*, 136; Nelson, *Anatomy of a Game*, 577–587.

45. Lloyd M. Garrison, *Echoes of the Harvard-Yale Football Game
of 1890* (Cambridge, MA: Charles H. Thurston, 1890), 6 (quote);
Kemp P. Battle, *History of the University of North Carolina* (Spartanburg, SC: Reprint Co., 1974), 477.

46. Daniel M. Pearson, *Baseball in 1889: Players vs. Owner*
(Bowling Green, OH: Bowling Green University Popular Press,
1993).

47. Ralph Stone Papers, Box 1, University of Michigan Archives;
Blanchard, *H. Book of Harvard Athletics*, 390; Thomas H. Bergin,
The Game: The Harvard-Yale Football Rivalry, 1875–1983 (New
Haven: Yale University Press, 1984), 84–50; Weyand, *Saga of Ameri-
can Football*, 44–49; Walter Camp, "Football of 1893: Its Lessons and
Results," *Harper's Weekly* (February 3, 1894), 117 (quote). Davis,
Football, 83; and Presbrey, *Athletics at Princeton*, 336, claim devel-
opment of the wedge as early as 1884.

48. Leonard Wood to Walter Camp, November 19, 1893, Reel 18,
Camp Papers. The Camp Papers contain numerous solicitations for
coaches. John Craig, "Football on the Pacific Slope," *Outing* (Septem-
ber 1893), 448–458; Lovick Pierce Miles, "Football in the South,"
Outing (December 1894), 257–264; Bicentennial Football Classic
Historical Brief, provided by James Cuthbertson of Johnson C. Smith
University; Brad Fuqua, *Glory of the Gridiron*, n.d., College Football
Hall of Fame Archives; Nelson, *Anatomy of a Game*, 85.

49. A. A. Stagg to William Rainey Harper, November 25, 1890; and
A. A. Stagg to William Rainey Harper, November 28, 1891, on the
contract negotiations, in Box 14, folder 38, Harper Papers, University of Chicago, Special Collections; Lester, *Stagg's University*, 1, 15,
17, 28–30.

50. *Chicago Tribune*, Nov. 29, 1891, 6; John Charles Hibner, *The Rose Bowl, 1902–1929* (Jefferson, NC: McFarland & Co., 1993), 3; Lou Maysel, *Here Come the Texas Longhorns, 1893–1970* (Fort Worth: Stadium Pub. Co., 1970), 1–4; Nelson, *Anatomy of a Game*, 69–70, indicates that Culbertson suggested that Pudge Heffelfinger, Yale All-American and a native Minnesotan, and Parke Davis, a Princeton rival, would grace the field.

51. Clyde Bolton, *War Eagle: A Story of Auburn Football* (Huntsville, AL: Strode Publishers, 1973), 30–32; Bert Randolph Sugar, *The SEC: A Pictorial History of Southeastern Conference Football* (Indianapolis: Bobbs-Merrill Co., 1979), 96, 118; Steven W. Pope, "God, Games, and National Glory: Thanksgiving and the Ritual of Sport in American Culture, 1876–1926," *International Journal of the History of Sport*, 10 (August 1993), 242–249.

52. Richard Harding Davis, "The Thanksgiving Day Game," *Harper's Weekly* (December 9, 1893), 1170.

53. Ibid.

54. Francis A. Walker, "College Athletics," Phi Beta Kappa Address, June 29, 1893, 1, 13, in *Harvard Graduates Magazine*, 2:5 (September 1893), 1–18.

55. Albert B. Crawford, ed., *Football Y Men, 1872–1919* (New Haven: Yale University, 1962), 10, provides biographical sketches and career choices. See Frederic Cople Jaher, *The Urban Establishment: Upper Strata in Boston, New York, Charleston, Chicago, and Los Angeles* (Urbana: University of Illinois Press, 1982), 265–267, 520, 551, 728; and Westby and Sack, "The Commercialization and Functional Rationalization of College Football," on the transition in elites' institutional allegiance. Smith, *Big-Time Football at Harvard*, xv; College Football Historical Society Records; and Lester, *Stagg's University*, 11; Presbrey, *Athletics at Princeton*, 398.

56. Bergin, *The Game: The Harvard-Yale Football Rivalry, 1875–1983*, 59; *Harvard Graduates Magazine*, 3:11 (March 1895), 366–379, 395 (quote); 3:12 (June 1895), 520; 4:14 (December 1895), 273–280, Bob Royce, "1894: Who's No. 1?" *College Football Historical Society*, 8:4 (August 1995), 2–3.

57. *Chicago Tribune* Nov. 25, 1887, 1; Walter Camp, *The Book of Football* (New York: The Century Co., 1910), 125; Nelson, *Anatomy of a Game*, 56, 63–66; Weyand, *Saga of American Football*, 37–46.

58. Walter Camp, "Interference in Football," *Harper's Weekly*, November 19, 1892, 1115; Smith, *Big Time Football at Harvard*, 4–5, n. 3; Nelson, *Anatomy of a Game*, 74–75; Danzig, *History of American Football*, 25–28.

59. Eugene L. Richards, Jr., "Football in America," *Outing* (April 1885), 62–66, 62 (quote).

60. Lester, *Stagg's University*, 42; Hal D. Sears, "The Moral Threat of Intercollegiate Sports: An 1893 Poll of Ten College Presidents, and the End of 'The Champion Football Team of the Great West,' " *Journal of Sport History*, 19:3 (Winter 1992), 211–226; Jim L. Sumner, "John Franklin Crowell, Methodism, and the Football Controversy at Trinity College, 1887–1894," *Journal of Sport History*, 17 (Spring 1990), 5–20; Andrew Doyle, " 'Foolish and Useless Sport': The Southern Methodist Crusade Against Intercollegiate Football, 1890–1914," presented at the North American Society for Sport History Convention, University of Saskatchewan, 1994.

In addition to Camp's *Football Facts and Figures: a Symposium of Expert Opinions on the Game's Place in American Athletics* (New York: Harper and Bros., 1894), see Walter Camp, "A Plea for the Wedge in Football," *Harper's Weekly* (January 21, 1893), 67; Walter Camp, "The Current Criticism of Football," *Century*, 47 (February 1894), 633–634; and "Football in the Hands of Players," *Spalding's Official Foot Ball Guide*, 1895, as examples.

The Camp Papers, Reels 6, 9, 14, 15, 29, and boxes 43–45, folders 161–177, and 178–204 cover the questionnaire in a more comprehensive fashion.

Lodge's speech is in *Harvard Graduates Magazine*, 5:17 (September 1896), 66–68.

61. *Chicago Tribune*, Feb. 4, 1894, 7; A. A. Stagg correspondence, A. A. Stagg Papers, Box 50, folder 21; A. A. Stagg to Camp, Jan. 30, 1896, Camp Papers, Reel 16; Davis, *Football*, 93, 101, 111–113; Danzig, *History of American Football*, 28; *Proceedings of Intercollegiate Conference of Faculty Representatives* (Minneapolis: University Press, 1901), 25–32, University of Illinois Archives, Record Group 28/1/805; "Smart Move," *Purdue University Perspective*, (Summer 1995), 10–11.

Nelson, *Anatomy of Game*, 70–79, 83, 105–113, 123–135; Howard Henry and Percy Haughton to Walter Camp, June 24, 1910, Reel 9; and Palmer Pierce to Walter Camp, November 25, 1913, Reel 13, give an indication of the ongoing struggle over the rules.

62. A Yale Player, "The Development of Football," *Outing* (November 1889), 144–150; Walter Camp, "Winning a Football Goal," *The Outlook*, May 30, 1896, 980; *Chicago Times Herald*, November 30, 1895, clipping; and Philip S. Allen, "Football in Ninety-Five," *Monthly Maroon*, 2:1 (November 1903), 1–8, in Stagg Papers, Box 24, folder 2 on Rockefeller; Weyand, *Saga of American Football*, 53.

63. Recruiting efforts are detailed in Stagg Papers, Box 12, folders 2–5, Box 13, folders 6, 8; Edward S. Jordan, "Buying Football Victories," *Collier's*, November 11, 1905, 19–20, 23; Stanley, *Before Big Blue*, 25–30, 36–37; Lester, *Stagg's University*, 47–55; Board in Control of Intercollegiate Athletics, Box 1, folders 3, 5, University of Michigan Archives; E. L. Richards to Walter Camp, November 14, 1899; and December 15, 1890, in Camp Papers, Reel 15; and William H. Corbin to Walter Camp, February 2, 1894, Reel 6.

On spying, see William H. Corbin to Walter Camp, November 11, 1890, in Camp Papers, Reel 6; and Walter S. Holden to Ward Hughes, November 19, 1897, Board in Control of Intercollegiate Athletics, Box 1, folder 5, University of Michigan Archives.

On trick plays, see Danzig, *History of American Football*, 25–26, 85–87, 98–99, 103; Umphlett, *Creating The Big Game*, 92–93.

64. Bill Reid, to H. E. von Kersburg, n.d., Harvard Archives.

65. Arthur L. Evans, *Fifty Years of Football at Syracuse University, 1889–1939* (Syracuse University: Football History Committee, 1939), 18; H. E. von Kersburg to Bill Reid, July 17, 1948, in Harvard Archives, HUD 8010.

66. Paine, "The National View in College Sports," *Century* (November 1905), 102–104, cited in "Dr. Angell on Athletics," *Michigan Alumnus*, 12:109 (December 1905), 101–102.

67. Danzig, *History of American Football*, 29; "Pres. Eliot on Football," *The Outlook*, February 11, 1905, 363–364.

68. Considerable correspondence on the White House meeting is in the Charles Eliot Papers, Box 244, Harvard Archives; Camp Papers, Reels 6, 14, and 15; H. P. Judson to L. B. R. Briggs, December 11, 1905, in HUD 8010, Harvard Archives; Smith, *Big Time Football at Harvard*, xiii, 192–196, 205; Lester, *Stagg's University*, 74–77; University Presidents' Papers, Box 15, folder 7; University of Chicago, Special Collections.

69. See Ronald A. Smith, "Harvard and Columbia and a Reconsideration of the 1905-06 Football Crisis," *Journal of Sport History*, 8 (Winter 1981), 5–19; and Roberta Park, "Football to Rugby and

Back," *Journal of Sport History*, 11 (1984), 15–40. University President's Papers, Box 15, folder 7, University of Chicago, Special Collections; and James Orin Murfin Papers, Box 8, folder 2, University of Michigan Archives, on the situation in the Midwest.

Ronald A. Smith, "Prelude to the NCAA: Early Failures of Faculty Intercollegiate Athletic Control," in David K. Wiggins, ed., *Sport in America: From Wicked Amusement to National Obsession* (Champaign, IL: Human Kinetics, 1995), 151–162, details previous attempts at regulation.

70. Walter Camp remained as secretary until his death in 1925. Walter Camp, "Football Reform in the West," *The Outlook*, February 3, 1906, 248–249; Nelson, *Anatomy of a Game*, 105–113, 123–125.

The ongoing deliberations over rule changes can be traced in the Stagg Papers, Box 50, folder 1, (including the Minutes of the Football Rules Committee for 1906), folders 21–22, University of Chicago.

71. Nelson, *Anatomy of a Game*, 90–91, 141, 144–148; Weyand, *Saga of American Football*, 93–94, 98; Camp, *The Book of Foot-ball*, 290–291; Caspar Whitney, "Is Football Worthwhile?" *Collier's*, December 18, 1909, 13, 24–25; John Hammond Moore, "Football's Ugly Decades, 1893–1913," *Smithsonian Journal of History*, 11 (Fall 1967), 49–68; John S. Watterson, "The Football Crisis of 1909–1910: The Response of the Eastern 'Big Three,'" *Journal of Sport History* 8 (Spring 1981), 33–49; John S. Watterson, "The Death of Archer Christian: College Presidents and the Reform of College Football," *Journal of Sport History*, 22:2 (Summer 1993), 149–167.

72. Steven W. Pope, *Patriotic Games: Sporting Traditions in the American Imagination, 1876–1926* (New York: Oxford University Press, 1997); John Rickard Betts, *American's Sporting Heritage, 1850–1950* (Reading, MA: Addison-Wesley Pub. Co., 1974); Paul Boyer, *Urban Masses and Moral Order in America, 1820–1920* (Cambridge, MA: Harvard University Press, 1978).

73. Walter Camp, "Football," *Outing*, February 1891, 102–104; Allan G. Bogue, *Frederick Jackson Turner: Strange Roads Going Down* (Norman: University of Oklahoma Press, 1998); Carl N. Degler, *Out of Our Past: The Forces That Shaped Modern America* (New York: Harper Colophon Books, 1970), 122–134; Frederick L. Paxson, "The Rise of Sport," *Mississippi Valley Historical Review*, 4 (1917), 143–168.

74. Basketball and volleyball, touted as uniquely American, originated in the 1890s, the latter by a Canadian, James Naismith at Springfield College. Baseball, with its similarities to rounders and

cricket, faced dubious ancestry until the fallacious rendering of the Mills Commission in 1907. See Nancy B. Bouchier and Robert Knight Barney, "A Critical Examination of a Source on Early Ontario Baseball: The Reminiscences of Adam E. Ford," *Journal of Sport History*, 15:1 (Spring 1988), 75–90 for a Canadian claim to baseball.

Ronald A. Smith, "The Historic Amateur–Professional Dilemma in American College Sport," *British Journal of Sport History* 2:3 (December 1985), 221–231.

On new equipment, see Camp, *The Book of Foot-Ball*, 240–242; Weyand, *Saga of American Football*, 17; Umphlett, *Creating the Big Game*, 21–22, 28.

On strategic innovations, see Camp, "The Game and Laws of American Football;" Walter Camp, "Football Studies for Captain and Coach," *Outing* (November, 1892), 104–107; Camp, "Personality in Foot-Ball: A Consideration of the Contributions to the Progress of the Game by Certain Players and Coaches," *Century*, 57 (January 1910), 442–457; Weyand, *Saga of American Football*, 19, 24, 29, 33; Danzig, *History of American Football*, 18, 25–26, 28.

75. Stephen H. Hardy, "Entrepreneurs, Organizations and the Sports Marketplace," In S. W. Pope, ed., *The New American Sport History* (Urbana: University of Illinois Press, 1997) 341–365; Weyand, *Saga of American Football*, 11, 13; see correspondence regarding book ventures between Walter Camp and Loren Deland, in Camp Papers, Reel 7; Caspar Whitney and Camp, Reel 9, Yale Archives; and A. A. Stagg to Henry Williams, Box 7, folder 8, Stagg Papers, University of Chicago.

Early Yale accounts, 1875–1893, are in Box 30, folder 819, Camp Papers, Reel 20. See George Woodruff to Camp, January 24, 1903, Reel 18, for a surplus at Penn. Site and market negotiation is contained in Board in Control of Intercollegiate Athletics, Box 1, folder 5; and Box 48, University of Michigan Archives.

76. *President's Report, 1906–07*, 104, and University President's Papers, Box 15, folder 3, University of Chicago, Board in Control of Intercollegiate Athletics, Box 1, folder 1; and C. K. Adams to Prof. A. H. Pattengill, November 22, 1899, in Box 48, University of Michigan Archives; Pope, *Patriotic Games*, 89, on Harvard; Elliott Gorn and Warren Goldstein, *A Brief History of American Sports* (New York: Hill and Wang, 1993), 165, on Yale.

77. Stagg Papers, Box 25, folder 7.

78. James R. H. Wagner to Charles Baird (graduate football manager), November 1, 1901; November 5, 1901, Board in Control of Intercollegiate Athletics, Box 1 folder 5, University of Michigan

Archives. Additional correspondence indicates guarantees of $1,000 to $2,000 for regular season games.

79. Wagner to Baird, December 6, 1901; December 10, 1901, Board in Control of Intercollegiate Athletics, Box 1, folder 5, University of Michigan Archives.

80. Presbrey, *Athletics at Princeton*, 40; Camp, *The Book of Foot-Ball*, 72–75; *Chicago Tribune*, November 25, 1887, 1 (quote).

81. *Chicago Tribune*, November 27, 1891, 1.

82. Charles Baird to H. B. Christiancy, November 24, 1903, indicates $800 for press tickets to the Chicago-Michigan game that year, in Board in Control of Intercollegiate Athletics, Box 1, folder 5, University of Michigan Archives.

For regional games, see *Chicago Tribune*, Nov. 28, 1890, 1; Stanley, *Before Big Blue*, 26–29; and Michael Hurd, *Black College Football; 1892–1992: One Hundred Years of History, Education, and Pride* (Virginia Beach, VA: Donning Co., 1993), 29. The latter indicates the inclusion of black, southern schools in such rituals.

Horace Butterworth to Ward Hughes, Sept. 13, 1897 (quote); Oct. 18, 1897; Nov. 4, 1897, Board of Control of Intercollegiate Athletics, Box 1, folder 5, University of Michigan.

83. George W. Patterson notes, Box 8, folder 2 of James Orin Murfin Papers, University of Michigan.

84. Eric Hobsbawm and Terence Ranger, eds., *The Invention of Tradition* (Cambridge: Cambridge University Press, 1983); Paul Connerton, *How Societies Remember* (Cambridge: Cambridge University Press, 1991). For particulars of the process in the United States, see Michael Kammen, *Mystic Chords of Memory: The Transformation of Tradition in American Culture* (New York: Alfred A. Knopf, 1991); and David Glassberg, *American Historical Pageantry: The Uses of Tradition in the Early Twentieth Century* (Chapel Hill: University of North Carolina Press, 1990).

Clarence Herschberger, the Chicago punter, became the school's first All-American; in Stagg Papers, Box 30, folder 2.

85. Walter Camp, "Team Play in Foot-Ball," *Harper's Weekly*, Oct. 31, 1891, 845, cited in Alexander Nemerov, *Frederic Remington & Turn-of-the-Century America* (New Haven: Yale University Press, 1995), 57.

86. Presbrey, *Athletics at Princeton*, 399.

87. Connerton, *How Societies Remember*, 44–50; Oriard, *Reading Football*, analyzes the interpretive role of the media.

C. Ian Bailey and George H. Sage, "Values Communicated by a Sports Event: The Case of the Super Bowl," *Journal of Sport Behavior*, 11:3 (September 1988), 126–143; Lawrence A. Wenner, "The Super Bowl Pregame Show: Cultural Fantasies and Political Subtext," in Lawrence A. Wenner, ed. *Media, Sports and Society* (Newbury Park, CA: Sage Pub., 1989), 157–179.

Chapter 2

Holding the Line: Football
and Feminism

By the turn of the century women posed both an enigma
and a problem for men. The "new woman," as she was labeled,
wanted greater social, political, economic, and domestic freedom. The extensive, though hardly united, independence
movement, encompassed numerous spheres and affected not
only a transition in social norms, but in the roles and responsibilities previously deemed to be male preserves.

The American feminist movement took flight shortly after
the war of independence. Women clamored for educational
rights by the 1790s. Social reforms, temperance issues, abolition, and legal equality provided themes throughout the first
half of the nineteenth century, highlighted by the Seneca Falls
Convention in 1848. Annual conventions thereafter called for
property rights, suffrage, higher education, and jobs. Women
no longer viewed themselves as property and began contesting
husbands' traditional marriage rights in court. Between 1870
and 1910 seventeen referenda aimed at women's suffrage and
the National American Woman Suffrage Association num-
bered 2 million members by 1917. By the late nineteenth
century American women were moving away from the Victorian model of domesticity in ever increasing numbers and
middle class males feared not only the feminization of culture
but their own emasculation.[1]

The decades after 1880 proved especially troublesome for
men. Women gained the vote in the western states, which men
feared as a harbinger of shared power. In the East women's
clubs organized, bringing them outside the home and into the
civic and political arena. One group in particular, the Woman's

Christian Temperance Union (WCTU), established in 1873, threatened a traditional male pleasure. The influx of European immigrants after 1880, mostly young, single males, only reinforced the established bachelor subculture in America that revolved around drinking, gambling, whoring, and sports. By 1890, 42 percent of men remained single, and a 1905 Chicago survey found that 50 percent of that city's residents visited saloons on a given day. Neighborhood bars served multiple functions, not only as providers of food and drink; but as employment agencies, political headquarters, sports centers, and male refuges. Frances Willard, president of the WCTU, urged women to march for the closure of such establishments, a movement which threatened to prohibit alcohol and, for many males, a way of life.[2]

Women increasingly engaged themselves in the roles of social activists thereafter. During the 1880s women, led by Jane Addams and Ellen Gates Starr in Chicago and, later, Lillian Wald in New York, founded settlement houses in urban immigrant neighborhoods to help assimilate ethnic residents. Such caretaking, nurturing, and teaching roles bridged traditional roles for women but also brought them into the political realm as they engaged urban poverty, family life, and labor issues. Women became labor organizers, sometimes uniting middle and working class females in their attempts to gain better working conditions, better working hours, and better salaries. Such legislation favored all workers, including men, but the presence of women in the workplace threatened masculine pride and privilege. Each year brought more women into the workplace even as the industrial process displaced males. Before 1860, 90 percent of men enjoyed self-employment; by 1910 less than 33 percent worked for themselves. Women slowly intruded upon the male preserves of medicine and law as well, affecting the status of white-collar males.[3]

Women accounted for one-third of all college students by 1880, and nearly a half by 1920. Throughout that period more radical activists proposed ideas that upset traditional notions of morality and subserviency. Charlotte Perkins Gilman railed against females' subordination, while Margaret Sanger promoted birth control, and the anarchist, Emma Goldman, even advocated "free love" that eschewed the legal bounds of marriage. Even within the mainstream, women had already gained dominance in literary circles and among the progressive Protestant religious leadership by the late nineteenth century. Middle class males felt beleaguered and besieged.[4]

As early as 1877 the *Harvard Advocate* reprinted the qualms of Amherst students, who testified that

> ...we appreciate (women's) excellent qualities,...peculiar powers, peculiar charms...; but we are hardly ready to admit that the opposite sex surpasses us in intellect, and it is not very flattering to our pride to have our professors continually stirring us up, by telling how much more the "Smith College girls" are doing ... and how much more readily they grasp difficult points.[5]

Female incursion into traditional male spheres brought a backlash. Males argued that women were incapable of real intellectual work, lest they tax their delicate constitutions. George Romanes, writing in *Popular Science Monthly*, argued "that the average brain weight of women is about five ounces less than that of men...we should be prepared to expect a marked inferiority of intellectual power in the former." Edward Clarke, a Harvard medical professor, claimed that intense study by women caused neurasthenia, the nineteenth century equivalent of a nervous breakdown. G. Stanley Hall, the most prominent psychologist of the era, agreed, stating that "it was a pity to spoil a good mother to make a grammarian."[6]

Perhaps most devastating to men was the emergence of women into the male domain of sports. Women had long been engaged in leisurely activities, such as gymnastics (calisthenics), croquet, skating, and archery, conducting a national championship in the latter in 1879. But transitional sports that brought an element of power, like tennis in the 1880s, signaled a further transgression into the male sphere. Women's participation in such sports not only challenged the physicians' and psychologists' notions of female debility; but devalued their worth for males. Any sport played by women lost its symbolism as a marker of masculinity. Women's participation in the power sports of cycling and track and field soon followed, and female baseball teams barnstormed the country. Active sports required new apparel and women shed the corsets, petticoats, and hoop skirts that had previously encumbered them. The athletic "Gibson Girl" symbolized a new spirit of independence and vitality. Bloomer girls and speeding cyclists challenged males both symbolically and literally. In Atlanta, a preacher declared female cyclists to be possessed by the devil; other municipalities simply banned them from the road, albeit unsuccessfully. By 1899 the *New York Times* reported that a woman would ride 700 miles, paced by men along the way. Author Patricia Marks presented the males' dilemma.

> The New Woman as a figure who had simply followed a new dress fad was ultimately acceptable, because her frivolity was expected. The New Woman whose dress indicated a real change in lifestyle was considerably more threatening, not only because once she shifted her place in society everyone else had to make accommodation, but because she held the physiological key to the next generation.[7]

While women, and feminists in particular, threatened American patriarchal society at the turn of the century, they had not yet succeeded in abolishing it. Men still had a period, a historical bloc between 1880–1920, in which to reintroduce their hegemony. College men found football to be an antidote to encroaching females. Males at hundreds of college campuses in all regions adopted the game by 1900. Males who resided in cities and towns without colleges formed athletic clubs and fielded teams. Proponents rationalized its brutality, and extolled its scientific strategy and character building qualities. Boxing attracted men for the same reasons; but the taint of professionalism, its close ties to the bachelor subculture mired in drinking, gambling, and vice, and the involvement of the least reputable women made it unacceptable for the most proper gentlemen. The *Chicago Tribune* stated that

> Prize fights between men are beastly exhibitions, but there is unutterable loathsomeness in the worse brutality of abandoned, wretched women beating each other almost to nudity, for the amusement of a group of blackguards, even lower in the scale of humanity than the women themselves.[8]

Football, therefore, served both class and gender functions. As played in colleges, athletic clubs, and high schools, it was restricted to the upper classes. By virtue of its scientific strategies, tests of strength, power, and endurance, it further limited play to males.

A typical commentator proclaimed that "The intellectual vigor of the race, to say nothing of its physical prowess, can be maintained only by availing ourselves of the instinct to play."[9] The physical as well as the intellectual benefited according to football's advocates. Parke Davis, a former player and later a historian of the game, claimed that "the unusual vigor and physical condition which I enjoy to day (sic), I attribute solely to football..."[10] William James, the Harvard philosopher, favored sport as an antidote to the sedentary life and effeminacy. Another observer maintained that "As a manly game there is none to compare with it. No Miss Nancy is ever found on a football field."[11] The commentator referred to effeminate men; but his words were literally true. Football, more so than any other game, marginalized women, restricting them to spectatorial roles in the symbolic maintenance of gender relations. Males even retained cheerleading duties for more than 50 years, because the role required leadership of other men.[12]

The male-dominated media reinforced traditional Victorian functions for female spectators. Narratives, written by men for other men, often minimized and devalued women. As early as 1874 a reporter remarked that "The Harvard men were stripped of their shirts again and again, which caused the few ladies present to flutter about in pretty agitation as to what they *should* do."[13] Similarly, media accounts described or pictured beautiful, emotional young women worshipping heroic football players, or nurturing their wounds.[14] Even the foremost psychologist of the day agreed that such heroes deserved trophies. G. Stanley Hall stated that

> Glory, which is the reward of victory and makes the brave deserve the fair, is...never so great as when it is the result of conflict...military prowess has a strange fascination for the weaker sex, perhaps ultimately and biologically because it demonstrates the power to protect and defend. Power... has played a great role in sexual attraction.[15]

Theodore Roosevelt rationalized that "men can fight in defense of their rights....This certainly makes a powerful argument against putting the ballot into hands unable to defend it...."[16] Thus, football provided strong evidence that women could not participate fully in the game, so they were not entitled to a full share of its benefits. They remained property, in the form of trophies, or, at best, witnesses and sustainers of masculine predominance.

The chivalrous attitude persisted throughout the twentieth century. Oregon State coeds fostered an inadvertent victory in 1911 when their undue attention paid rival Oregon players incensed their male classmates, who reclaimed their honor and their perceived territory with a 16–0 win. The 1918 Rose Bowl game featured two military service contingents, the Mare Island Marines and the Camp Lewis Army team. A woman, garbed as the Goddess of Liberty and escorted by military officers, sang the "Star Spangled Banner" before the Marines prevailed in a game of "old-time football with mass plays." After turning over the proceeds to the Red Cross they were feted in a victory party at which they earned a kiss from the wife of the commanding officer.[17]

Nearly twenty years later the high school championship of Chicago brought the largest crowd ever to witness a football game, as 120,000 jammed Soldier Field. Star players received due adulation from the media, which also emphasized the twin drum majorettes and a girlfriend, mother, and grandmother, in supporting roles.[18] At the end of the twentieth century little has changed. In H. G. Bissinger's study of a Texas high school team, girls considered it an honor to be chosen a Pepette, one assigned to individual players in order to cater, serve, and glorify them.[19]

Football enabled men to define a limited role for women, as it defined the characteristics of true manhood. As women intruded into male spheres, the traditional traits of masculinity subsided and new ones emerged. That transition proved most difficult for middle class men. The working class, engaged in physically demanding occupations and more active or homosocial leisure lifestyles that centered on neighborhood saloons, remained closer to the physicality and prowess that had traditionally defined manhood. The growing middle class, however, assumed more sedentary, white collar positions devoid of activity. In a search for lost values, antimodernism and antiintellectualism prevailed, symbolically portrayed in football. W. H. Harper, a Yale alumnus who would become the editor of *Chicago Commerce*, wrote to Walter Camp in 1891, stating that "A man is doing a good deal who helps to popularize the manliest sport in Christendom."[20] Three years later, John Poe, a lawyer and former Princeton player, stated that "the game is a thorough education in all the qualities that go to make a manly man. It teaches obedience, self-restraint, unselfishness + (sic) calls for the greatest amount of pluck, self denial (sic) quickness of thought + action."[21] Men of action superseded scholars, and feats of physical prowess glorified the body. Body culture duly exhibited by the likes of Eugen Sandow and Bernarr MacFadden, won acclaim. The art of Frederic Remington and Thomas Eakins portrayed cowboys and muscular athletes and Gilbert Patten's Frank Merriwell novels taught boys to become men.[22]

As classical Greek sculpture portrayed morphological ideals so, too, did football represent exemplary models. Football players stood distinct from common, less active men by their dress. Canvas jackets, jerseys, and protective equipment marked their participation in the arena of courage. Theodore Roosevelt remarked that

> The credit belongs to the man who is actually in the arena, whose face is marred by dust, and sweat, and blood; who strives valiantly, who errs and comes short again and again because there is no effort without error and short-comings; but who actually strives to do the deed, who knows the great devotion; who spends himself in a worthy cause, who at the best knows in the end the high achievement of triumph and who at worst, if he fails while daring greatly knows his peace shall never be with those timid and cold souls who know neither victory nor defeat.[23]

By the 1890s football players wore their hair long to serve as extra padding, for helmets were not required until 1939. Lettermen's sweaters provided added distinction and further public display of honored status. Athletes enjoyed a particular esteem among fellow students and a football player became a

"man among men" and a "big man on campus." Lest anyone
harbor doubts, any trace of femininity earned exclusion. Although Syracuse defeated Hamilton in an 1889 field day, their
pink and blue uniforms brought derision. Athletes, students,
and alumni quickly decided that such colors were inconsistent
with prowess and opted for orange as a replacement to the
pink. Likewise the University of Chicago replaced its original
yellow uniforms with a bloody maroon. Coach Stagg admitted
that the yellow "had a regrettable symbolism." In 1895, David-
son, which had also sported the pink and blue, changed to a
more virile and sanguine black and red. Men thus consciously
constructed for themselves and other men both the meanings
and symbols of masculinity.[24]

Men proclaimed that it required strong male leadership, in
the form of captains or coaches, to elicit results; a cultural
precedent to contemporary debates over same-sex marriages
and male role models in the African-American community. W.
Cameron Forbes, the grandson of Ralph Waldo Emerson, felt
awe for football coaches, whom he considered the "greatest
men on earth" as a young man. He assumed coaching duties
at Harvard before embarking on a diplomatic career as gov-
ernor-general of the Philippines and ambassador to Japan.[25]
When Amos Alonzo Stagg indicated an interest in Leo De Tray,
a local football star in Chicago, his high school principal
responded that

> De Tray possessed (sic) of a tremendous nervous energy....
> Frankly there has been too much of the "eternal feminine"
> in his life. By that I mean the persons who have most
> influenced his life thus far have been women. Now I feel that
> he needs the influence of strong, manly men....He is emo-
> tional, impulsive, with high strung nerves and as many
> moods as a French verb.[26]

With Stagg's guidance De Tray gained All-American status,
but lost an eye in the process. To become men boys had to
endure such physical and emotional pain. At Harvard, Coach
Cameron Forbes eschewed doctors, medicine, and even time-
outs, lest his men become "babies." Despite debilitation and
painful injuries players were admonished to "show their sand"
in an attempt to beat Yale. A Yale professor assured Coach

Walter Camp that injured athletes would play "if I have to stand over (sic) with a whip."[27] Peer pressure, perhaps more so than adulation, spurred such efforts. A St. Louis teacher maintained that "boys (were) forced onto teams by strong public sentiment which declared it his 'duty' to play or be called a 'mollycoddle' or a 'sissy-boy.'"[28]

Boys and men thus proved their manhood to other males and football served as a public stage. Losses meant dishonor and impugned one's masculinity. When Harvard defeated Yale in 1898 students staged a bonfire "to burn the remnants of the losing period."[29] Despite its academic prestige Harvard still felt the need for football glory. After suffering three straight shutout losses to Yale it offered Bill Reid $7,000 to become its coach and reclaim its dignity in 1905. Reid put priorities in order by stating that "I don't care how much of a student a fellow cares to be....I don't see how a man can help feeling that hardly anything is more important than to beat Yale."[30] Also, as the United States pondered entry into World War I, Tad Jones, the Yale coach, implored his charges in all earnestness before the 1916 engagement. "You are now going out to play football against Harvard, never again in your whole life will you do anything so important."[31] Notre Dame students mocked unmanly behavior before 120,000 at the 1927 contest against the University of Southern California in Chicago in a satirical halftime show that featured teams clad in tutus prancing about the field in a game of tag football. The farce clearly defined real football as a rugged, heterosexual activity played by true men.[32]

Aggressive, even violent manhood served as a counterpoint to effeminacy. A popular ditty of the 1890s described game preparations:

> Just bring along the ambulance,
> And call the Red Cross nurse,
> Then ring the undertaker up,
> And make him bring a hearse;
> Have all the surgeons ready there,
> For they'll have work today,
> Oh, can't you see the football teams
> Are lining up to play.[33]

The most aggressive players earned the highest praise. All-American Hector Cowan, a Princeton divinity student who scored seventy-nine touchdowns, was said to "fear God and no one else."[34] Frank Hinkey of Yale weighed only about 150 pounds but became a media star. One newspaper claimed that he was a "brutal fellow, born slugger without the smallest pretension to gentlemanhood."[35] Most, however, lionized his fierce and punishing performances. Hinkey's play on the field exhibited homicidal tendencies; but was characterized by the media as public acts of bravado. Even his own teammates feared practice sessions; yet they twice elected him captain, and he made Camp's All-America team four straight years.

Within such an atmosphere the death toll inevitably mounted. Still, males extolled its virtues. One college president opined that "I would rather see our youth playing football with the danger of a broken collar-bone occasionally than to see them dedicated to croquet."[36] Another claimed that "an able bodied young man who cannot fight physically can hardly have a true sense of honor, and is generally a milksop, a lady-boy or a sneak. He lacks virility, his masculinity does not ring true."[37]

When mounting casualties engendered calls for reform opponents of the game faced ostracism. A proponent remarked that

> the sport can never suffer...unless it is legislated against by Presidents of colleges, who I am sorry to say have missed their gender, and should be at the head of some seminary, where their ideas would be more in keeping with those entrusted to their care.[38]

When a few brave presidents actually moved to address the issue, Coach Bill Reid reported to Walter Camp from California, "As you probably know, the universities of this coast have become so effeminate as to adopt Rugby football in place of our own game."[39] The perceived correlation of effeminacy with a lack of leadership again reinforced gender stereotypes.

Given the budding of feminism over the past 200 years and its impending bloom at the turn of the century the process of male predominance and its cultural entrenchment in the

values of football could hardly have been one of passive com-
pliance. Women reacted to football in various ways. In the late
nineteenth century women were just beginning to define their
own sporting culture. In 1894 Mary Taylor Bissell, a female
physician, wrote that

> ...so long as baseball and football and the boat race stand
> for the national expression of athletics, the experience of
> girls in any similar department will seem like comparing
> moonlight unto sunlight, and water unto wine....The spirit
> for physical recreation has invaded the atmosphere of the
> girl's life as well as that of the boy, and demands considera-
> tion from her standpoint.[40]

The new sport of basketball, rather than football, sparked
women's play in the 1890s and fostered both philosophical and
physiological debates over the nature of competitive and
strenuous athletics for women. Doctors contended that hu-
mans had limited vital energy and that women needed to
conserve theirs for reproductive functions, while female physical educators allowed for moderate exertion. The focus of
female leaders and mostly male physicians on basketball and
the cycling craze of the 1890s provided males with a relative
lack of feminine opposition to football, and a historical bloc in
which to establish its viability and its inherent cultural symbolism.[41]

Not all women assumed disinterested or passive roles however. Both Alice Camp and Stella Stagg, coaches' wives, fulfilled responsibilities that would merit assistant coach status
today. Mrs. Camp observed the Yale practices, then reported
her findings to her busy husband, who directed the team
captains. Mrs. Stagg even charted plays from the press box
for her spouse. In 1913 Charlene Burckhart, who had participated in sports at Vassar College, became the acknowledged
assistant coach of a football team. Bonnie Rockne later became a chief hagiographer in promoting her husband's legend.
None of these women could be considered feminists; their
actions upheld the status quo.[42]

Other women might have been expected to address the
numerous moral issues associated with football, such as brutality, cheating, and the intemperate revelry that accompa-

nied games. On the few occasions when female reporters covered football they offered no chastisement, and even reinforced some Victorian chivalric attitudes. In one case the reporter was saved from a team prank by the gallant captain, while another concerned herself with socialites attending the game and girls who wanted to hug a gladiator.[43] Such narratives only reinforced the stereotypes of the defenseless, frivolous, and romantic female.

Women served as recipients or the audience for male actors, who played the game both on and off the field. Though confined to spectatorial roles at male performances, participation of any kind brought gradual change in Victorian tenets of decorum. Football, like other forms of commercialized amusement, removed women from assigned domesticity. By the late nineteenth century women attended stage plays, vaudeville shows, public lecture halls, and sporting events. By the 1870s, art exhibitions by Thomas Eakins featured lightly clad, muscular athletes. George Bellows's boxers shed even more clothing, and by the turn of the century sculptors showcased reproductions of classical Greek nudes. Literature, too, offered such forbidden pleasures, as in Jack London's *The Game*, where the fiancé of a boxer is both repulsed and attracted by his body and brutal occupation. London rationalized the paradox as a Darwinian impulse to attract a strong mate.[44]

Sporting events, when combined with the introduction of cinema in the 1890s, produced a virtual assault on Victorian mores, and demonstrated that women were not immune to erotic impulses. Boxing films, which showed nearly naked men, produced titillation and an aspect of voyeurism previously denied women. Newspapers noted the sizable number of women attending such performances and theater owners scheduled matinees to accommodate them. Physical culture performances, too, like those of strongmen Eugen Sandow and Bernarr MacFadden, exposed the nearly naked male form to female view. Women bought nude photos of Sandow, requested private exhibitions, and paid to feel his muscles. Such performances, ironically, produced male sex objects, and the media idolization of football players cast them in the same light.[45]

Women, like men, solicited tickets for the biggest games, where the newspapers gave women uncommon recognition amidst the social spectacle. High school girls showed their school spirit by attendance at league games in Chicago during the 1880s. Despite any philosophical differences with Amos Alonzo Stagg at Chicago, Marion Talbot and Agnes Wayman proved major supporters of the football team. Wayman, a member of the women's physical education department, led rallies for the players; while Talbot, as Dean of Women, organized cheers for the women's separate rooting section, even offering money prizes for the best lyrics. Nor was Chicago unique. Southern women fervently supported their teams and even young girls bet on games in Kentucky. In an 1892 game against Georgia "One charming and gentle lady from Auburn in her excitement broke her parasol over the head and shoulders of a gentlemen in front of her whom she had never seen before." At Oregon State female students provided the post-game musical entertainment, and Bessie Smith served as secretary of the first students' athletic union. Football games provided one of the few means to limited inclusion in campus activities for some women at Berkeley, where they sang and cheered, albeit in segregated cheering sections. At Harvard Margaret Farlow started her football scrapbook in 1892 in which she kept preseason forecasts, players' pictures, notes, and biographies as she followed their careers over the years. In that same year female students sewed the uniforms for the Livingstone players when they opposed Biddle in the first game between black colleges. Even Mabel Lee, a physical educator, idolized the football coach as an undergraduate at Coe College. She thrilled upon meeting Ted Coy, the Yale star, when she attended Wellesley. Such women did not share the feminist concerns of the pioneering leaders during football's formative years.[46]

The brutality of the game created horrid injuries that repulsed most women, further reinforcing Victorian perceptions of the weaker sex. Newspapers recorded the increasing number of football deaths in sensational fashion, including the mournings of the grieving mothers. But even some of these upheld the game. When Richard "Von" Gammon was killed in a game between Georgia and Virginia in 1897, his own mother protested the Georgia legislature's attempt to ban football. In 1910 the mother of the Texas manager hosted a posh post-season dinner for the team. *Outlook* published an article by Grace Sharp that same year, entitled "Mothers and the Game," and admitted "that the mother side has not been heard" after four players died in separate incidents on the same day in 1909. Sharp criticized the emphasis on football, the antiintellectualism on college campuses, and college presidents' concern over increasing enrollments and football victories. Yet the editors ran an introduction to the piece indicating their disagreement, but allowing for its "maternal" concerns.[47]

Sharp's was practically the lone voice of feminine opposition acknowledged by the press. Such marginalization of the female voice was an old tactic, employed often by ancient Greek dramatists. While editors printed an abundance of muckraking articles on football to increase sales, they overwhelmingly favored male viewpoints, and influential proponents of football presented decidedly biased accounts. In his 1894 book, *Football Facts and Figures*, Walter Camp published only supportive testimonials; and when Caspar Whitney asked "Is Football Worth While?" after the 1909 carnage, only one of eighteen printed responses opposed the game.[48]

While such men undoubtedly posed a barrier to any feminist voice, social class precluded any uniform resistance to male hegemony. Many, if not most, of the feminist leaders held bourgeois roots and values. Despite its negative features, football's organization, specialization, and commercialization reinforced the capitalist structure and any thorough criticism of the game may have endangered their own self-interest. For many of the early college women social class took precedence over gender.[49]

Another possibility for the lack of feminine opposition rests in the sheer volume of social reform on the feminists' agenda. Temperance, suffrage, equal rights, education, and labor issues left no time for the rehabilitation of male sports. Reform-minded female physical educators simply proposed their own noncompetitive model and left the men to squabble over football. Wives of some Harvard professors joined the vanguard of the women's movement but did not oppose their husbands' endorsement of the aggressive, violent, and all-male activity. Although they questioned biological determinism and culturally assigned gender roles, it is unlikely that such women even perceived the game as a cultural threat.[50]

The Woman's Christian Temperance Union even used football to promote its cause. Except for one editorial, written by a man, which opposed brutality and antiintellectualism, the WCTU made no formal opposition to the game. To the contrary, it solicited and printed testimonials from the major football powers as to the benefits of temperance for athletes.[51]

While working class women fought the social system over labor and educational issues, they too saw no threat in football. Congruent with their own lives mired in physicality, football valued prowess, and accorded their husbands and sons much needed income opportunities on the fledging professional circuits. When two Pennsylvania teams played in 1895, a newspaper reported that

> Not a female in the burg could be seen who did not wear the colors of the football team...noisy delegations of Greensburgers invaded the powerful village, but...loyal female Latrobists glanced disdainfully at the shouting marchers, and some even grew livid with rage. This was the case among old and young. An old lady turned her back after spitting at a Greensburg crowd and then defiantly waved a yard or more of red and blue ribbon.[52]

At least one neophyte pro team disbanded, however, when the young women of Warren, Ohio took a stand in 1904. The newspaper reported that "The sweethearts of some of the players told them if they played they need not call on them again."[53] It left unclear their motive, whether opposition to professionalism, brutality, or injury to potential husbands is unknown.

Perhaps the ultimate test of masculine allegiance to football occurred amidst the brutality controversy in 1907. Anna T. Jeanes, a millionaire heiress, died without relatives and bequeathed her coal and mineral rights to Swarthmore College on the condition that it abolish its intercollegiate athletic program. It marked the most significant effort by a woman to change the aggressive, commercial, patriarchal ideology of sport in the United States. The gift could have provided

millions to the school's endowment; and President Joseph
Swain consulted twenty-five of his peers for advice. Only two
years before a Swarthmore game triggered a movement to
abolish football when Penn triple-teamed its All-American
lineman, Robert Maxwell. A photo of Maxwell's face, covered
in blood, with a broken nose, and both eyes swollen shut even
brought a call for reform from President Theodore Roosevelt.
Swain suspended play for one season; but ultimately he declined acceptance, rather than forego athletic competition.[54]

Other women supported football for religious reasons. For
Catholics, football served as a holy crusade. Father John
O'Hara declared that

> Notre Dame football is a spiritual service because it is
> played for the honor and glory of God and of his Blessed
> Mother. When St. Paul said "Whether you eat or drink, or
> whatever else you do, do all for the glory of God," he included
> football.[55]

Despite such ahistorical exegesis, nuns supported the team
wholeheartedly. They taught Catholic school children to pray
for victory each week, while the nuns offered rosaries for a
win. They even sang the victory march before the game and
expounded in "a verbal rhapsody over some of the players" at
one convent. A participant theorized "...isn't it to the glory of
the Church to prove that her system of Catholic education can
produce men strong in body and in mind?"[56] In such cases,
religion proved stronger than gender.

Given limited evidence one cannot conclude that women
abdicated control of football issues to men, nor did they
necessarily endorse male cultural constructs in the shaping
of the football culture. Most feminists seemingly ignored the
relatively innocuous activity; while those who challenged it
were muted by male command of the media. Some may have
accepted football as the scientific arena that tested the pre-
cepts of Social Darwinism. Class and religion further faction-
alized any potential for uniform resistance, and the evidence
suggests a degree of female support for football that transcended age cohorts. The failure to present a concerted resistance, however, produced an inevitable result. As feminism

eroded male dominance in social, political, economic, and educational domains, football provided compensation for males.

The absence of a unified female opposition to the development and growth of football and its inherent value system allowed for its entrenchment in American culture. Football coaches, in conjunction with male political leaders, male physicians, and male psychologists reacted to the perceived feminization of culture by creating a new definition of masculinity as tough, aggressive, competitive, virile, and violent. G. Stanley Hall asserted that "too much association with girls diverts the youth from developing his full manhood."[57] Men taught boys and other men the desired qualities, and were paid handsomely for their efforts. Many coaches received and still receive higher salaries than college professors; but at the turn of the century such payments covered only the three month football season. Women, perceived as culprits in the process of emasculation, lost what little intellectual value they had gained. By 1908 Amos Alonzo Stagg earned $3,500; while Gertrude Dudley, the women's physical education director at Chicago, got only $50. While women continued their struggle in other social spheres, Theodore Roosevelt observed that the "football field is the only place where masculine supremacy is incontestable."[58] Succeeding generations perpetuated the cult and the process of masculinity. In 1931 E. K. Hall, chairman of the football rules committee, demanded that "In these soft days of movies, autos and mushy social weekends let's preserve in all its virility the ruggedest game we have left."[59] Such male socialization patterns thus taught beliefs and behaviors that reinforced patriarchy and dominance rationalized as mental, physical, and moral development.[60] Such character building and leadership qualities were deemed essential as the United States embarked on its own quest for empire at the turn of the century and thereafter as it engaged in worldwide conflict.

Notes

1. Nancy Woloch, "Feminist Movement," in Eric Foner and John Garraty, eds., *The Reader's Companion to American History* (Boston: Houghton Mifflin, 1991), 391–394; E. Anthony Rotundo, *American*

Manhood: Transformations in Masculinity from the Revolution to the Modern Era (New York: Basic Books, 1993); Ann Douglas, *The Feminization of American Culture* (New York: Anchor Books, 1977); Lynn D. Gordon, *Gender and Higher Education in the Progressive Era* (New Haven: Yale University, 1990), 13–51; Hendrik Hartog, "Lawyering, Husbands' Rights, and the 'Unwritten Law' in Nineteenth Century America," *Journal of American History* 84 (June 1997), 67–96; Stanley Coben, *Rebellion Against Victorianism: The Impetus for Cultural Change in 1920s America* (New York: Oxford University Press, 1991), 94.

2. Marion Talbot, *The Education of Women* (Chicago: University of Chicago, 1910), 48–49, indicates women's suffrage in Colorado, Idaho, Utah, and Wyoming. See Sarah Barringer Gordon, "The Liberty of Self-Degradation: Polygamy, Woman Suffrage, and Consent in Nineteenth Century America," *Journal of American History* (Dec. 1996), 815–847, on the particular dilemma in Utah. Jon M. Kingsdale, " 'The Poor Man's Club': Social Functions of the Urban Working-Class Saloon," *American Quarterly,* 25 (October 1973), 472–489; Perry Duis, *The Saloon: Public Drinking in Chicago and Boston, 1880–1920* (Urbana: University of Illinois Press, 1983).

3. Mina Carson, *Settlement Folk: Social Thought and the American Settlement Movement, 1885–1930* (Chicago: University of Chicago Press, 1990); Patricia Marks, *Bicycles, Bangs, and Bloomers: The New Woman in the Popular Press* (Lexington: University Press of Kentucky, 1990), 116–146; Michael S. Kimmel, "Men's Response to Feminism at the Turn of the Century," *Gender and Society,* 1–3 (Sept. 1987), 261–283; See Mark C. Carnes and Clyde Griffen, eds., *Meanings for Manhood: Constructions of Masculinity in Victorian America* (Chicago: University of Chicago Press, 1990), 195, on males' attempt to bar women from the professions.

4. Gordon, *Gender and Higher Education,* 2; Rotundo, *American Manhood,* 209–246; Michael Oriard, *Reading Football,* 250; Douglas, *The Feminization of American Culture,* 80–117.

5. *Harvard Advocate,* 24:7 (Dec. 14, 1877), 80.

6. George J. Romanes, "Mental Differences of Women and Men," *Popular Science Monthly* (August 1887), 383–401, cited in Marks, *Bicycles, Bangs, and Bloomers,* 103; Kim Townsend, *Manhood at Harvard: William James and Others* (New York: W.W. Norton), 1996, 203–209, (quote, 207).

7. Illustrator Charles Dana Gibson began portraying the new woman as an athlete in the 1890s. *Boston Globe,* July 4, 1883; n.p.;

Mar. 18, 1894, n.p.; *Outing* (Sept. 1884), 477; "Lawn Tennis in the South," in *Outing* (March 1889), 496–504; C. R. Yates, "Lawn Tennis on the Pacific Coast," *Outing* (July 1890), 271–279; "Lawn Tennis in California," *Overland Monthly* (Oct. 1892), 363–376; *Sporting and Theatrical Journal,* August 16, 1884, 217–219; June 20, 1885, 9; *Atlanta Constitution,* July 14, 1895, 14; *Chicago Tribune,* July 8, 1884, 6; July 31, 1895, 6; Nov. 19, 1895; *New York Times,* Sept. 18, 1899, 4; Bryson, "Sport and the Maintenance of Masculine Hegemony," 349–360; Roberta J. Park, "Physiologists, Physicians, and Physical Educators: Nineteenth Century Biology and Exercise, Hygienic and Educative," *Journal of Sport History,* 14 (Spring 1987), 28–60; Marks, *Bicycles, Bangs, and Bloomers,* 147, 208 (quote).

8. *Tribune* cited in Bessie Louise Pierce, *A History of Chicago* (New York: Alfred A. Knopf, 1940), Vol. 2, 468; Brad Fuqua, *Glory of the Gridiron,* n.d., College Football Hall of Fame Archives, South Bend, IN; Oriard, *Reading Football,* 248.

9. John Corbin, "The Modern Chivalry," *Atlantic Monthly,* 89 (May 1902), 601–611 (quote, 603).

10. Parke Davis to Walter Camp, Mar. 18, 1894, Reel 7, Camp Papers.

11. Townsend, *Manhood at Harvard,* 171–172; Frank R. Peters to Walter Camp, Mar. 29, 1894, Reel 14, Camp Papers, (quote).

12. Catriona M. Parratt, "From the History of Women in Sport to Women's Sport History: A Research Agenda," in D. Margaret Costa and Sharon R. Guthrie, eds., *Women in Sport: Inter-Disciplinary Perspectives* (Champaign, IL: Human Kinetics, 1994), 11; College Football Historical Society, 8:2 (Feb. 1995), 11, lists Marian Draper as the first female cheerleader for Tulane in 1924. Mary Ellen Hanson, *Go! Fight! Win! Cheerleading in American Culture* (Bowling Green, OH: Bowling Green University Popular Press, 1995), 15, states that Trinity (San Antonio) had 15 women on its 1923 pep squad.

13. *Yale Record,* May 27, 1874, 419–420.

14. Richard Harding Davis, "The Thanksgiving Day Game," *Harper's Weekly,* Dec. 9, 1893, 1170; Walter Camp, *The Book of Foot-ball* (New York: Century, 1910), 72–76; Oriard, *Reading Football,* 109–110, 247–276.

15. Hall, cited in Robin Lester, *Stagg's University,* 36–37.

16. Theodore Roosevelt, "Practicality of Equalizing Men and Women Before the Law," June 30, 1880, in Charles W. Eliot Papers, Harvard University, HUC 6879.62.

17. OSU Football: Celebrating 100 Years. 1893–1993, 9; Hibner, *The Rose Bowl,* 34–41.

18. *Chicago Tribune,* Nov. 26, 1937, 19; Nov. 28, 1937, 1.

19. H. G. Bissinger, *Friday Night Lights,* 45–6, 136–7.

20. W. H. Harper to Walter Camp, Nov. 25, 1891, Camp Papers, Reel 9.

21. John P. Poe to Walter Camp, Mar. 15, 1894, Camp Papers, Reel 14.

22. Townsend, *Manhood at Harvard;* Mark C. Carnes and Clyde Griffen, eds., *Meanings for Manhood: Constructions of Masculinity in Victorian America* (Chicago: University of Chicago Press, 1990); Jon M. Kingsdale, "The Poor Man's Club"; T. J. Jackson Lears, *No Place of Grace: Antimodernism and the Transformation of American Culture, 1880–1920* (New York: Pantheon, 1981); David L. Chapman, *Sandow the Magnificent: Eugen Sandow and the Beginnings of Bodybuilding* (Urbana: University of Illinois Press, 1994); Robert Ernst, *Weakness is a Crime: The Life of Bernarr MacFadden* (Syracuse, NY: Syracuse University Press, 1991); Michael Hatt, "Thomas Eakins' Salutat," in Kathleen Adlee and Marcia Pointon, eds., *The Body Imaged: The Human Form and Visual Culture Since the Renaissance* (New York: Cambridge University Press, 1993), 57–69; John Levi Cutler, *Gilbert Patten and His Frank Merriwell Saga: A Study in Sub-Literary Fiction, 1896–1913* (Orono, ME: University of Maine Press, 1934).

23. *Harvard Graduates Magazine,* 2:5 (Sept. 1893) 17–18, draws the connection between Greek art, sport, and the body; Theodore Roosevelt address at Sorbonne, 1910, in Mario R. DiNunzio, ed., *Theodore Roosevelt: An American Mind* (New York: St. Martin's Press, 1994), xiii.

24. Evans, *Fifty Years of Football at Syracuse,* 16, 167–169; Lester, *Stagg's University,* 22; Patrick B. Miller, "The Manly, the Moral, and the Proficient: College Sport in the New South," *Journal of Sport History,* 24:3 (Fall 1997), 285–316.

25. W. Cameron Forbes, *Football Notebook,* 1901, 2, in Harvard Archives, HUD 10897.24; Pope, *Patriotic Games,* 100.

26. Lewis A. Wilcox to A. A. Stagg, Stagg Papers, Box 13, folder 6, University of Chicago.

27. Lester, *Stagg's University,* 253–254, fn. 45; Forbes, *Football Notebook,* 1901, Harvard Archives,1–2, 9, 12, 17; Eugene L. Richards to Walter Camp, Oct. 30, 1889, Reel 15, Camp Papers.

28. Calvin Milton Woodward, "An Estimate of the Value of Football," Jan. 1910, in Camp Papers, Box 51, folder 1, Yale University.

29. *Boston Globe,* Nov. 22, 1898 (clipping), Harvard Archives, HUD 10898.

30. Smith, *Big Time Football at Harvard,* xiii, xv.

31. Tom Perrin, *Football: A College History* (Jefferson, NC: McFarland & Co., 1987), 89.

32. Sperber, *Shake Down the Thunder,* 151–152.

33. Michael D. Smith, "A Typology of Sports Violence," in Stanley Eitzen, ed., *Sport in Contemporary Society* (New York: St. Martin's Press, 1993), 87–88.

34. Alexander M. Weyand, *The Saga of American Football,* 34.

35. Ronald A. Smith, ed., *Big-Time Football at Harvard,* 313.

36. Father John Cavanaugh of Notre Dame, cited in Caspar Whitney, "Is Football Worth While?" *Collier's,* Dec. 18, 1909, 25.

37. H. Addington Bruce, "The Psychology of Football," *Outlook,* 96 (Nov. 5, 1910), 541–545.

38. Frank R. Peters to Walter Camp, March 29, 1894, Camp Papers, Reel 14, Yale University Archives.

39. William Reid, Jr., to Walter Camp, Feb. 28, 1908, Camp Papers, Reel 14.

40. Mary Taylor Bissell, "Athletics of City Girls," *Popular Science Monthly* (Dec. 1894), 145–153.

41. Patricia Vertinsky, *The Eternally Wounded Woman: Women, Exercise and Doctors in the Late Nineteenth Century* (Manchester: Manchester University Press, 1990); Susan Cahn, *Coming on Strong: Gender and Sexuality in Twentieth-Century Women's Sport* (New York: Free Press, 1994), 23–30; Jack Berryman, ed., "Sport, Exercise, and American Medicine," *Journal of Sport History,* 14:1 (Spring 1987), 5–76; Roberta J. Park, "Physiology and Anatomy are Destiny!?: Brains, Bodies and Exercise in Nineteenth Century American

54. Smith, *Sports and Freedom*, 209–212; Richard Pagano, "Robert 'Tiny' Maxwell," *College Football Historical Society*, 1:4 (May 1988), 1–3.

55. Murray Sperber, *Shake Down the Thunder*, 399–400.

56. Sister M. Helen, "The Power Behind the Team," *Notre Dame Alum.ius* (March 1936), 156, 160. See Gerald R. Gems, "The Prep Bowl: Football and Religious Acculturation in Chicago," *Journal of Sport History* (Fall 1996), 74–92, on the phenomenon of Catholic football.

57. Hall, *World's Work*, 1908, cited in Townsend, *Manhood at Harvard*, 207.

58. David Glassberg, *American Historical Pageantry*, 2; Chantal Mouffe, "Hegemony and New Political Subjects: Toward a New Concept of Democracy," in Cary Nelson and Lawrence Grossberg, eds., *Marxism and the Interpretation of Culture* (Urbana: University of Illinois Press, 1988), 89–104; Stagg Papers, Box 21, folder 7, University of Chicago; Joan S. Hult, "The Story of Women's Athletics: Manipulating a Dream, 1890–1985," in D. Margaret Costa and Sharon R. Guthrie, eds., *Women and Sport*, 84 (quote).

59. See "Mr. Hooley on Debrutalized Football," *University of Chicago Magazine*, 3 (Dec. 1910), 108–111, for a satirization of overregulated and less masculine football rules. Hall cited in Nelson, *Anatomy of a Game*, 197.

60. Don Sabo, "Sport Patriarchy, and Male Identity: New Questions About Men and Sport," *Arena Review*, 9:3 (1985), 1–15.

Chapter 3

Calling Signals: Militarism and Leadership Training

During the nineteenth century Europeans sought to extend their power and influence beyond their national borders. Great Britain's colonies spanned the globe, the Dutch controlled the East Indies, and other European countries carved up Africa to acquire overseas possessions. Russia still ruled over the remnants of its expansive feudal empire, while, in Asia, China and Turkey held a more tenuous grip on their vast dominions.

An English philosopher, Herbert Spencer, preached the "survival of the fittest" throughout the latter half of the nineteenth century and Social Darwinism proved pervasive in the *fin de seicle* world. Europeans fought each other in the Balkan Wars and as they colonized Africa and the Far East. Africans retaliated with the Zulu and Boer Wars, as did the Chinese in the Boxer Rebellion. Asians faced one another in the Sino-Japanese War, which was followed by a Russo-Japanese conflict.[1]

Spencer's beliefs had even greater influence in the United States, where capitalists strove to monopolize commercial interests against competitors and laborers engaged in pitched battles against employers; while the teeming urban masses struggled for existence. Strife and contention seemed normal and necessary, an evolutionary process also rationalized by American psychologist G. Stanley Hall's recapitulation theory, which proposed that men passed through several learning stages, including savagery, before achieving the civilized state appropriate to governance.

Europeans espoused the rhetoric of progress and the "white man's burden" as they imposed their own values, beliefs, and systems of governance on conquered peoples in the survival of the fittest. Once the United States had conquered its own western frontier it joined the imperial quest, expanding its commercial markets, and promoting its democratic republic as a better form of governance for subject populations. Americans seized Hawaii in 1893, confronted Great Britain over its boundary dispute with Venezuela in 1895, and then extended its control over Cuba, Puerto Rico, Guam, and the Philippines in the Spanish-American War of 1898. It then secured the Panama Canal Zone and pushed its influence throughout the Caribbean and Mexico thereafter.[2]

Such imperial ambitions required soldiers, military leaders, and governors. Sport, and football in particular, fit the need well. Chroniclers of the game at Princeton declared that "the aim of the American University is not merely the production of scholars, but the development of men."[3] In the survival of the fittest the game prepared one not only for national glory but international competition.

Since the first America's Cup challenge in 1851, Americans had tried themselves against the British empire in various sporting contests. Boxing matches between the two had started as early as 1810, when the former slave, Tom Molyneux, contested for the English championship. After John C. Stevens's America's Cup yachting victory, American thoroughbred owners raced for British stakes, or nationalistic glory, as did individual track stars, tennis players, and college crews. Beginning in 1896 the modern Olympics provided an international stage for the athletic wars.[4]

Football produced the tough men, discipline, martial spirit, and strategic tactics necessary for conquest. In the period between the Civil War and the short-lived Spanish-American campaign, young American men had little else in which to prove their mettle. The Indian "wars" and Custer's ignominious defeat did little to regain the sense of lost masculinity. For the college men who expected to become the nation's leaders, football served an essential function as a surrogate war. Walter Camp assured Americans that "this outdoor game is doing for our college-bred men, in a peaceful way, what the

experiences of war did for so many of their predecessors in
1861–65...."[5] Governor Wolcott of Massachusetts considered
football as preparation for the "country's call...as did our
fathers and brothers in '61...."[6]

Sons of veterans suffered constant reminders of their own
shortcoming in the parades, festivals, memorials, and paeans
that honored combatants in the Civil War throughout the last
quarter of the nineteenth century. Whereas before the war,
scholars, orators, and clergymen won esteem; physicality
ruled thereafter as men of action replaced men of intellect.
Throughout the era the art of Frederic Remington, Thomas
Eakins, and George Bellows glorified the heroic, active, and
virile man, such as cowboys, soldiers, and athletes.[7]

Within the climate of antiintellectualism physical prowess
defined manhood. John L. Sullivan, a boxer, became the first
great sports hero to win national acclaim. Football accorded
players opportunities for public acts of bravado with less
chance of death than actual combat; yet commentators often
saw little difference in the two. Caspar Whitney described
football as a "mimic battlefield, on which players reconnoiter,
skirmish, advance, attack, and retreat in good order."[8] Another observer claimed that the teams symbolized "two armies, managed on military principles." The quarterback, who
delivered the ball, served as quartermaster to the infantry,
while halfbacks dashed into the line like "calvary," and full-
backs supplied the "artillery," all of which required courage in
the presence of physical dangers.[9]

The physical dangers proved real enough as teams received
instructions to eliminate the opponents' best players in the
first five minutes of the game. In the 1905 season alone,
Harvard suffered 145 injuries to its 70 players, including 29
fractures, 29 dislocations, and 19 concussions. Players expected as much, and wore their injuries as badges of honor.
Harvard players had been taught that "a good game of football
is a good fight," and that ball carriers should "strike for the
face of a would-be tackler." A blocker encountering an unsus-
pecting opponent from the side "should make his head bump
twice before anything else touches the ground."[10]

Both the images and language of war and football became closely intertwined. In describing Princeton's new V-formation in 1888, a writer stated that

> It is Napoleon's method of assault which you will find in Hugo's description of Waterloo. He sent a flying column at an angle to the point he meant to attack, and another from the other side at an angle to the same point in front of his main column, which then went forward to the same point, now an opening, marching at right angles to the enemy's line.[11]

A Harvard scouting report of 1906 stated that "...we must follow up any gain with an offensive campaign....It will be a case of carrying the war into the enemy's country and keeping it there...."[12] During World Wars I and II sports terminology had become commonplace in media reports of battles. The parallel between football and war has become even more firmly entrenched in the latter half of the twentieth century, as quarterbacks throw "the bomb" to "flankers," while linebackers "blitz," and linemen fight it out "in the trenches." John Teerlinck, then defensive line coach for the Detroit Lions in 1995, described play more recently

> We're asking them to storm the beachhead. Hit the beach with fixed bayonets. Over the top. We're the first wave coming on. We always say you can't ease into a knife fight. You've got to come out swinging because it can be over that quick. It's a gung-ho, marine-type thing; let's go. You're in a trench, and you've got to fight yourself out of that pit.[13]

Such sanctioned fighting allegedly built better men and better government, and rationalized as such football took on the mantle of moral justification. At Syracuse, "no less than seven candidates for the ministry were on the Varsity, each one rated as a 'scrapper,' with John A. Hamilton, later a distinguished clergyman and Doctor of Divinity, conceded to be the hardest fighter of them all."[14] George Hares, another Syracuse player, confided that "Football served my religion well and my religion came in handy as a restraining influence versus fistic encounters and swearing."[15] In light of such testimonials, Billy Sunday, the baseball player turned evangelist, proclaimed that "Jesus was the greatest scrapper that ever lived."[16]

The merger of football, militarism, and morality sanctified players in a holy cause against allegedly immoral opponents, and eventually, evil enemies in real wars. Coach Forbes, of Harvard, stated that

> It is often the case that Yale men will go on the field and begin dirty work at the start, using their fists and knees, and kicking feet and shins, and playing for the eyes with their fingers or for the throat with the elbow or worse. A good, sharp blow will usually stop that in the first two minutes.[17]

Such retribution and self-appointed justice rested on the presumption of a higher moral order, not unlike the assumptions that led to American interventions in the Pacific and Caribbean.

Harvard had already tied football to righteous causes when Henry Lee Higginson endowed Soldier's Field in 1890 as a memorial to his classmates who had died in the Civil War. Harvard further eulogized its 1,200 sons who answered "their country's call in the great war of rebellion," as well as those martyred in the recent Spanish-American War at its victory party after a 17–0 win over Yale in 1898. Theodore Roosevelt, a leader of the Rough Riders, praised General Leonard Wood's abilities not only as a commander, but as a football player, and acknowledged the Harvard coaches who had joined his volunteer regiment. Massachusetts Governor Wolcott stated that "the thing that makes a man a strong, fearless, clean athlete makes him also a good citizen of his country, a gallant soldier, a brave son of Harvard." Roosevelt likened the football victory to the "prize of death in battle," and drew further correlations between the Harvard players and their counterparts in the Civil War. The players, symbolically seated above the others, sang "General Grant," a Civil War tribute, "America," and a football song adapted to the tune of "John Brown's Body" to end the festivities.[18]

Harvard had followed Rousseau's formula for instilling pride and a sense of tradition by organizing patriotic festivals around historical monuments linked with heroes. It continued to enjoy several winning seasons under coaches Bill Reid and Percy Haughton; and Harvard was not alone in such commemorations. More than fifty years later a Penn publication recalled Win Osgood, the star runner who had defeated Princeton in 1894, then gave his life in the Spanish-American War. Harvey McAlister, hero of the 1895 Oregon State team, also served in the war; but returned to his farm afterward. Nearly a century later he still earned praise in a football centennial published by the university for his role in the capture of Manila.[19]

Literary works of the period extolled such men of action in the works of Owen Wister and Jack London. Wister, a friend of Theodore Roosevelt, characterized the rugged, outdoor, masculine hero in *The Virginian*, which went through fifteen reprints in 1902, its first year of publication. Frederic Remington, a former Yale player, illustrated the book, and contributed his own sculptures of the frontier experience that Americans believed had set them apart. Stephen Crane's *The Red Badge of Courage* drew on his experiences as a football player; and he later influenced youths with his athletic stories in *St. Nicholas* magazine.[20]

Perhaps most influential was Gilbert Patten's *Merriwell* series, which ran for twenty years in *Tip Top Weekly* beginning in 1896, and resulted in 208 full-length novels. The Frank Merriwell character, supposedly modeled on Walter Camp, always proved to be a paragon of virtue, self-sacrifice, and athletic success. At its height the Merriwell series sold more than 500,000 copies a week and engendered numerous spin-offs. Owen Johnson's *Dink Stover at Yale* represented the All-American, Frank Hinkey; and John Tunis's athletic novels followed the same formula well into the twentieth century. Walter Camp praised real-life football heroes in his books, articles, and stories for juveniles. Such works, aimed at boys and men, further excluded females from the masculine world of football, war, and leadership.[21]

Football bred the martial spirit, discipline, and self-sacrifice necessary for such endeavors. Brooks Adams, the grandson of former president John Quincy Adams, praised the martial spirit of the great civilizations in his 1896 book, *The*

Law of Civilization and Decay. Captain Alfred Thayer Mahan campaigned for a bigger, stronger navy, and Theodore Roosevelt continually linked athletics with physical and moral strength. In an address at Harvard Union he stated that

> ...I emphatically disbelieve in seeing Harvard or any other college turn out molly coddles instead of vigorous men....I do not in the least object to sport because it is rough....We cannot afford to turn out of college men who shrink from physical effort or from a little physical pain. In any republic, courage is a prime necessity for the average citizen if he is to be a good citizen; and he needs physical courage no less than moral courage, the courage that endures, the courage that will fight valiantly alike against the foe of the soul and the foes of the body. Athletics are good, especially in their rougher forms, because they tend to develop such courage. They are good also because they encourage a true democratic spirit, for in the athletic field, the man must be judged not with reference to outside and accidental attributes but by that combination of bodily vigor and moral quality which to go make up prowess.[22]

Roosevelt sought such men of action for his Rough Riders, composed largely of cowboys and athletes. As the Rough Riders stormed the San Juan heights, *Outing* published an article entitled "Sports Place in the Nation's Well Being," which compared Englishmen and Americans to the French, Spanish, Italians and Chinese, with the Anglos favored because of the sports they played.

> Sport is merely artificial work, artificial adventure, artificial colonizing, artificial war....Those were hard games we played against the Indians, against fierce nature, against England, and against one another in the sixties.[23]

Warlike nature, if not inbred, would be nurtured, and self-sacrifice for the team and country instilled.

Coaches insured that players practiced self-denial and discipline for the good of the team, which would make them better citizens in the larger democracy. Percy Haughton, Harvard coach from 1908–1917, asserted that "discipline is the foundation for all our work. It is a campaign conducted on military principles...not only in discipline, but also in organization of forces. There is absolute subordination of the individual for the good of the team."[24] Another Harvard coach, Cameron Forbes, had often played the game with a broken nose and expected his men to be as tough, but admitted that players were overworked in four-hour practices. One who couldn't walk a flight of stairs or get any sleep due to pain, and another with water on both hips and both knees tried to beg off, but were denied. Forbes allowed no time-outs, and kept doctors, massagers, and medicines out of sight.[25] A few years later Coach Bill Reid admired a player who returned a month after appendicitis and continued to play with a rupture, although he vomited daily at practice. Reid remarked that "the fact that he is willing to undergo this punishment every day shows... his desire to play."[26]

Such virility became the hallmark of "real men," with heroic examples provided in popular culture. Theatrical productions portrayed the martial spirit in gladiatorial combat, and the Spanish-American War induced an intense patriotic fervor seemingly unsatiated by a multitude of war films produced in the post-war years. The western art of Frederic Remington, who, as a Yale football player, had dipped his uniform in blood to make it more "business-like," enjoyed great popularity; as did the martial music of John Philip Sousa. On college campuses Sousa's rousing tunes were matched by "fight" songs, such as "The Victors," played at the University of Michigan in 1898. The Chicago band played "William Tell's Overture" and other dynamic pieces by 1900. "Yale Boola," "The Eyes of Texas," the "Notre Dame Victory March," "Anchors Aweigh," and "On Wisconsin" followed, with most compositions appearing by 1910. At Syracuse, "The Saltine Warrior" likened football players to medieval warrior-heroes.[27]

The Army-Navy game, initiated in 1890, symbolized the merger of football, militarism, and patriotism as it became a national tradition. Songs, cheers, chrysanthemums, and pennants accompanied the 35,000 who attended the 1914 game in Philadelphia. The army band played the "Star Spangled Banner" (not yet the national anthem) as its number one ranked team administered a 20–0 beating. A member of the 1912 team, Dwight Eisenhower, later explained that "football ...tends to instill the feeling that victory comes through hard—almost slavish—work, team play, self-confidence, and an enthusiasm that amounts to dedication."[28]

By World War I football players had become thoroughly indoctrinated with such perceptions. While many professional baseball players demurred from military service, college football players readily enlisted. While Babe Ruth, and boxer Jack Dempsey opted to stay home, the Harvard, Yale, and Princeton football teams were among the first to enlist, with all of Harvard's 1916 lettermen doing so. Princeton's former captain and an All-American, the legendary multisport athlete, Hobey Baker, entered military service in 1916. The handsome, popular, and modest Baker reified the fictional Frank Merriwell both on and off the athletic field, as a consummate gentleman and protector of the weak. As a squadron commander with the Lafayette Escadrille, Baker won the Croix de Guerre, but died after a plane crash that only secured his stature as the heroic ideal.[29]

Such heroes, socially constructed by media reports and oral storytellers, compensated for the lost qualities of the past and helped Americans to define a collective identity in times of social transition. Others soon followed Baker and paid the ultimate sacrifice. Nearly half of the thirty-two players in the 1918 Rose Bowl game, played between two service teams, gave their lives in World Wars I or II. The 1918 Rose Bowl pageant celebrated such patriotism in its parade banquet, military bands, and American flags. Army and Marine officers escorted the singer of the "Star Spangled Banner," and the promoters dutifully turned over nearly $5,000 of the proceeds to the Red Cross. The 1920 parade acknowledged the transition to modernity when the procession followed an auto rather than a horse; but maintained more traditional values with the inclusion of the Salvation Army band, and the Woman's Christian Temperance Union. A "victory" float celebrated the win in Europe and airplane pilots dropped footballs as they passed over the stadium crowd. Ten thousand returning servicemen among them saw the game free of charge, as guests of the city.[30]

By the 1920s war and football had become so romanticized that "men...were suckled on stories of valor and heroism and of war as a rite of passage." War became "some form of ultimate athletic contest."[31] As commandant of West Point following World War I, Douglas MacArthur, who had been the student manager of the 1903 football team, required sports for cadets. His inscription on the gym read:

> Upon the fields of friendly strife,
> Are sown the seeds
> That, upon other fields, on other days,
> Will bear the fruits of victory.[32]

Athletics became a primary means by which men usurped the traditional feminine role in the upbringing of boys. Under the guidance of coaches effeminate boys would be turned into strong, virile, aggressive men, capable of conquering enemies or colonizing lands, bestowing capitalism and American democracy. With the founding of the Boy Scouts, a quasimilitary organization, in 1912, and the extension of public education and its interscholastic athletic programs in the early twentieth century, such values permeated the middle class.[33]

By that time Americans needed such men to govern its overseas possessions and to teach such lessons to the masses both at home and abroad. Endicott Peabody, headmaster at Groton, had included athletics for leadership training even before the Spanish-American War. Shortly thereafter an American writer advocated both baseball and football for Cubans and Filipinos as well. Proponents had long claimed that football "is the best test and cultivator of courage, judgment, perseverance and physical and intellectual quickness, that exists,"[34] and that "the game is a thorough education in all the qualities that go to make a manly man."[35] Philip King, Princeton captain in 1892, asserted that football "helped me when and how to act in a crisis...(it) better fitted me to take up the battle of life."[36] In his numerous writings, Walter Camp emphasized the leadership opportunities and responsibilities congruent with football.[37]

Camp and others often pointed to former football players as role models and success stories. Thomas "Bum" McClung,

Yale captain in 1891, became the United States treasurer in 1909, and Vance McCormick, another Yale player, served as mayor of Harrisburg, Pennsylvania. George R. Carter, a member of the 1888 team governed Hawaii from 1903–1907, and Gifford Pinchot served as Chief Forester of the United States. His teammate, Amos Alonzo Stagg, while coaching at Chicago, served as a presidential elector and for twenty-six years on the Olympic committee. Another teammate from 1889, George Woodruff, coached at Penn before becoming Assistant Attorney General of the nation, and later, Attorney General of Pennsylvania. Others served in the U.S. Congress and in state legislatures. A Yale survey of 514 former players found that 75 percent of those with law degrees were partners or judges; 80 percent of financiers held top bank or business positions; and of those engaged in business, 50 percent were chief executive officers.[38]

Harvard could point to its biggest fan, President Theodore Roosevelt, or former players, such as General Leonard Wood, or Cameron Forbes, all of whom went into public service. Another, Robert Bacon, became Secretary of State during Roosevelt's presidency. Other Harvard athletes won election to Congress or appointment to Washington posts. Princeton's one-time mentor, Woodrow Wilson, became governor of New Jersey, and then president of the country. One of Penn's players, Harry Mackey, officiated as mayor of Philadelphia, while John Bell served as the State Attorney General. Amherst claimed a Chief Justice, and New York City College a U.S. Senator. Former players clearly prospered; but promoters seemingly forgot that most Ivy Leaguers were already blessed with advantageous wealth and social networks conducive to advancement.[39]

Players from more humble origins also made their mark. Walter Steffen, an All-American at Chicago, also became a superior court judge, a position shared by Michael McKinley, a former Iowa end, and John Karel, who played at Wisconsin. In the South, Robert E. Lee Roy, a Texas player in 1893, became district judge of Fort Worth, while Louisiana and North Carolina claimed governors, as did Purdue in the Midwest. Lynn Frazier, North Dakota captain in 1899, governed his state before becoming its senator.

Perhaps most noteworthy of the judicial appointments was that of William Henry Lewis. An African-American who gained All-American honors during the 1890s, Lewis followed Harvard Law School with election to the Cambridge city council in 1899, and the state legislature in 1901. Appointed assistant U.S. Attorney General in 1903, he still found time to coach the football team during ensuing years. In 1910 Lewis became an assistant attorney general of the United States. Even in the South, blacks gained some recognition. W. J. Trent, halfback and manager of Livingstone's first football team in 1892, eventually became the college's president.[40]

During a time when professional baseball consciously excluded African-Americans from its major leagues, and the *Plessy v. Ferguson* Supreme Court decision rendered segregation of the races legal, football appeared to uphold more egalitarian principles and opportunities for all citizens in the American democracy. The masking of reality led W. E. B. DuBois to make his own assessment. As a contemporary of Lewis he stated that he was "in Harvard but not of it."[41]

While football appeared to provide opportunities for some blacks, whites still held a virtual monopoly on power. Maintenance of the status quo proved apparent in the relationship between football and the military leadership. Peyton C. Marsh, Lafayette fullback in 1883, became the Army's Chief of Staff, as did Malin Craig, who quarterbacked West Point in 1896. Edwin Denby, a Michigan center in 1895, served both presidents Harding and Coolidge as Secretary of the Navy. A Nebraska halfback of the 1890s, George H. Dern, went to Washington as Secretary of War from 1933–1936. Both West Point and Annapolis held positions on the football rules committee, and the Navy's Paul Dashiell remained on that governing body for twenty-eight years, eight of them as chairman. Army Captain Palmer Pierce filled even more important roles, serving two terms as president of the National Collegiate Athletic Association, the governing body for all intercollegiate sports. Pierce also ruled the Amateur Athletic Union, another national regulating organization, as its president.[42]

Pierce managed the first team at West Point in 1890 and acted as the graduate manager from 1902–1907. During the abolition movement of 1905, Pierce and his army colleague,

Lieutenant Colonel Howze, controlled the December 28, 1905, meeting of sixty-eight colleges in New York. Though a number of prominent colleges decided to ban football as too violent, Pierce insisted "that the U.S. Military Academy would continue to play the game whether other colleges did or not." The Army considered football to be "an excellent test of character." Pierce secured the necessary votes, and along with the promised reforms fostered by Roosevelt's White House meeting, the sport survived. Pierce's role in football governance brought him national recognition and he retired as a general.[43]

Paul Dashiell, a chemistry professor at the Naval Academy, did not fare as well. As umpire of the 1905 Harvard-Yale game, Dashiell failed to call a foul on an apparent fair catch, which cost Francis Burr a broken nose, and possibly the game for Harvard. President Theodore Roosevelt, a keen observer of the sport and fan of his alma mater, called Harvard's coach, Bill Reid, to the White House to hear his version of the story. Roosevelt's son, Ted, also had his nose broken against the Yale freshmen, though he absolved them of any blame. Despite Dashiell's pleas and a request for his own hearing, Roosevelt delayed his imminent promotion at Annapolis for six months and he never again officiated a Harvard-Yale game.[44]

The violent play continued throughout the decade, and a commentator lamented that "a student who has broken somebody's nose at football stands higher than a master of arts."[45] In a world still absorbed with imperial domination and international tensions, football had military value. Despite the death of one of his own players in 1909, University of Virginia president Edwin Alderman refused to ban the sport, stating that "In dealing with this game you are dealing with our national characteristics."[46]

Football proponents had long made the case for more than just the belligerence inherent in the game. Media, psychologists, educators, coaches, and players all touted the character building qualities of sports participation. Coaches superseded student captains and graduate managers, as schools moved to secure greater control over extracurricular activities at the turn of the century. In the process, the coaching profession overcame the negative stereotypes often associated with "professional" trainers hired by the students. As school staff or faculty members they assumed an equal measure of responsibility for students' guidance, with the expectation that they would serve as role models who taught young men to be manly, yet Christian gentlemen.

Coaching positions emerged from alumni still filled with school spirit and eager to see their alma mater conquer opponents in general, and traditional rivals in particular. After leaving Yale as a student, Walter Camp continued to guide the football team as a graduate advisor, systematizing its organization, schedules, strategies, and financing. Most colleges were far less structured and formal. Recalling the 1880s at Princeton, observers claimed that there was "little or no graduate coaching;" and that it was

> confined to criticism from the sidelines by any old player (or) ...some recently graduated player, who, feeling strong in newly acquired avoirdupois and more or less egotistical in his recollections of how he used to do it; would don football togs, and amidst the plaudits of the college crowd, enter the scrub line...he would proceed for a period of about ten minutes to vigorously tear up the Varsity. As strength and enthusiasm diminished and muscles weakened, his voice would increase in strength until you would see him entirely out of the play...yelling, coaxing, exhorting, pleading and commanding in no uncertain tones or mild language, he would urge the men on...This was doubtless quite exciting to the old player and somewhat amusing to the crowd, but of little benefit to the team.[47]

With Yale's success other schools began adopting its organizational and business-like features. Former players served as individual coaches at smaller institutions or organized a staff of assistants at larger ones to elicit the best results. Such training encompassed character building beyond that encountered on the playing field. By the late 1880s a commentator recognized that

> the game asks a larger amount of self-control, there is no better school for developing a man or boy's command of his passions and his powers...If a man is timid...football...will... rouse his sense of manhood....The pluck needed in the competitions of life is just the pluck demanded by football.[48]

"Pudge" Heffelfinger, the Yale All-American, maintained that "football training removes temptations...which every young man is subjected to."[49] A Harvard report concurred "that the man who trains is left stronger in mind and body, as also in that moral strength which enables him to resist temptation to vice."[50] More than twenty years later, even at the height of the football abolition movement, Edwin Alderman, president of the University of Virginia, rationalized that "football encouraged courage, self-denial, self-restraint, and unselfish loyalty to a cause. It required skill, daring, and pluck, and it established "ideals of bodily cleanliness."[51]

Football thus carried the banner of muscular Christianity promoted by the Young Men's Christian Association and similar white, Anglo-Saxon Protestant organizations. Some coaches and players had close ties to the YMCA. Stagg, for example, served as YMCA secretary at Yale, spent summers with Dwight Moody's evangelical movement, and joined the initial class of the YMCA's training school in Springfield, Massachusetts before accepting the coaching position at Chicago. Football players at many colleges, especially those with religious affiliations, submitted to temperance pledges. By 1895 the *Wesleyan University Bulletin* announced that "... these (athletic) contests play their part in making sturdy citizens, and training men in the invaluable qualities of loyalty, self-sacrifice, obedience and temperance."[52]

Proponents of the game assured parents that under the watchful eye and careful guidance of coaches their boys would become honorable gentlemen, fitted for life and service to the nation. The prestigious and oldest American quarterly, the *North American Review*, gave the following account.

A young student who has left home and a parent's watchful care, especially if the home be at some distance from a large city, arrives under the shades of the college...in a peculiar state of mind...and full of animal spirits....Each one who offers himself (to a sport) must be on the field at a certain time every day, must stop smoking...must stop drinking... Order and regularity is the first principle of the team. The trainer insists upon this, and the candidate does not object, because it is a point of honor with him to do his best in the defence (sic) of the larger honor of his college. ... He may put off the team...he has the opportunity of joining others (for) the perpetration of some outlandish prank....They are both the overflow of this new sense of freedom, of naturally buoyant spirits that can be turned into athletic sports as easily as into cards or something worse.

Close upon the restraint of training comes that which is the first essential of education, and which has greatly been said to be next to godliness. After two hours of strong, vigorous exercise comes a hot and cold bath, a "rub down" with all sorts of healthy liniments, and a phenomenal dinner of soup, roast beef, potatoes, and custard pudding; what could be a better preparation for morality and health and success?...[53]

Some schools tried to enforce morality with strict regulations for players during the 1890s. At Mississippi team members endured a daily four-mile run before a cold bath, and had to eschew not only tobacco, but tea and coffee as well. Michigan players could be banned from the athletic field for using profanity. At Chicago, Stagg required a 9:30 check-in and 10 p.m. bedtime. By the 1920s, Coach Howard Jones of Iowa even objected to dancing because it caused players to stay up too date, thus losing vital sleep and eating late due to the obligatory midnight snack required by their dates. Coaches seemingly regulated every hour of a player's day and night.[54]

National leaders welcomed and encouraged such regulation and training as necessary not only to building stronger men, but a stronger country as well. Woodrow Wilson claimed that "It (football) develops more moral qualities than any other game of athletics."[55] Theodore Roosevelt often equated athletics with leadership and morality during his rise to power. In 1893 Roosevelt wrote on the "Value of an Athletic Training," in *Harper's Weekly*. He extolled the benefits of sport, football in particular, in creating "the virtues which go to make up a race of statesmen and soldiers, of pioneers and explorers...of bridge-builders and road-makers, of commonwealth builders...." He further claimed that "athletic sports... minimize dissipation...and fight against debauchery;" and that former athletes "do their duty well, both to the State and to their own families"; and "Of all these sports there is no better sport than football."[56] In another speech during his presidency, Roosevelt stated that

> ...athletics encourage a true democratic spirit...man must be judged by that combination of bodily vigor and moral quality which go to make up prowess....The weakling and the coward are out of place in a strong and free community ...the governing class is composed of strong men...if you are too timid...you become one of the governed...one of the driven cattle of the political arena.[57]

Such messages delivered by national leaders, and reinforced by popular writers for most of the next century, sent clear notice that football produced strong, moral leaders for society. The numerous works of Walter Camp and the prolific boys literature often offered such players as role models for emulation by youth. The absence of similar female heroines in such literary works and, even more emphatically, the game itself, assured that such roles were reserved for men.[58]

Men, as coaches, began to assume the traditional Victorian role of nurturer previously reserved for women, and along with the new responsibilities for guidance acquired the spiritual characteristics usually attributed to women. Amos Alonzo Stagg viewed the coaching profession as

> one of the noblest and most far-reaching in building manhood...Not to drink, not to gamble, not to smoke, not to swear ...to be fair minded...to deal justly...to be honest in thinking and square in dealing...not to bear personal malice or to harbor hatred against rivals...not to be swell-headed ...to be sportsman and gentleman at all times...these should be the ideals of a coach.[59]

When Clark Hetherington, director of the University of Missouri athletic department, recommended David Fultz to Michigan as a coach, he stated that Fultz "never swears...does not smoke and never drinks. I consider him a strong man in every way. His habits are the result of strong character and not of effeminacy."[60] College presidents, most of whom supported the sport despite its brutality, appreciated strong leaders who could turn boys into men. President Alderman at

Virginia stated that he would rather "see a boy of mine on the rush line fighting for his team than on the sideline smoking a cigarette."[61]

Woodrow Wilson, shortly after resigning the Princeton presidency to become governor of New Jersey, told the Princeton football team that "honor should outweigh all considerations of success....The spirit in which Princeton teams have often met defeat is more heroic and really greater than victories might have been." He hoped for a return to traditional values when honor and courage were extolled above material success and called for universities to be "leaders in this great movement, if they are to properly serve the nation."[62] Despite the rhetoric, Wilson had himself contributed to the commercialized atmosphere that rewarded coaches for winning games, bringing athletic prestige, and filling university coffers as a team advisor, member of the faculty athletic committee, and president of Princeton.[63]

Universities began paying coaches large salaries to ensure success, which effected the transient nature of the profession as both schools and coaches sought better opportunities on an annual basis, a practice that has continued over the past century. As early as 1893, friends tried to secure a $3,500 salary for Walter Camp at Yale; equal to a professor's salary. In actuality, as manager of the school's athletic funds, Camp had personal access to far greater amounts. By 1900, President Arthur Hadley suggested that Camp's position was similar to that of a dean, and that his salary was paid by private subscription (i.e., alumni support). Other major institutions allowed similar arrangements to obtain or keep the best coaches. At Chicago, President Harper announced an official salary of $2,500 for Stagg; but supplemented that with another $3,500 from the athletic revenue. The $6,000 placed Stagg above most of the school's distinguished full professors. Similarily at Harvard, top professors earned $5,500; but coach Bill Reid, only 27 years old in 1905, got $7,000, half of it from subscription.[64]

Only a year earlier, a minister praised the qualities developed by such coaches, concluding that

Physical perfection is the final analysis....Thus we gladly
pay our tribute to the great game which is doing as much
for developing our young men physically and morally, preparing them for the hard grinding battles of coming days.[65]

Despite such testimonials football faced continual struggles for acceptance. At the University of North Carolina the
president and board of trustees initially endorsed sports,

which have grown to be not only a means of physical and
moral culture but a great source of strength to the university
and a great rallying point for college enthusiasm...that
drunkenness among the young men has almost entirely
disappeared.

By 1895, however, the trustees reconsidered, due to the
gambling and drinking that accompanied football games.

I regret very much to report that there was immorality and
rowdyism...that several kegs of beer were brought into college...that much liquor drinking was indulged in...that
many students were practicing the vice of gambling, that
much debauchery was indulged in after the match game of
football in Richmond on Thanksgiving Day.[66]

They reasoned that older men had led younger ones astray
and restricted future games to the campus under the watchful
eyes of faculty. Faced with a student revolt, they eventually
relented by allowing the team to travel; but required parental
consent and pledges of good conduct from both players and
spectators.

Similar issues confronted administrators as football spread
from its eastern roots. Authorities at Trinity College (now
Duke University) faced the dilemma of weighing the benefits
of football against its accompanying evils. The presumed
temptations particularly vexed Methodist schools in the
South, eventually leading to a split between the church and
Vanderbilt University in 1914. The game prevailed, however,
partly due to the military tradition of southerners, which
easily transferred to the football field. By the early twentieth
century southern football teams symbolized the Lost Cause,
as they increasingly tested themselves against intersectional

opponents. Southern teams promoted regional pride and upheld its racially exclusive ideology by refusing to play integrated opponents.[67]

Kansas lacked such tradition, and harbored a strong temperance movement that militated against the game. In 1894 Methodist ministers appealed to all institutions in the Kansas conference to ban football. The ministers feared exposure to alcohol, as well as travel that might violate the Sabbath. Despite Baker University's three state titles in four years, a claim to the "western championship" with an undefeated 1893 team, and little evidence of wrongdoing, the ministers succeeded in effecting a ban for fifteen years. The school's president, who favored the game, and all of its players left the institution in 1894.[68]

Even in places where the game was firmly entrenched, such as the East or other areas of the Midwest, football faced opposition. Intercollegiate sports, based on the British ideal of amateurism, assumed mutual trust and honesty among gentlemen. In America the early teams, managed by students or team captains, resolved issues by mutual agreement with opponents. Even after school administrators and faculty assumed greater control over the extracurricular activities of students, each school assumed responsibility for its own operating policies. The most troublesome issue revolved around players' eligibility. Rivalries, an emphasis on winning, and charges of professionalism pointed to different standards of acceptability even within the same conference. Schools argued over the eligibility of freshmen, graduate, part-time, and transfer students, and some schools refused to play others for years due to such differences.

Professional teams emerged by 1892, and quite possibly before that date, among athletic clubs unaffiliated with colleges and independently controlled by their members. College teams often faced criticism for employing one or more "professionals" for a big game or a season. The definition of a "professional" proved debatable, but generally meant anyone who received compensation for physical abilities. Technically, that definition included the whole working class, which reserved intercollegiate football for the working middle class and the wealthy who had the time and money to pursue higher education. Such a definition would prove problematic in a democratic society that offered free public education, particularly when that education and its extracurricular components were more fully extended to all Americans and immigrants in the twentieth century. The erosion of the amateur ideal began before that, however, with the organization of the National Association of Professional Baseball Players in 1871. The National League started play in 1876, and professional track stars and crews proliferated by the 1880s.

Football players saw little reason to miss out on opportunities for profit in a land of entrepreneurs. As early as 1890 there is evidence of Yale players accepting gold watches for a game played in New York. Such gifts were easily pawned for cash, while others received "expense" money as a form of reimbursement. In 1892 the Yale All-American, "Pudge" Heffelfinger, quit a railroad job in Omaha to play football "for expenses" with the Chicago Athletic Association, which had split from the Chicago University Club team a year earlier over the reimbursement issue. Although the Amateur Athletic Union allowed reimbursement for travel expenses, the faculty at Northwestern University refused to allow its team to play against the Chicago "professionals." Heffelfinger became the first documented professional player when he accepted $500 to play for the Allegheny Athletic Association against its Pittsburgh rival later that season. Within five years professionalism spread across the country, and the Butte, Montana team openly acknowledged such payment in games against West Coast teams in 1897.[69]

Despite the arrival of A. A. Stagg and his devout Christianity and avowed amateurism at Chicago, the football program faced consistent criticism over the issue of professionalism. As early as 1898, Chicago's president, William Rainey Harper, normally a staunch supporter of Stagg, showed concern over the use of athletes who were not in good academic standing. Only three years later Stagg and George Woodruff, the Penn coach, conspired to defraud the public by hiding Penn's weaknesses for their match in Chicago because such media exposure might limit gate receipts.[70] The commercialization of football thus clouded the professional ethics of coaches who were supposed to develop character in their charges.

Ethics became a larger issue when Stagg could not hide the professional activities of his players. One of Stagg's players, Hugo Bezdek, allegedly engaged in professional boxing matches in 1904. Despite convincing evidence, including account books showing the disbursements, and a warning by Assistant Athletic Director Joseph Raycroft "that Hugo hasn't been telling the whole truth," Stagg chose to accept Bezdek's denial. Irritated at the University of Illinois for publicizing the affair and accusing Chicago despite its own violations, Raycroft explained, shortly after Christmas of 1904: "This isn't a very good Holiday (sic) spirit, is it? But it's in accord with the first law of nature (a reference to survival of the fittest). You know what that is." Even after Stagg admitted "that we probably have been fooled in this matter," he continued to allow Bezdek to play through the 1905 season in which Chicago beat Michigan and Bezdek gained All-American recognition.[71]

Walter Eckersall proved even more problematic for Stagg. A high school sensation at nearby Hyde Park High School and holder of the state record in the 100-yard dash, both Michigan and Chicago coveted his abilities. By that time alumni and some coaches already offered significant inducements and Stagg allegedly intercepted Eckersall before he could leave the city for Michigan. Admitted to the university despite a lack of its academic criteria, Eckersall had also been suspended by the AAU amidst charges of professionalism while still in high school for playing baseball with the Spalding team of the Interstate League. Once enrolled, Eckersall's academic problems continued. He often missed classes, failed exams, did not pay his bills, and borrowed money to buy expensive clothes. Stagg interceded with faculty members, and even the president, to keep him eligible for competition. By 1907 then-President Harry Pratt Judson threatened to expel Eckersall. A friend, writing in defense of the athlete, admitted "many deplorable and unfortunate actions...knowledge of his loose morals...an absolute lack of a sense of responsibility...he has been a grafter as well as a monumental liar."[72]

Eckersall left the school, less than halfway to a degree, when his football eligibility expired after the 1906 season. Nearly twenty years later he had not yet repaid a $20 loan from his mentor, Stagg, despite a substantial income as a national promoter for cigarettes and in his dual roles as a famous sportswriter and highly paid football official. Both Stagg and the university had clearly failed to build character in Eckersall's case; but one might never learn the truth from the succeeding reports.[73]

The university whitewashed the Eckersall affair amidst charges of their own wrongdoing in exploiting the three-time All-American for publicity purposes. Newspapers lionized his feats on the football field, and magazines, poems, and songs immortalized his stature as a national football hero. At the end of his Chicago career a school rally acknowledged his uncommon distinction. Students cheered as the dean praised Eckersall's character and the faculty presented him with a gold watch. Eckersall responded with equal praise for his coach. "I cannot tell you how great a privilege it has been to spend four years under Coach Stagg. I owe what success I have had to him. He not only trains his men in athletics but he trains their character."[74] Such honors for player and coach continued throughout the century as Eckersall was selected the greatest quarterback of the half-century and the city of Chicago named a stadium in his memory as late as 1949, nearly two decades after his death. A 1957 biography stopped little short of canonization, and in 1969 Eckersall still made the All-Time All-American listing. Despite his character flaws the singular focus on his athletic abilities allowed for the media manufacture of a hero.[75]

At Michigan, All-American Willie Heston, earned similar rave reviews for his play, and his exposure of a betting scandal in 1902 solidified the character image that enabled Heston to become a judge. Heston refused $500 to throw a game with Minnesota; yet he was not above requesting that same amount from Ohio pro teams in a bidding war for his services the next year, when still a student at Michigan.[76]

Heston played seven years of college football, having come to Michigan from San Jose State with Coach Fielding Yost, when the latter left Stanford. Yost's recruiting tactics had cost him his job at Kansas in 1899. Similar efforts resulted in his dismissal from Stanford, where President David Starr Jordan stated apologetically that "... All of us who have ever had a

Yost or any Yost-like man about are not to be counted as sinless."[77] Nevertheless, the Michigan football team, still run by alumni in 1901, offered Yost $2,750 plus room and board for his services from September 1 through the last game. Yost soon produced the first Rose Bowl rout, perhaps vindictively in a 49–0 win over his last employer, Stanford, along with a national championship claim and his famous point-a-minute teams.[78]

Yost's questionable recruiting, as well as those of Stagg and others throughout the Western Conference led to charges and countercharges of professionalism. Rampant and widespread violations led to a series of exposés. In 1905 *Collier's* charged that "the University of Chicago (was) first among the violators," and that Eckersall was no more than "an athletic ward," as Stagg manipulated an $80,000 scholarship fund for "needy students." Leo De Tray's father acted as his agent, allegedly declining all expenses for his son and a companion at a California school for a better deal at Chicago. Nor could Northwestern match the offer that included theater tickets and dinner parties. Walter Steffen, another local sensation, refused lucrative offers from Lafayette, Wisconsin, and Northwestern by informing the latter that

> You fellows can't get me at Northwestern, and they can't get me at Wisconsin. You haven't got the money. I am going to Chicago. I tell you they won't get me there for what they gave De Tray. I know what he got.

Chicago, however, ultimately lost the services of a fellow named Borg, the center at Nebraska. Though he enrolled and began practice with Stagg's team, coach Booth at Nebraska retrieved him after appealing to his sense of responsibility. Though a Chicago agent allegedly paid him $600, he had already been "taken care of" by Nebraska alumni and had not yet repaid his debt to that institution.[79]

President James B. Angell of Michigan tried to achieve reforms by calling a conference meeting in January 1906; but failed to even control his own institution, where faculty voted to release Yost, but a student rally and his alumni supporters succeeded in installing him as the athletic director. Other conference teams refused to play against Michigan, which left the association in 1908, partly over a ban on intersectional games, which produced major sources of revenue. Michigan's secession lasted until 1917.[80]

Challenges to the character building process in football occurred throughout the country. Columbia offered George Foster Sanford $5,000 to coach in 1899; but the former Yale player lasted only three years. His teams defeated Yale, Princeton, and Penn; but did so with professional players. Columbia dismissed Sanford after discovering that he paid athletes, but he soon appeared on the Yale staff. In Georgia too, the alumni hired four pros to defeat rival Georgia Tech in 1907 with the collusion of coach W. S. "Bull" Whitney. Georgia students bet large sums on the outcome; but the scheme backfired when the pros, each of whom was promised a bonus for scoring, argued over ball-carrying duties. Professionalism even extended to Texas, where the Baylor trustees voted to ban football in 1906. Students there staged a mock funeral with a bonfire and buried a football under a headstone marked with floral arrangements. The headstone inscription read

> Here lies our dear foot-ball,
> Long may his ashes rest;
> He died by vote of the trustees,
> And not by our request.

Students enacted a resurrection at the gravesite when the trustees reinstated the game in 1907.[81]

At Harvard Coach Bill Reid avoided a football interdiction through subterfuge. When the Harvard overseers planned to announce a ban, Reid preempted their intentions with a national letter calling for reforms in the game to be initiated by Harvard. Believing in his sincerity, the governing boards relented. Reid later admitted that "Our ruse worked, and the announcement of the vote was deferred...."[82]

Reid played a similar hoax on Walter Camp while the latter edited the *Spalding Football Rules Book*. Reid offered to do the editing work, but allowed Camp's name to continue on the publication. Reid explained that

> ...it was a mass of incongruities and contradictions...Mr.
> Camp and the Yale coaches took advantage of these ambi-
> guities for Yale, and when challenged would justify their
> position by pointing to the rule that favored them...My
> ostensible reason was to save Mr. Camp's time, but it was
> not the real one....I went to work and eliminated all the
> discrepancies...so that there could be no question...[83]

Such duplicity may have achieved a degree of justice, but
the means could hardly have been considered character building. As a coach, Reid did, however, advocate that his players
quit smoking, drinking, and shirking practice duties. He also
encouraged them to cut classes for practice or on the day
before a game. He perpetuated yet another masquerade to
retain the good will of the faculty by sending selected players
to lectures, while others went sailing, boating, fishing, or just
listened to a gramophone.[84]

Reid's conduct paled in comparison to that of Richard Webb,
assistant coach at Kentucky in 1912. Webb used his social
connections to regain his coaching position after having been
fired for taking the team to a brothel. When the team came
under investigation for professionalism, Webb destroyed the
eligibility records by committing arson.[85]

Lesser crimes, like gambling, continually tarnished football's reputation. Students had long bet on their team's performance, but players too placed wagers on games in which
they played. Syracuse players even pooled their money for
such purposes in 1919. A few years later Fielding Yost complained that players had lost their ideals and only played "for
mercenary incentives of friends."[86] Such influences were easily blamed on the rise of professional football, and college
coaches continued to extol the virtues of the game and their
guidance.[87]

During the half-century between the Civil War and World
War I, few middle or upper class American males had any
opportunity to prove themselves in combat as their forefathers
had done. Distressed by a perception of progressive effeminacy and a need for the United States to take its place among
the imperial powers, football provided an alternative training
ground for restoring masculinity and aggressiveness, and

helped to define national characteristics. As early as 1890, *The Nation* recognized that

> The spirit of the American youth, as of the man, is to win, to "get there," by fair means or foul; and the lack of moral scruple which pervades the struggle of the business world meets with temptations equally irresistible in the miniature contests of the football field.[88]

The game fostered an aggressive, masculine culture that taught military strategy, self-sacrifice, discipline, and loyalty to a cause. Mass plays and wedge formations adapted textbook military tactics, and Stagg's experiments even presaged the future. In preparing for the Penn game of 1899 he asked "Could not our ends let Penn's ends through & (sic) charge them from behind (sic)." Such guerrilla tactics soon appeared in the Philippine insurrection. His orders to "Have plays go like lightning ..." anticipated the blitzkrieg of World War II. Also, the passing attack developed by Stagg and others soon found fruition in the aerial warfare of World War I.[89]

Football plays also paralleled the scientific precision found in industry. Coaches had determined that the relay from the quarterback to the punter took 2.5 seconds and adopted the direct snap from center as a more efficient alternative by 1897. Coaches, such as Glenn "Pop" Warner and Knute Rockne, won games and popular support with the machine-like precision of their backfield shifts, which produced favorable blocking angles and numerical superiority at the point of attack.[90]

Over that period of time, physical prowess and competitiveness, traits previously ascribed to the working class, became rationalized as a Social Darwinian necessity for middle class and elite males threatened by effeminacy and masses of ethnic immigrants. Football violence was rationalized as a catharsis and even a necessity, a compensatory theory espoused in 1903, and later, by Sigmund Freud in his *Civilization and Its Discontents*. Cameron Forbes explained that "Football is the expression of strength of the Anglo-Saxon. It is the dominant spirit of a dominant race, and to this it owes its popularity and its hopes of preeminence."[91] When Indiana dropped its football program during World War I, the other Big Ten teams persisted "because they had decided that athletics are essential to put men in shape for real warfare."[92]

World War I strengthened the bond between football and the military. The character building qualities of sport were perceived to be a wholesome alternative to the drinking and prostitution that too often filled servicemen's leisure time. Dr. Joseph Raycroft, Stagg's former assistant and Princeton athletic director, led an army commission, while the navy hired Walter Camp for its commission on athletics. Camp produced the daily dozen set of calisthenics and both groups initiated a comprehensive sports program, including football, for training and recreational purposes.[93]

Postwar political developments only intensified American fears and the need for military preparedness. The Russian revolution produced an irrational "Red Scare" that tainted European immigrants and brought a xenophobic repression. Over the next two decades Fascist takeovers in Italy and Germany threatened American democracy and led to a civil war in Spain.

The favorable relationship between football and the military was clearly accentuated by World War II, as sport became associated with fitness, patriotism, and morale, both within the ranks and on the homefront. Jimmy Conzelman, coach of the Chicago Cardinals professional team, and a Navy commander in World War I, stated:

> For years we've (football coaches) been on the defensive against attacks from reformers who regard us as muscle-bound mentalities....Football has been under fire because it involves body contact and it teaches violence. But that's all over now. The bleeding hearts haven't the courtesy to apologize to us, but they're coming around and asking our help in the national emergency...because the college commencement classes...find the customary challenge of life a pale prelude to the demands of a world at war...the graduates suddenly have become defenders of a familiar way of life, of an ideology, a religion and of a nation. They have been taught to build. Now they must learn to destroy....The young man must...become accustomed to violence. Football is the No. 1 medium for attuning a man to body contact and violent physical shock. It teaches that after all there isn't anything so terrifying about a punch in the puss.[94]

George Halas, owner-coach of the professional Chicago Bears, had already served in World War I; but reenlisted as a lieutenant commander in the South Pacific. Frank Leahy, the Notre Dame coach, urged his players to become marines. Within five months of the bombing at Pearl Harbor, 32 percent of the National Football League's professional players had already enlisted, and 638 would eventually join during the war. Commissioner Elmer Layden, who had been one of Notre Dame's famed Four Horsemen in 1924, claimed that "Naturally, we're proud of that record, and I believe it's additional proof of the worthwhileness of football. Action on the playing field has fitted these boys with something special."[95]

After the Second World War football no longer faced any serious opposition. Top commanders, such as Navy admirals Ernest J. King, William "Bull" Halsey, Jonas Ingram, and Chester Nimitz, along with the Army's Chief of Staff, General George C. Marshall, had been football players, as were generals Dwight Eisenhower, Omar Bradley, Joseph Stilwell, Robert Porter, James Van Fleet, and Earnest "Iron Mike" Massad. Eisenhower, commander of the Allied forces in Europe, "would prefer his entire staff to be composed of ex-footballers as they were the men who he could be sure would fill the leadership roles demanded of them in the army."[96]

Football training seemed essential to the war effort. Coach Harry Stuhldreher of Wisconsin, and another of the Four Horsemen, claimed that the "stamina, teamwork, and coordination football men are getting on the gridiron will help make them better soldiers."[97] General Marshall agreed, stating that "The American standard of discipline (is) cheerful and understanding subordination of the individual to the good of the team."[98] Football became a fixture on military bases at home and abroad. Even pilots needed exposure to the game. At George Field in Illinois, Captain Joe Fernandes announced that "Football is not a game for sissies and any man who is afraid of getting hurt or going through some vigorous training periods need not come out for the team."[99] Claire Chennault even trained his Flying Tigers in the Far East like a football team, providing a training table, special quarters, and daily football games to prepare for flying missions.[100]

By 1950 the navy counted eighty former players as admirals, while ninety-eight generals had played the game.[101] One of them, General Robert Neyland, conveniently stationed in Knoxville, coached the University of Tennessee for more than 20 years, while still on active duty with the army. Influenced by Douglas MacArthur at West Point, whom he served as an assistant, Neyland brought military organization and discipline, as well as army assistant coaches to his duties at Tennessee. In comparing football and war, Neyland said that "The same Cardinal (sic) rules apply to both."[102] When the post-war platoon system allowed for free substitution and greater specialization, Neyland called it "chicken shit" and not "real football." Another traditionalist, Coach Larry Mullins, stated that "Endurance should play a vital part....Why should we develop boys to be just half football players....There are some quarterbacks in particular who haven't made a dozen tackles during their collegiate careers. That is not football."[103] Ensuing conflicts in Korea, the Cold War, and Vietnam assured the necessity of such training for American men. Scholastic surveys throughout the twentieth century indicated the centrality of sports in student life and even concluded that the "highest honor" a senior boy can have is captaincy of the football or basketball team.[104]

That ideology of male leadership, dominance, and white elitism symbolized in football and the culture of the Northeast underwent transition, adoption and adaptation as the game spread to the West and South. At the 1908 commencement Massachusetts' Governor Curtis Guild pronounced that "... Harvard is not merely Massachusetts, Harvard is not merely New England, Harvard is the ideal of America." The following year Harvard counted 5 blacks, 8 Italians, 19 Chinese, 50 Irish, and 89 Jews among its students.[105] The complexion of America was changing, and so would football as the children of ethnic immigrants assimilated with the game.

Notes

1. Blum, et al., *The National Experience,* 464–466; Thomas Pakenham, *The Scramble for Africa: The White Man's Conquest of the Dark Continent from 1876 to 1912* (New York: Random House, 1991).

2. Alan Dawley, *Struggles for Justice: Social Responsibility and the Liberal State* (Cambridge, MA: Harvard University Press, 1991), 48–55, 105–109, 152–153, 179–180; Walter Millis, *The Martial Spirit* (Chicago: Elephant Paperbacks, 1989), 2–6, 20–24, 36–37.

3. Presbrey and Moffatt, *Athletics at Princeton,* 16.

4. George Kirsch, ed., *Sports in North America: A Documentary History, vol. 3: The Rise of Modern Sports, 1840–1860* (Gulf Breeze, FL: Academic International Press, 1992), 55–59, 141–152, 211–214, 327–329; and Gerald R. Gems, ed., vol.5, *Sports Organized, 1880–1900* (1996), 398–400, 414–416.

5. Roberta J. Park, "We're Killing Our Sons—But We're Making Men: A Tolerance for Football Injuries in Britain and America, 1874–1914," North American Society for Sport History Convention, Auburn, Alabama, May 25, 1996; Lt. Richard Morse Hodge, "American College Football," *Outing,* 40:6 (March 1888), 483–498; Walter Camp, "Football of 1893: Its Lessons and Results," *Harper's Weekly* (Feb. 3, 1894), 117–118.

6. *Boston Globe,* Dec. 4, 1898, clipping in HUD 10898, Harvard Archives.

7. Kammen, *Mystic Chords of Memory,* 101–131; Gerald F. Linderman, *Embattled Courage: The Experience of Combat in the American Civil War* (New York: The Free Press, 1987), 275–297; Francis A. Walker, "College Athletics," in *Harvard Graduates Magazine,* 2:5, (Sept. 1893), 1–18. See Oriard, *Reading Football,* 174, 206, 213, 228, on football and Darwinism.

Nemerov, *Frederic Remington;* Helen A. Cooper, *Thomas Eakins: The Rowing Pictures* (New Haven: Yale University Press, 1996); Marianne Doezema, *George Bellows and Urban America* (New Haven: Yale University Press, 1992).

8. See Michael T. Isenberg, *John L. Sullivan and His America* (Urbana: University of Illinois Press, 1988); Caspar Whitney, "The Athletic Development at West Point and Annapolis," *Harper's Weekly,* 36 (May 21, 1892), 496, cited in Reiss, "Sport and the Redefinition of American Middle-class Masculinity," 19.

9. Alexander Johnston, "The American Game of Football."

10. Lester, *Stagg's University,* 74; See Smith, *Big Time Football at Harvard,* 241, for an example of deliberate injury. Park, "We're Killing Our Sons;" Smith, *Big Time Football at Harvard,* 314–317;

W. Cameron Forbes, *Football Notebook,* 1901, Harvard Archives, HUD 10897.29, 39, 41, 81, 85, 134.

11. Presbrey and Moffatt, *Athletics at Princeton,* 336.

12. James L. Kuo to Bill Reid, Nov. 5, 1906, in Harvard Archives, HUD 8010.

13. See Wanda Ellen Wakefield, *Playing to Win: Sports and the American Military, 1898–1945* (Albany: State University of New York Press, 1997), 35–57; Teerlinck, quoted in *Aurora Beacon-News,* Sept. 8, 1995, F23.

14. Evans, *Fifty Years of Football at Syracuse University,* 31–32.

15. Ibid., 231–232.

16. Robert J. Higgs, *God in the Stadium: Sports and Religion in America* (Lexington: University Press of Kentucky, 1995), 255–256.

17. Forbes, *Football Notebook,* 1901, 39.

18. Reiss, "Sport and the Redefinition of American Middle-class Masculinity," 18; *Boston Globe,* Dec. 4, 1898, clipping in Harvard Archives, HUD 10898 (quote).

19. Kammen, *Mystic Chords of Memory,* 290; Ed Pollock, "Pennsylvania Football History," in *Franklin Field Illustrated,* 1951, Penn Archives; "Football Centennial, 1893–1993," *The Oregon Stater,* 11.

20. Townsend, *Manhood at Harvard,* 263–274; Christian K. Messenger, *Sport and the Spirit of Play in American Fiction: Hawthorne to Faulkner* (New York: Columbia University Press, 1981), 143–146.

21. John Levi Cutler, *Gilbert Patten and His Frank Merriwell Saga: A Study in Sub-Literary Fiction, 1896–1913* (Orono, ME: University of Maine Press, 1934); Messenger, *Sport and the Spirit of Play in American Fiction,* 165–176; Reiss, "Sport and the Redefinition of American Middle-class Masculinity," 20; Walter Camp, *The Book of Foot-ball,* 1910, 139–183; Camp, "Personality in Football," *Century* 57, (Jan. 1910), 442–457.

22. H. W. Brands, *Bound to Empire: The United States and the Philippines* (New York: Oxford University Press, 1992), 12–16; Roosevelt quoted in *NCAA News,* Jan. 6, 1993, 4.

23. Price Collier, "Sport's Place in the Nation's Well-Being," *Outing* (July 1898), 382–388. See "American Military Efficiency," *Chicago Tribune,* Nov. 16, 1902, 17, for British criticism of U. S. forces.

24. P. D. Haughton, "Football Coaching," address presented at Harvard Athletic Conference, May 27, 1916, in *Harvard Alumni Bulletin,* 684–685, in Harvard Archives, HUD 10915.

25. Forbes, *Football Notebook,* 1901, 7, 9, 12.

26. Smith, *Big Time Football at Harvard,* 1905, 209.

27. Arthur Inkersley, "Graeco-Roman Games in California," *Outing* (Feb. 1895), 409–416; Nasaw, *Going Out,* 146–151; 40th Reunion booklet of 1898 University of Michigan Football Squad, Board in Control of Intercollegiate Athletics, Box 39, Bentley Historical Library, University of Michigan; *Chicago Tribune,* Nov. 3, 1900, 6; William E. Studwell, "American College Fight Songs: History and Historiography," *Journal of American History,* 19 (Fall 1995), 125–130; Evans, *Fifty Years of Football at Syracuse University,* 202.

28. Gene Schoor, *100 Years of Army-Navy Football* (New York: Henry Holt, 1989), 48 (quote)–51. The "Star Spangled Banner" became the official national anthem in 1931.

29. Charles Fountain, *Sportswriter: The Life and Times of Grantland Rice* (New York: Oxford University Press, 1993), 141–142, 162; Bob Royce, "Hobey Baker: He Lived for Excitement," *College Football Historical Society,* 7:3 (May 1994), 16–18. Hibner, *Rose Bowl,* 58, claims all 107 candidates for the 1919 Harvard team as war veterans.

30. Janet C. Harris, *Athletes and the American Hero Dilemma* (Champaign: Human Kinetics, 1994), 1–18; Hibner, *The Rose Bowl,* 38–42, 54, 69–70. See James Mennell, "The Service Football Program of World War I: Its Impact on the Popularity of the Game," *Journal of Sport History,* 16:3 (Winter 1989), 248–260, for an informative, but speculative analysis of military teams.

31. Fountain, *Sportswriter,* 137–138.

32. Pope, *Patriotic Games,* 140–143; Higgs, *God in the Stadium,* 229 (quote). See Steven W. Pope, "An Army of Athletes: Playing Fields, Battlefields, and the American Military Sporting Experience, 1890–1920," *Journal of Military History,* 59 (July 1995), 435–456, for developments during that period.

33. Rotundo, *American Manhood,* 236–246. See Hardy, *How Boston Played;* Gerald R. Gems, *Windy City Wars: Labor, Leisure, and Sport in the Making of Chicago* (Lanham, MD: Scarecrow Press, 1997); and J. Thomas Jable, "The Public Schools Athletic League of New York City: Organized Athletics for City School Children, 1903–

1914," in Steven A. Riess, ed., *The American Sporting Experience: An Historical Anthology* (West Point, NY: Leisure Press, 1984), 219–238.

34. Riess, *Sport in Industrial America,* 48; John Corbin, "The Modern Chivalry," *Atlantic Monthly,* 89 (May 1902), 601–611. Sugar, *The SEC,* 146, indicates a University of Mississippi loss at the University of Havana in 1921. Eugene L. Richards to Walter Camp, March 5, 1894, Camp Papers, Reel 15.

35. John P. Poe to Walter Camp, March 15, 1894, Camp Papers, Reel 14.

36. King cited in Camp, *Football Facts and Figures,* 85.

37. See Camp, "Football Studies for Captain and Coach," *Outing* (Nov. 1892), 102–107; and Camp, *The Book of Foot-ball,* 202–226, 323–340, for examples.

38. Camp, *The Book of Foot-ball,* 139–183; Thomas Lee McClurg to "Mr. Mayor," Mar. 5, 1902, in Camp Papers, Reel 12; Albert B. Crawford, *Football Y Men, 1872–1919* (New Haven: Yale University Press, 1962).

39. Theodore Roosevelt to Walter Camp, Mar. 11, 1895, Camp Papers, Reel 15; William T. Reid, Jr., *H.V.F.B.A. Notes, 1905,* Vol. 2, n.p. Harvard Archives. Umphlett, *Creating the Big Game,* 21; Weyand, *Saga of American Football,* 43, 53–54. Roosevelt's role in Wood's promotion to colonel can be found in Theodore Roosevelt to Charles W. Eliot, Sept. 28, 1906, Eliot Papers, Harvard Archives.

40. *The Order of the C, 1937,* n.p., Stagg Papers; Ralph Cannon, "Football Training Helped Two Judges Shape Career," *News,* Oct. 11, 1932 clipping, both in Box 16, folder 9; Maysel, *Here Come the Texas Longhorns,* 4; Weyand, *Saga of American Football,* 60, 78, 114, Evans, *Fifty Years of Football at Syracuse University,* 6–7, judged almost all of its past 1800 players successful.

41. Arthur R. Ashe, Jr., *A Hard Road to Glory: Football* (New York: Amistad, 1993), 2–3; Bealle, *The History of Football at Harvard,* 534–536; Hurd, *Black College Football,* 27; Townsend, *Manhood at Harvard,* 247, quote.

42. Weyand, *Saga of American Football,* 53–54, 56; Nelson, *Anatomy of a Game,* 533–551; Higgs, *God in the Stadium,* 220–221.

43. Higgs, *God in the Stadium,* 220. Columbia, New York University, Union, Stanford, California, and Northwestern banned football, albeit temporarily.

44. Reid, *H.U.F.B.A. Notes, 1905,* n.p.; Theodore Roosevelt to Pres. Charles W. Eliot, Dec. 9, 1905, Eliot Papers, Harvard Archives; Smith, *Big Time Football at Harvard,* 135, 317; Theodore Roosevelt to Walter Camp, Nov. 24, 1905, Camp Papers, Reel 15.

45. Watterson, "The Death of Archer Christian," 159.

46. Ibid., 163. See William E. Hicks, "The Military Worthlessness of Football," *Independent,* 67 (Nov 25, 1909), 1201–1204, for a minority opinion.

47. Westby and Sack, "The Commercialization and Functional Rationalization of College Football;" Presbrey and Moffatt, *Athletics at Princeton,* 399 (quote).

48. Hodge, "American College Football," 498.

49. W. W. Heffelfinger to Walter Camp, Mar. 5, 1894, Camp Papers, Reel 9.

50. *Harvard College Report Upon Athletics,* 52.

51. Watterson, "The Death of Archer Christian," 158.

52. Lester, *Stagg's University,* 11–13; Nora Campbell Chaffin, *Trinity College, 1839–1892: The Beginnings of Duke University* (Durham, NC: Duke University Press, 1950), 446–447; Wesleyan quote cited in Michael Messner, *Power at Play: Sport and the Problem of Masculinity* (Boston: Beacon Press, 1992), 7.

53. Oriard, *Reading Football,* 140–141; Joseph Sears, "Foot-Ball: Sport and Training," *North American Review,* 53 (1891), 750–753.

54. "Ole Miss Rebels," article provided by University of Mississippi Archives, 23; Board in Control of Intercollegiate Athletic Minutes, Dec. 16, 1895, Michigan Archives; Stagg Papers, Box 30, folder 5; Nelson, *Anatomy of a Game,* 175, on Jones.

55. See Mrozek, *Sport and American Mentality, 1880–1920,* 28–66, for a discussion of several influential leaders. "Woodrow Wilson Supports Football and Its Promotion of Manliness," *New York Times,* Feb. 18, 1894, cited in Steven Riess, ed., *Major Problems in American Sport History* (Boston: Houghton Mifflin, 1997), 245–246.

56. Theodore Roosevelt, "The Value of Athletic Training," *Harper's Weekly* (Dec. 23, 1893), 1236.

57. Roosevelt's speech at Harvard, Feb. 23, 1907, in Camp Papers, Reel 15.

58. An example of Camp's pieces on role models can be found in "Personality in Foot-ball: A Consideration of the Contributions to the Progress of the Game by Certain Players and Coaches," *Century,* 57 (January 1910), 442–457.

59. Nelson, *Anatomy of a Game,* 94–95 (quote). See Smith, *Sports and Freedom,* 147–164, on the advent of professional coaches.

60. Clark W. Hetherington to Charles Baird, Jan. 24, 1901, Board in Control of Intercollegiate Athletics, folder 5, Michigan Archives. Hetherington later became a national leader of physical education in public schools.

61. Watterson, "The Death of Archer Christian," 155.

62. Arthur S. Link, ed., *The Papers of Woodrow Wilson, 1910–1911,* vol. 22 (Princeton: Princeton University Press, 1976), 4–5.

63. Weyand, *Saga of American Football,* 18; Presbrey and Moffatt, *Athletics at Princeton,* 57. Some football historians list Wilson as a Princeton coach, but his role probably would not fit current definitions.

64. Eugene L. Richards to Walter Camp, Nov. 14, 1893, Camp Papers, Reel 15; Arthur T. Hadley to Mr. Bertron, June 29, 1900; Camp Papers, Reel 18; Lester, *Stagg's University,* 87–88.

65. Rev. A. E. Colton, "What Football Does," *Independent,* 57, (Sept. 15, 1904), 605–607 (quote).

66. Board of Trustees, Ex. Comm., Jan. 3, 1891, vol. 9, 6; Jan. 5, 1894, 361, 470, 484 (quotes), 486. A previous ban had occurred in 1890, see Trustee Minutes, vol. 8, 459–61, University of North Carolina Archives. See Eugene L. Richards to Walter Camp, Nov. 9, 1896, Camp Papers, Reel 15, for complaints at Yale.

67. See Sumner, "John Franklin Crowell, Methodism, and the Football Controversy at Trinity College, 1887–1894," for similar problems leading to a ban at Duke; Doyle, "Foolish and Useless Sport: The Southern Methodist Crusade Against Intercollegiate Football, 1890–1914."

68. Hal D. Sears, "The Moral Threat of Intercollegiate Sports: An 1893 Poll of Ten College Presidents, and the End of 'The Champion Football Team of the Great West,'" *Journal of Sport History,* 19:3 (Winter 1992), 211–226.

69. Eugene L. Richards to Walter Camp, Dec. 15, 1890, Camp Papers, Reel 15; Bob Braunwart and Bob Carroll, *The Alphabet Wars:*

The Birth of Professional Football, 1890–1892 (Professional Football Researchers Assn., 1981), 42; J. Thomas Jable, "The Birth of Professional Football: Pittsburgh Athletic Clubs Ring in Professionals in 1892," *The Western Pennsylvania Historical Magazine,* 62:2 (April 1979), 131–147. The Pro Football Hall of Fame in Canton, Ohio, contains the Allegheny Athletic Association ledger showing the payment to Heffelfinger. *Butte Miner,* Dec. 27, 1896, 1; Jan. 12, 1897, 1.

70. William Rainey Harper to A. A. Stagg, n.d., Stagg Papers, Box 9, folder 3; George W. Woodruff to A. A. Stagg, Mar. 28, 1901; A. A. Stagg to George Woodruff, Apr. 2, 1901, Stagg Papers, Box 42, folder 6.

71. Dr. J. E. Raycroft to A. A. Stagg, Dec. 8, 1904; Herbert Barton to Dr. Raycroft, Dec. 9, 1904; J. E. Raycroft to A. A. Stagg, Dec. 19, 1904; Raycroft to Stagg, Dec. 28, 1904, (quotes); Stagg to Raycroft, Dec. 31, 1904 (quote), Stagg Papers, Box 12, folder 1.

72. Eckersall's high-school teammates, the Hammond brothers, became All-Americans at Michigan. The Stagg Papers contain much correspondence on Eckersall's problems. See *Record-Herald,* Oct. 30, 1903 clipping in Box 16, folder 10; Palmer E. Pierce to Stagg, Mar. 6, 1903; and Stagg to Pierce, Nov. 10, 1903; Jan. 19, 1904, Box 42, folder 15; Charles S. Slichter to Stagg, Oct. 2, 1903; Joseph Curtis Sloane to Stagg, Nov. 9, 1903; F. L. Beebe To Whom It May Concern, Mar. 22, 1905; John R. Seidenbecker To Whom It May Concern, Mar. 22, 1905; Box 78, folder 1.
Chicago Tribune, Nov. 21, 1903, 6, details a meeting between Edwin G. Cooley, Superintendent of Chicago's Public Schools and the Universities of Chicago, Michigan, and Northwestern over their efforts to induce high-school athletes to enroll before graduation.
George Buckley to Pres. Judson, Mar. 14, 1907 (quote), University of Chicago Presidential Papers, Box 15, folder 7; A. A. Stagg to Joseph E. Raycroft, June 12, 1905, Stagg Papers, Box 12, folder 1.

73. Lester, *Stagg's University,* 55–64, provides a succinct but thorough review of Eckersall's career and problems at Chicago.

74. Buckley to Judson, Mar. 14, 1907; Lester, *Stagg's University,* 58–59 (quote), 61–62.

75. *Chicago Tribune,* Sept. 8, 1949; Sept. 18, 1949; *Herald American,* Mar. 6, 1950, clippings in Stagg Papers, Box 16, folder 10; James Peterson, *Eckersall of Chicago* (Chicago: Hinckley and Schmitt, 1957); Lester, *Stagg's University,* 233, fn. 71.

76. *Chicago Tribune,* Dec. 7, 1902, 9; Fred H. Sypher to A. A. Stagg, Feb. 3, 1905, Stagg Papers, Box 78, folder 4.

77. Rader, *American Sports,* 139–140 (quote).

78. Yost's 1901 contract is contained in Box 1, folder 5, Board in Control of Intercollegiate Athletics, University of Michigan Archives.

79. Jordan, "Buying Football Victories."

80. James Orin Murfin Papers, Box 8, folder 1; George W. Patterson Notes, Box 8, folder 2; "The Conference Question," *Michigan Daily,* 1913; *Michigan Alumnus* (June 1913), 453–454; "Dr. Angell on Athletics," *Michigan Alumnus,* 12:109 (Dec. 1905), 101–102, Michigan Archives. See Lester, *Stagg's University,* 83–91, on the reform movement at Chicago.

81. John Watterson, "The Rehabilitation of a Football Coach: Alienation, Race and 'Mucker' Football," North American Society for Sport History Convention, Long Beach, Ca., May 26–29, 1995; Sugar, *The SEC,* 81; Kent Keith, *Looking Back at Baylor,* reprints from *The Baylor Line,* 1975–1985, supplied by Baylor Archives, 66–67 (quote).

82. William T. Reid to H. E. von Kersburg, undated, HUD 8010, Harvard Archives.

83. Ibid.

84. Smith, *Big-Time Football at Harvard,* 84–86, 291, 310–311, 334.

85. Stanley, *Before Big Blue,* 61–73.

86. Evans, *Fifty Years of Football at Syracuse,* 233–234; Fielding H. Yost, "Loyalty and Betting," 1922 Manuscript, Stagg Papers, Box 2, folder 22.

87. Fielding H. Yost, "Professionalism in Collegiate Athletics," undated manuscript, Board in Control of Intercollegiate Athletics, Box 39, Michigan Archives; Fielding H. Yost, "The Function of College Athletics," undated manuscript, Stagg Papers, Box 2, folder 22.

88. *The Nation,* Nov. 20, 1890, 895.

89. 1899 Notes for Penn game, Stagg Papers, Box 30, folder 4.

90. Forbes, *Football Notebook,* 70.

91. G. L. W. Patrick, "The Psychology of Football," *American Journal of Psychology,* 14 (July–Oct. 1903), 104–117; Mark Edmundson, "The Doctor in the Dungeon," *Civilization,* 3:1 (Jan.–Feb.

1996), 70–72; Pope, *Patriotic Games,* 155; Oriard, *Reading Football,* 229 (quote).

92. Wakefield, *Playing to Win,* 20.

93. Ibid., 6–57; Pope, "An Army of Athletes."

94. Robert W. Peterson, *Pigskin: The Early Years of Pro Football* (New York: Oxford University Press, 1997), 139.

95. Ibid., 138 (quote)–143.

96. Danzig, *History of American Football,* v; Robert J. Higgs, *Sports: A Reference Guide* (Westport, CT: Greenwood Press, 1982), 172; Wakefield, *Playing to Win,* 61 (quote)–66.

97. Wakefield, *Playing to Win,* 98.

98. Cited in Benjamin L. Alpers, "This Is the Army: Imagining a Democratic Military in World War II," *Journal of American History,* 85:1 (June 1998), 129–163, 141 (quote).

99. Wakefield, *Playing to Win,* 180 fn. 39.

100. Ibid., 103.

101. Higgs, *Sports: A Reference Guide,* 172.

102. Andrew J. Kozar, "And the Big Orange Caissons Went Rolling Along: R. R. Neyland: Engineer, Soldier, Football Coach," *College Football Historical Society,* 8:1 (November 1994), 17–18; Higgs, *God in the Stadium,* 273 (quote).

103. Nelson, *Anatomy of a Game,* 267, 296–298.

104. Andrew W. Miracle, Jr., and C. Roger Rees, *Lessons of the Locker Room: The Myth of School Sports* (Amherst, NY: Prometheus Books, 1994), 66–67.

105. Townsend, *Manhood at Harvard,* 16 (quote), 92.

Chapter 4

The Huddle:
Multicultural Football

Immigrants came to the United States in search of greater opportunities, and they did so in overwhelming numbers that threatened the established Anglo leadership. The Irish and Germans began their large scale exodus in the 1840s with southern and eastern European ethnics largely arriving after 1880. A steady stream of refugees continued until Congress enacted restrictive legislation in 1924 curtailing the flow by quotas.

One way in which progressive reformers hoped to Americanize the foreigners rested upon the adoption of American sports. Even though most immigrants initially lacked English language skills, they might be taught the values of capitalism and democracy through competition and teamwork. The reformers had little success with working class adults who had little time and less interest in such diversions as they clung to more traditional and familiar leisure pursuits. Comprehensive sport programs in the settlement houses, schools, parks, and playgrounds held great attraction for the immigrants' offspring however. Football played a prominent role in that process, for its physicality appealed to the working class's sense of prowess as well as the middle class's need for a sense of masculinity and growing leadership in the evolving American society.[1]

A game that had started among and for the northeastern elites could not remain so as it spread westward and southward. Students at land grant colleges, the burgeoning public high schools, and even boys' sandlot teams adopted the game by the 1880s, eventually bringing greater democratization to the sport. The consequent inclusion of disparate social, ethnic, racial, and religious groups, though relatively small in the nineteenth century, carried great symbolic meaning to American promises of equality and opportunity thereafter.

Exclusion from the ranks of leadership and the football field had been painful for many non-WASPS. If sport taught character and leadership, nonparticipants would be relegated to inferior status. George Santayana, a Spanish Catholic student of William James at Harvard, and later a professor of philosophy, explained in a letter to his mentor: "I wonder if you realize the years of suppressed irritation which I have passed in the midst of an unintelligible sanctimonious and often disingenuous Protestantism."[2] In Santayana's novel, *The Last Puritan*, a Harvard Catholic is considered a social failure and criticized by his Protestant peers because "he hadn't distinguished himself in any sport."[3] Football had become the most prominent of all sports on college campuses by the 1890s.

Although Social Darwinists of the time assumed white, Anglo, upper class superiority they did not fully intend to test James's pragmatism on the football field. Walter Camp claimed that

> ... it is a gentleman's game— that, as the "Dandy" gentlemen regiments in the war outmarched, out fought, and out plucked the "bloody rebs," so gentlemen teams and gentlemen players will always hold the foot ball field. Brutes haven't the pluck....[4]

When Camp and Caspar Whitney planned to publish a football book, Whitney made clear the intended audience in a letter to Camp. "What do we care for...the men in the Fall River Mills or in the silk mills at Paterson...the only Foot Ball in America is the Inter-Collegiate game."[5]

The elites' own insistence on winning dismantled the amateur code and its pretensions of gentlemanly posture. Victories required talent, regardless of lineage, and the spread of the game induced an inevitable leveling effect. As early as 1894, a proponent of the game extolled that it "dissapated (sic) bigotry and intolerance."[6] Within a generation a Norwegian immigrant, Knut Rockne, supplanted Walter Camp as America's greatest football figure. Rockne declared that "Western supremacy in football is a triumph of the middle class over the rich."[7]

Among the first to challenge the myths of Social Darwinism were native and African-Americans, who held a marginal existence in American society. Characterized as "others," whites portrayed Indians as uncivilized savages, and blacks as primitive brutes. Football provided both groups with the opportunity to dispel such notions of inferiority.

Systematically excluded from the upper echelons of professional baseball after 1884, boxing, for a time, offered blacks the opportunity to challenge the belief in white superiority. When George Dixon, the black featherweight champ, bloodied and knocked out Jack Skelly in an 1892 New Orleans title fight, however, a racist backlash ensued in a move to ban interracial bouts. Heavyweights refused to give the black Peter Jackson a deserved chance at the crown, and when Jack Johnson finally wrested it from Tommy Burns in Australia in 1908, it engendered the search for the "Great White Hope," Johnson's flight from federal prosecution, race riots, and his eventual imprisonment. It remained for the more docile Joe Louis to rekindle African-American hopes in the 1930s. Until that time football provided the only continuous, highly visible, integrated athletic enterprise for African-American athletes. Moreover, whereas boxing pitted black against white in an individual and hostile encounter, football included black players within the cooperative framework of the team.[8]

Within that framework blacks seemed less threatening than in the singular encounters of the boxing ring; yet stellar play might be recognized by all. Given the game's similarity to military combat, football may have served a surrogate function for African-American players, allowing them to attain a measure of the hero status denied them, though they had served with distinction in the Civil War, as Buffalo Soldiers, and in the Spanish-American War. Such disregard for black contributions to war efforts continued throughout World Wars I and II.[9]

On the football field, however, African-American players literally fought for and earned a measure of respect. George

Jewett, star of the Ann Arbor High School team in 1889, entered the University of Michigan the next year. As a half-back and kicker, Jewett scored six touchdowns in one game against the Detroit Athletic Club; but his play in a 56–10 win over Albion resulted in a riot as opponents and fans tried to "kill the nigger." Police restored order and Jewett remained in the game. A teammate admitted that Jewett was "very fast ...He undoubtedly was the best player on the Michigan team of 1890." When an Indianapolis hotel manager refused his stay, white teammates caused the man to retract his decision. Despite such support, Jewett left Michigan the following year, and reappeared in 1893 on the Northwestern team, whose fans apparently appreciated his play. In the game against Michigan that year a "special student train with all kinds of money to bet on their team" traveled to Ann Arbor. When Jewett scored the first touchdown they doubled their bets, only to be humiliated 72–6.[10]

While Jewett's fame proved transitory, he led the way for others. The year after his appearance two African-Americans played for the Amherst team. William Tecumseh Sherman Jackson starred at halfback, and William Henry Lewis captained the team at center. Lewis, the son of former slaves, entered Harvard Law School and earned All-America honors at center in 1892 and 1893, the first black to gain such distinction. Lewis coached Harvard teams in later years and won election to the Cambridge city council and state legislature. He then served as Assistant United States Attorney General for Boston and held that national office during the Taft administration.[11]

Lewis earned respect beyond the football field; but it was due at least initially and in no small part to his prowess on it. When a local barber refused service to Lewis fellow students boycotted his shop. Yet they took no action when Monroe Trotter, Harvard's first black Phi Beta Kappa, suffered a similar fate. Blacks' physical abilities were apparently more meaningful than their intellectual attainments. W. E. B. DuBois, who obtained his bachelor's, master's, and doctoral degrees at the institution during the same period stated that he did not feel a part of the school.[12]

In the South segregation laws required African-Americans to play each other, and they did so by 1890 when Biddle began intramural football. Two years later it engaged in the first black intercollegiate game with Livingstone at Salisbury, North Carolina. The Lincoln-Howard series, initiated in 1894, became a Thanksgiving spectacle in Washington, D.C., that paralleled white festivities in New York. The Tuskegee and Atlanta series opened in 1897 and black sandlot teams competed in the south by the mid-1890s. Where excluded, African-Americans thus constructed a parallel sporting culture and thereby gained some sense of inclusion in the mainstream sporting activities.[13]

Somewhat more fluid social conditions allowed greater opportunities for African-Americans in the North. In 1902 Minnesota featured a multiracial front line with an Indian, an African-American, a German, two Englishmen, and two Irishmen, all led by a Jewish quarterback. Such cosmopolitanism gradually appeared throughout urban areas where the children of ethnic immigrants and African-American migrants increasingly attended the public schools after the turn of the century. In Chicago the Pollard brothers began earning athletic laurels in the 1890s. By 1902 Chicago newspapers regularly praised Sam Ransom, a multisport star and teammate of Walter Eckersall at Hyde Park High School. When Hyde Park arranged a post-season game in Louisville with Manual Training School in November of 1902, the southerners refused to let Ransom play. He later showcased his brilliance in a "national championship" game against a Brooklyn team in which he scored seven touchdowns. Despite future All-Americans, including Eckersall, who also played, the *Chicago Tribune* asserted that

> Ransom was the particular star of the game. It was Sammy who was always in evidence, running now around one end and now the other, gaining twenty, thirty, forty yards with ease, always on hand when a fumble was made ready to fall on the ball. Ransom it was who made touchdown after touchdown, Ransom the irresistible.[14]

Despite such ability, relatively few African-Americans got to showcase their talents on the collegiate level. Both Stagg and Yost fought over Eckersall; but neither apparently tried to recruit Ransom, who ended up at tiny Beloit College. Yost paid no heed in 1904 when a Michigan supporter wrote about Abner Powell, a black schoolboy sensation in Salt Lake City. At 180 pounds Powell allegedly ran 100 yards in 10 seconds. "This young man is a *human whirlwind*...the equal of Heston ...a thorough gentleman, always knows his place...fine punter...." Such attributes proved to no avail.[15]

Stagg also bypassed the numerous black stars on local high school teams. When Dan McGugin, the Vanderbilt coach, requested a game with Chicago he wanted assurances that Chicago had no blacks on its team. Stagg replied,

> No, we have no negroes (sic) on the University of Chicago football team, and there is no chance of there being any candidates for the team next fall. Up to date there has never been a negro on a University of Chicago team. In twenty-four years only three negroes have competed...in track athletics.[16]

Some coaches thus negated the promise of education and equal opportunity by limiting the complexion of their squads. African-Americans might compete in individual sports, such as track, but could not be part of the team on or off the field. Only in professional baseball were black athletes able to organize their own leagues. Football players, however, continued to contest white contentions of racial superiority on integrated gridirons.

Those athletes who got a chance made the most of it. Bob Marshall earned All-America recognition at Minnesota in 1905 and 1906, as did Edward Gray at Amherst in the latter year. Archie Alexander gained All-Missouri Valley honors for Iowa in 1910, even though opponents in Missouri refused to let him play. Alexander worked as hard in the classroom, earning a degree in civil engineering. Two years later, Roy Young coached linemen at Northwestern, one of the few blacks accorded a leadership role. Fritz Pollard, in 1916 and Paul Robeson, in 1917 and 1918, became the first African-Americans to make the All-American first team, thereby becoming national heroes in the black community.[17]

The *Chicago Defender*, perhaps the most prominent of all African-American newspapers, charged that football had become an "obsession" in black colleges as early as 1910. The craze included the trustees, alumni, faculty, and women. The paper claimed that players experienced tremendous pressure to bring glory to their schools and their female fans, for whom they risked injury and death. Failure to win brought disgrace, and players considered such matters seriously.[18]

Jack Trice, the first black athlete to attend Iowa State, wrote himself a note before a game with Minnesota in 1923. After Nebraska and St. Louis refused to let him play in the previous two games, Trice wrote "The honor of my race, family and self is at stake. Everyone is expecting me to do big things. I wil ...."[19] Despite a first-half injury, Trice continued to play, and he suffered further harm in the third quarter. Against his protests Trice was removed from the field and died two days later.

By that time Lincoln University of Pennsylvania had already joined three southern schools to form the Colored Intercollegiate Athletic Conference in 1912. Greater racial consciousness and race pride surfaced when the *Pittsburgh Courier* began naming a black national champion in 1920 and a black All-American team in 1927. Six years later Florida A&M hosted the Orange Blossom Classic in Jacksonville; an African-American bowl game that served as the unofficial national championship game. Still laboring under the Jim Crow laws that forced segregation, African-Americans adopted the game as their own within their own administrative framework and commercialized structure. By that time dozens of black players had competed with and against whites on northern teams, slowly dismantling the assumptions of Social Darwinism and providing the African-American community with continued hope in the promise of democracy. Blacks demonstrated that trust by donating the proceeds of the 1942 Tuskegee-Wilberforce game, held in Chicago's Soldier Field, to the army emergency relief fund.[20]

Ironically, it was often in the small towns and among the less educated working class that black players won begrudging respect for their prowess on the burgeoning professional circuit. Professionalism spread from western Pennsylvania to eastern Ohio after the turn of the century when Massillon hired four Pittsburgh pros for its state championship game with East Akron in 1903. It then divided its winning shares among the whole team. At least six other towns hired players the next year. Shelby, Ohio, signed Charles Follis, previously a star black running back for the Wooster Athletic Association, to a contract for a full season and provided him with a job in the local hardware store. Such insurance moves secured the loyalty of Follis through the 1906 season, for it was common practice for players to switch teams weekly, following the highest bidder for their services.[21]

Community pride and enormous bets required securing the best talent as professionalism spread to the East and westward, and African-American players benefited. Akron signed Charles "Doc" Baker in 1906, and Henry McDonald began a long career among various New York teams in 1911. Gideon "Charlie" Smith played for Canton in 1915, and Bobby Marshall, the Minnesota All-American, was still playing professionally in 1927 at the age of 47 with the Duluth, Minnesota, Eskimos in the National Football League. The emergence of Fritz Pollard on the professional scene in 1919 signaled the heyday of early black pros in the 1920s. Pollard enjoyed one of the highest salaries in the new professional league and a measure of prestige as the first African-American to serve as a head coach. Fred "Duke" Slater, an Iowa standout, and All-Pro lineman for the Chicago Cardinals in the 1920s, later became a judge. Such leadership roles enabled blacks to encroach upon the boundaries of white power. More than a dozen black players appeared on six different pro teams before white owners followed the lead of baseball and banned them after 1933. Numerous others played for semipro, college, club, and high school squads throughout the country, enabling whites and some blacks to perceive a degree of racial progress.[22]

For more than 50 years, while major league baseball excluded African-Americans, football provided hope, opportunity, and a measure of recognition and esteem for black athletes. Though more democratic, at least until 1934, black pioneers still faced racism from both opponents, teammates, and fans. Racial slurs and intentional injuries were constant threats; but as African-Americans prevailed they further damaged the restrictive barriers of Jim Crow and Social Darwinism. In the process they developed a greater sense of identity, racial consciousness, and racial pride.[23]

Football also highlighted the limited inclusion of native Americans in white society. In 1879 the Carlisle school for Indians, one of six nationally, opened its doors in abandoned army barracks in Pennsylvania with the purpose of converting the Indians to white notions of civilization. The program of assimilation taught English, vocational skills, and WASP values; but the football team represented its most visible success. Although the team began play in 1890, injuries resulted in a two-year hiatus, until resurrected in 1893. Within two years the school embarked on a national schedule by challenging the eastern powers. In 1898 quarterback Frank Hudson became the first of many Indian players to win All-American recognition.[24]

The school housed individuals from 70 different tribes, and the 1901 football team even included an Eskimo, Nikifer Shouchuk. The school, and the team in particular, represented a showcase of government assimilation efforts. With no home field the team traveled the length of the country, including West Coast tours in 1899 and 1903 to play against universities, middle class athletic clubs, and other Indian schools. In 1912 Carlisle even went to Canada to play a combined rugby-football game against Toronto University, in which Carlisle prevailed 49–1. Such exposure, and victories, garnered acclaim and power. Carlisle nearly defeated Harvard and Yale in the 1896 season, and beat Penn in 1899. Sportswriters ranked Carlisle among the best teams in the nation between 1904–1914, and its 1912 team, with ten tribal groups represented, led the nation in scoring with 504 points. Jim Thorpe accounted for 25 of the team's 66 touchdowns.[25]

Such a visible symbol of democracy at work proved a commercial bonanza for opponents and provided a measure of power for the institution. As early as 1900, Coach Stagg at Chicago acknowledged the possibility of "a great financial success"; but ultimately decided not to play the Indians because a loss might "jeopardize chances for (the) western championship."[26] Carlisle got a $2000 guarantee from Michigan for a 1901 game in Detroit, and Chicago gave up $17,000 for a 1907 contest, which Carlisle won 18–4.[27]

Winning at the box office and on the field may have gone a long way in resurrecting the image of native Americans, except that "Pop" Warner, Carlisle's coach from 1899–1903, and again from 1907–1914, got most of the credit. The innovative formations and trick plays which the Indians featured were attributed to Warner's genius and only reinforced the Social Darwinian perception of the necessity for white leadership. When Carlisle hid the ball under a player's jersey and nearly defeated mighty Harvard in 1903, Warner reinforced the prevailing stereotypes by asserting that "The public expects the Indians to employ trickery and we try to oblige."[28] Warner also capitalized on the nativist sentiment that all Indians looked alike and "that 'Redskins' are hard to distinguish" by refusing to number players' jerseys.[29]

The white press continued to represent Indians as primitives, or at best, noble savages, despite the fact that the Indians' sportsmanship exceeded that of their white opponents. When kneed by an antagonist, Pete Hauser, a 1907 standout, retaliated with a simple question, "Who's the savage now?"[30] Often characterized as tricksters who won by deviousness or "massacre" if they scored a lot of points, such media descriptions reinforced white notions of Anglo moral superiority. Football taught Indians rules, discipline, and civilization; but ultimately they served as "good losers," as they had in the Anglo land quest for Manifest Destiny.

The game meant much more to the Indians, however, and provided them with a means to exhibit racial pride and a measure of vengeance. "Pop" Warner admitted approaching games as a frontier conflict and inciting his players in a continuation of the Indian wars. The Indians knew that such battles had been fought on unequal terms and proved anxious to show "what they could do when the odds were even." The importance of winning for the Indians can be deduced from Warner's remark that, if the team lost more than one game in a season "they felt like painting their faces black and throwing ashes over their head." When Dickinson's pregame festivities included a cowboy scalping an Indian in 1905, Carlisle retaliated with a Dickinson dummy and proceeded to shoot arrows into its chest with each score in a 36–0 rout. In 1911 when Syracuse players smashed the nose of a Carlisle guard, they were amazed to witness his second half return under a mask of tape. Only after the game did they realize that Carlisle's assistant coach, Emil Hauser (also known as Wauseka), had posed as an impostor to gain a measure of revenge.[31]

The Indians took particular pride in defeating Army, winning two of three games against the symbol of U.S. military might. A Carlisle historian noted that against the Army, "Redskins play football as if they were possessed."[32] Before the 1912 contest Warner allegedly told the Indians: "These are the long knives. You are Indians. Tonight we will know whether or not you are warriors."[33] When Jim Thorpe was ruled out of bounds on a kickoff that he presumably had returned for a touchdown, he avenged the decision by scoring another on the ensuing play. Carlisle won 27–6.

Carlisle players also found particular joy in outsmarting elite institutions with trick plays. The 1907 rules disallowed a pass completion out of bounds, so Albert Exendine ran around the Chicago bench before returning to the field to catch a touchdown pass in an 18–4 win. Trick plays were commonplace against Harvard; but unnecessary in 1911 when Thorpe scored a touchdown and four field goals in an 18–15 Carlisle win. After such games players "had a lot of fun parodying the Cambridge accent, even those with very little English attempting the broad A." After a win over Penn, one Carlisle player concluded that "Maybe white men better with cannon and guns, but Indian just as good in brains to think with."[34]

Football served the native American players as a means to both resist and adapt to the dominant culture that was imposed on them. Their entrance into the outlaw world of professional football continued that evolution into a gradual and limited adoption of commercialism. Green Bay reportedly paid Tom Skenandore, an Oneida Indian at Carlisle, as early as 1896, and two players as well as coaches Warner and Pierce played in a New York tournament in 1902. John Mathews, a former Carlisle player, got paid by the Franklin, Pennsylvania, team that same year. Carlisle players gained greater exposure to the renegade brand of football when interim coach, Edward Rogers, scheduled a Wednesday game against the Massillon, Ohio, team in Cleveland in 1904. Despite the weekday they drew 3,600 patrons and thousands of dollars in bets, won by the Massillon pros, 8–4.[35]

Forced to return his 1912 Olympic medals for violating the amateur ideal by playing professional baseball, Jim Thorpe openly adopted professional football in 1915, earning as much as $250 a game from the Pine Village, Indiana and Canton, Ohio teams. Others soon found employment in the professional ranks after their college days. Joe Guyon starred at Carlisle before helping Georgia Tech to the national championship in 1917. As an All-American he soon enjoyed a lucrative salary as a professional. Thorpe served, nominally, as the first president of the new professional league upon its founding in 1920. Both Thorpe and Guyon played for the all-Indian Oorang team on the professional circuit in 1922 and 1923, with Thorpe as player-manager of the 12 different tribes represented on the roster.[36]

Other Indians earned a measure of fame and status as football coaches too. Bemus Pierce, a Carlisle star from 1894–1898, became Warner's assistant thereafter before assuming head coaching responsibilities at several schools. Albert Exendine won All-America recognition in 1906 and 1907 before starting a long coaching career in 1908 that took him to both coasts and Oklahoma, where he retired to serve as a lawyer with the Bureau of Indian Affairs. Lone Star Dietz, a teammate of Thorpe's from 1907–1911, enjoyed an equally prestigious career as a coach, leading Washington State to an undefeated season and a 1916 Rose Bowl win. Dietz coached several collegiate squads before accepting the position of head coach of the professional Boston Braves in 1933 (later Washington Redskins). Dietz returned to the collegiate ranks in 1935 and a career as an artist.[37]

The athletic tradition spawned by Carlisle ended in scandal when financial mismanagement by white administrators caused the school's closure in 1918. Indian players continued to earn acclaim and money in the professional ranks for another decade, and Mayes McLain, of the Haskell Indian Institute in Kansas, led the country in scoring with 253 points in 1926. Haskell garnered a 12-0-1 record that year, but the white media and NCAA record books subsequently diminished both team and individual achievements. Haskell had attempted to "attain a position among the foot ball teams of the west similar to that occupied by the Carlisle team among those of the east..." as early as 1900.[38] The most prominent teams, however, declined to schedule Haskell, thus limiting the Indian presence in the more elite circles. Despite Carlisle's success the white media continued to reinforce old stereotypes a quarter century later. In the 1926 battle of unbeatens Haskell and Boston College tied 21–21 in Boston. The *Boston Globe* declared the Indians "more powerful"; but the Bostonians "smarter." When Haskell then defeated an unbeaten Xavier squad the *Cincinnati Enquirer* called it "the modernized version of warfare of the Indian empire of the past." Perhaps it was such designation as "others," or perhaps the prowess of its players that caused the Missouri Valley Conference to shun Haskell when scheduling, ensuring that there would be no more Carlisles.[39]

The perception of integration and assimilation fostered by the Carlisle teams masked the reality of limited inclusion in American society. Football allowed diverse tribes to obtain a sense of collective racial identity, combat Social Darwinian stereotypes, and develop pride in Indian athletic heroes. A select few gained socioeconomic status exemplifying the American dream. Whites, however, chose to arrest the development of full incorporation in American society by maintaining the separate and unequal reservation system that continues to plague Indian populations with poverty and the mixed blessing of limited autonomy.

Other ethnic groups fared better, and the physicality of football held particular appeal to the children of working class immigrants who measured their self-esteem by toughness and prowess. By the turn of the century the explosive growth of the game across the country brought greater representation on the football fields that seemed to portend a fuller inclusion in the American democracy.

Irish-Americans fled the potato famine of the 1840s in their homeland, and more than 4 million found their way to America thereafter. Restricted, for the most part, to manual labor, and urban ghettoes, the bachelor subculture produced the first American sports heroes in the form of boxers. John

Morrissey won acclaim in the New York Irish community by the 1850s and parlayed his popularity into political office and a gambling fortune. By 1860 another Irish-American, John C. Heenan, challenged the British champion, Tom Sayers, in a controversial draw. In the 1880s John L. Sullivan won a national reputation and a following that crossed ethnic and class lines. Such pugnacity served the Irish well on the football field as they gained social status and access to college educations.[40]

Men of Irish extraction proliferated in the game by the 1890s and they soon progressed off the field as well. Ben "Sport" Donnelly, scion of a wealthy Chicago printer, attended Princeton in 1889, and earned a reputation as a "slugger." Walter Camp selected him as an alternate on the first All-American team; but Donnelly returned to Chicago, where he joined an athletic club team and emerged as one of the first professional players in 1892. Both Vance McCormick and Thomas "Bum" McClung starred for Yale in the 1890s. McCormick became mayor of Harrisburg, Pennsylvania and McClung served as United States treasurer from 1909–1912. James Hogan, born in Ireland, and a three-time All-American, captained the Yale team in 1904. The Yale Athletic Association not only covered his room, board, and tuition; but provided him with a Cuban vacation. He also received commissions on baseball programs sold at games and on all cigarettes sold in New Haven; yet somehow retained his amateur status.[41]

The Irish also proved adept as coaches and promoters of the game. Mike Donahue, born in Killarney, Ireland, in 1879, came to the United States at the age of 14. After a stint as the Yale quarterback, Donahue served as the Auburn football coach from 1904–1922 and compiled a record of 97-35-4. Even more remarkably, he did so as an Irish immigrant Catholic during the crest of Ku Klux Klan power in the deep South. Dan McGugin, perhaps the South's most famous coach, led Vanderbilt from 1904-1934. In more cosmopolitan New York City Thomas O'Rourke, manager of Madison Square Garden, staged the first professional football tournaments starting in 1902. His 1903 invitational included a Gaelic football game.[42]

Starting as the Morgan Athletic Club, a sandlot team, in 1898, Chris O'Brien developed a neighborhood organization into the professional Chicago Cardinals. Numerous other Irishmen managed early pro teams. Both Connie Mack and Jimmy O'Donnell fielded clubs, though both became more famous as baseball managers. Walter Flanigan directed the Rock Island (Illinois) Independents, a charter member of the National Football League, and John "Paddy" Driscoll starred for O'Brien's entry in the new professional circuit before assuming full-time responsibilities as a coach. Edward "Slip" Madigan played center at Notre Dame and coached the South Bend Arrows pro team before leading little St. Mary's of California to national prominence from 1921–1939. After Tim Mara, owner of the New York Giants, and Art Rooney, with his Pittsburgh Pirates (later Steelers), joined the NFL the league took on the appearance of an Irish Catholic club. Sport, like politics, allowed Irish-Americans an entrée into the mainstream culture.[43]

More than 6 million Germans made the European exodus to America, and their descendants became well represented on the football fields by the 1890s. Frank Hinkey, the son of a German immigrant, and the greatest player of his day as a four-time All-American, led Yale from 1891–1894. Arthur Hillebrand captained the Princeton team of 1898 and twice won All-American honors. In 1898 Clarence Hershberger of the University of Chicago earned the distinction of becoming the first noneasterner selected to the All-America team. During the next decade Chicago produced one of college football's great quarterbacks in Walter Steffen, who later became a coach at Carnegie Tech and an alderman, U.S. attorney, and superior court judge in Chicago. Michigan's Adolph "Germany" Schulz earned All-American honors in 1907, and his brother, Guy, appeared as an Ohio professional three years later. The six Nesser brothers, boilermakers for the Columbus Panhandle branch of the Pennsylvania Railroad, terrorized the Ohio league for two decades. The sons of German-Americans who had settled in central Texas also played on the university team, and German-born John Heber played four years at Kentucky, starting in 1916. The most famous of the German-born, however, was not a player but a coach, Bob Zuppke. In 1881 the Zuppke family arrived in Milwaukee, where their son attended high school before entering the

University of Wisconsin. He began his career as a high school coach in 1906. After his Oak Park, Illinois team defeated Everett, Massachusetts for the national interscholastic championship in 1912, Zuppke became a sought-after coach by Midwestern universities. He coached at the University of Illinois until 1941, producing four national championship teams.[44]

Another German-American, Jay Berwanger, a halfback at the University of Chicago, won the first Heisman trophy awarded in 1935. Alan Bergner, the son of German immigrants, captained the 1939 Navy team. Canadian-born Arnie Weinmeister, of German descent, played at the University of Washington before an All-Pro career from 1949-1955. German-born Ernie Stautner continued that tradition as an All-Pro lineman and National Football League coach. Almost from its inception German-Americans accompanied and gloried in the growth of football.[45]

Eastern Europeans arrived in America; but most did so after 1880. Their children, too, began to grace the football fields thereafter, with the best-known appearing after 1900. Hugo Bezdek, born in Prague in 1884, came to Chicago, where he played fullback from 1902–1905 for Amos Alonzo Stagg. Bezdek earned All-America recognition in his final year before becoming a coach at Oregon, Arkansas, and Penn State, where he also served as Dean of Physical Education. Bezdek took three different teams to the Rose Bowl during his career, and he managed the Pittsburgh Pirates professional baseball team from 1917–1919. He coached the Cleveland Rams of the National Football League in 1937 and 1938. Bezdek lost his position at Penn State when he tried to abolish athletic scholarships, and students and alumni protested the decline in football prominence.[46]

Another Czech who bridged the amateur-professional world of football, and had an even more lasting influence upon it, also grew up on Chicago's South Side. George Halas, the son of immigrants, read the idealistic Merriwell stories but forged his own path to fame and fortune. A high school star, Halas followed his brothers into industrial league and semi-pro play before attending the University of Illinois. As a member of the Great Lakes naval team in the 1919 Rose Bowl

Halas won the most valuable player honors in a 17–0 win over the Mare Island Marines. He played pro baseball with the New York Yankees later that year and pro football with the Hammond, Indiana team before accepting a job with the A. E. Staley Company in Decatur, Illinois. As player-manager of its football team he participated in the founding of the American Professional Football Association, which soon became the NFL. The larger urban crowds of Chicago drew the team back to Chicago, where Halas eventually took ownership of the Bears. He remained a driving influence in professional football for a half-century and still retains heroic status in Chicago, where he personified the American dream.[47]

Although many played, no other player of Czech heritage rivaled Halas's stature. But Chuck Bednarik, the son of working-class immigrants, won particular esteem in Philadelphia. An All-American at Penn in 1947–1948, and an All-Pro for the Eagles through 1960, Bednarik was the last of the full-time players who never left the field. On the offensive line and as a defensive linebacker he exhibited the tenacity, toughness, and stamina with which the working class identified and held dear.[48]

Poles, although typically working class and sheltered within their Catholic parishes, also adopted football by the turn of the century. Sports provided a means to a larger social network and middle class status for some. A Polish team from St. Stanislaus Kostka Parish in Chicago allegedly defeated Stagg's university squad by the confusing use of their native tongue when calling signals. The first Polish alderman in Chicago, August Kowalski, doubled as the team quarterback. They remained undefeated from 1900–1903 against formidable competition. Polish players began appearing on college teams about the same time.[49]

Thomas A. Butkiewicz played at center for Penn from 1900–1904. He was joined on the line by Frank A. Piekarski, from the Pennsylvania coal region, in 1902. By 1906 Dan Policowski, playing under the alias "Riley," joined the professional team in Massillon, Ohio. Within a decade entrepreneurs John Smogor and "Slicie" Neizgodzski had their own pro team in South Bend, Indiana. Frank Rydzewski, a Notre Dame center and 1916 All-American, joined the pro ranks, and other area professional teams included John Klosinski and Tommy Grzegorek. Polish players figured prominently on the nearby Notre Dame team by the 1920s. In the 1930s "Ace" Gutowski quarterbacked the professional Portsmouth, Ohio team, and Ed Danowski filled the same role for the New York Giants, while Ed Skoronski enjoyed All-American honors at Purdue before engaging in a pro career. The greatest of all, however, proved to be "Bronko" Nagurski, born to Polish-Ukrainian parents in Canada in 1908. Four years later they moved to Minnesota, where Nagurski became an All-American at the state university. After his graduation in 1930 Nagurski starred with the Chicago Bears for nine seasons as a powerful fullback. Poles maintained their religious loyalties by playing for Notre Dame in the 1940s, where "Ziggy" Czarobski starred and Johnny Lujack won the Heisman trophy.[50] Such religious links proved important, for they allowed nationalistic ethnic groups to assimilate on their own terms.

Other eastern Europeans adopted the game as well. A Romanian team played in Aurora, Illinois, as early as 1921, and Lithuanians pointed to the three Wistert brothers, sons of an immigrant, all of whom starred for Michigan from 1933–1949. Al Wistert then played for the professional Philadelphia Eagles from 1943–1951. Frank Filchock, born to Slovak parents, led the NFL in passing in 1944, and later coached the Denver Broncos. The Baltimore Colts plucked Johnny Unitas, of Lithuanian descent, from the sandlots to lead them to glory in the 1950s.[51]

Scandinavians produced their share of football heroes, particularly on the Minnesota teams after the turn of the century. The greatest, however, belonged to Notre Dame, where Norwegian-born Knute Rockne played and coached his way to fame and prosperity before a plane crash secured his status as an American icon.

Among the southern Europeans more than 5 million Italians entered America, mostly after 1880. They adopted football by the 1890s with an Italian, only identified as Boggiano, on the 1894 Memphis Athletic Club team. Giovanni F. Villa played for Michigan in 1898. Ed Abbaticchio competed for Latrobe, Pennsylvania in 1895, one of the early pro teams, before turning to professional baseball. Lou Little, whose real name was Luigi Piccolo, played tackle on Penn's 1917 Rose Bowl team before a brief pro career in Ohio during the 1920s. He became more famous as a coach at Georgetown (1924–1929) and Columbia (1929–1956).[52]

Italian boys had become so enamored of football by the 1920s, and football heroes so prevalent during the period, that at least one contrived to capitalize on such interest. Emanuel Steffano, born in Florence in 1904, came to the United States in 1908 and later joined his high school team. But by the early 1920s he had taken to impersonating Johnny Mohardt, the Notre Dame star, and capitalizing on such celebrity by bilking unwary idolizers, resulting in an indictment for fraud in 1923.[53]

Italians had no need to search for heroes however, particularly in the urban centers where they proliferated on sandlot, high school, and college teams. Frank Carideo, the son of an Italian immigrant laborer, quarterbacked Notre Dame from 1928–1930, where teammate Joe Savoldi starred at fullback in 1929–1930, creating an Italian-American bond with the Irish Catholic institution. Flavio Tosi, a Boston College star, earned $100 a game when he turned pro with the Redskins in 1934. Henry Stella, another second generation Italian, captained the 1939 Army team; while Chicagoan Tony Canadeo traveled cross country to play for Gonzaga before returning to a pro career in the Midwest with the Green Bay Packers from 1941–1952. During the same period Johnny Del Isola, Dom Principe, and Nello Falaschi played for the New York Giants, and Angelo Bertelli won the 1943 Heisman trophy as a quarterback at Notre Dame, a feat repeated by Joe Bellino of Navy in 1960.[54]

By the 1950s Italian-born Leo Nomellini dominated opponents for the San Francisco 49ers, on both the offensive and defensive lines. Gino Marchetti also starred as a defensive end for the Baltimore Colts into the 1960s, as did Andy Robustelli with the New York Giants; and in later years, quarterbacks Joe Montana and Dan Marino enjoyed Hall of Fame careers. Coach Joe Paterno at Penn State won national acclaim, and Vince Lombardi joined the pantheon of American coaches when his Green Bay teams conquered all in the realization of the biblical David and Goliath tale.[55]

Other southern Europeans joined the football world as well, with Alex Karras representing Greeks as a stalwart All-Pro lineman for the Detroit Lions from 1958–1970. Latin Americans appeared even earlier, with Rafael Hernandez serving as an assistant coach for the early Syracuse teams. Jesse Rodriguez, born in Spain in 1901, won all-state honors at his West Virginia high school before becoming an outstanding punter at Salem College from 1925–1928. His brother, Kelly, played for West Virginia Wesleyan, and both went on to brief pro careers after their college days. Waldo Don Carlos, a second generation Spaniard, played for Drake from 1927–1930 before joining the Green Bay Packers as a center on the 1931 NFL championship team.[56]

Other early immigrants, such as Asian-Americans, proved less visible in football. But in 1923 William and Mary's Japanese quarterback, Arthur Matsu, did provide the lone highlight, a field goal, in a 61–3 loss to Syracuse. He later coached at Rutgers. More recently, Dat Nguyen, a Vietnamese linebacker for Texas A&M, won the Lombardi Trophy as one of the country's top defensive players in 1998.[57]

Proponents of assimilation and Americanization could point to such singular instances as a success, and the pattern of ethnic inclusion over three generations during the twentieth century proved continuous and fluid for white European groups. In the American melting pot ethnicity proved a more fluid synthesis than race. By the 1930s multiethnic sandlot, high school, and college teams became commonplace. Austin High School, Chicago city champions in 1937, featured an ethnic melange of Swedes, Germans, Irish, Italian, Greeks, Poles, Anglos, Jews, and other eastern Europeans all on the same team. Their opponents in the championship game, Leo High School from the separate Catholic League, proved that religion still remained an exclusive factor in American society.[58]

The media and institutions themselves have continued to draw such distinctions. As early as 1910 Texas labeled its Louisiana State opponents "creoles," and proclaimed its secular status against the Baylor "Baptists" and Southwestern "Methodists" the following year. Notre Dame faced continual rebuffs in its early attempts to join the Big Ten but now revels in its independent Catholicism. Similarly, Brigham Young University carries the banner for American Mormons.[59]

With no similar institution and no European homeland to fracture their loyalties, American Jews adopted the game as a means to instill ethnic pride and combat anti-Semitism. Cohen's Tigers, one of the top teams in Canton, Ohio, from 1909–1911, may have been an entrepreneurial venture; but early Jewish teams in Chicago were meant to gain respect. The Chicago Hebrew Institute organized in 1903 by German Jews to assimilate their more recently arrived and largely Orthodox eastern European brethren without losing their religion. Its monthly newspaper stated that "These results once accomplished much of the prejudice against our people will be removed and the Jew will then possess those traits and characteristics held in common by the other peoples of the community, and still not lose his inborn Judaism, of which he is so justly proud."[60]

Throughout the latter nineteenth century and into the 1930s scientists claimed that Jewish males had wide hips, narrow shoulders, and a diminished sex drives. In the early twentieth century doctors and psychologists asserted that Jews had a greater tendency toward homosexuality, and other ethnic groups often stereotyped them as feeble. In such cases Jewish masculinity came into question.[61]

Sports teams served to overcome the stereotype of Jews as cerebral and weak, with football, wrestling, and boxing figuring prominently in that process. The Chicago Hebrew Institute fielded its first football team in 1912, and gloried in its undefeated season, a lone 6–6 tie coming against the Medorah Athletic Club, which claimed to be the lightweight champions of Chicago. The following year, Labe Safro, known as the "Jewish Lion," appeared as a halfback on the Minneapolis Marines, a working class team organized in 1905. In 1921 the Marines joined the newly formed pro football league.[62]

By 1920 Chicagoans Arnold and Ralph Horween played for Harvard in the Rose Bowl. Fully assimilated in the American culture, the family had changed its name from the original Horowitz. The brothers then took advantage of professional opportunities with the Chicago Cardinals, playing under Irish aliases, until Arnie was named head coach in 1923. He assumed that role for Harvard from 1925–1930.[63]

Bennie Friedman, the Jewish-American quarterback for the University of Michigan from 1924–1926, attracted widespread media attention and All-American honors. The child of Russian immigrants, Friedman's collegiate experience made him a hero in the Jewish community. The *American Hebrew* newspaper proclaimed him "a Jewish prodigy of America's greatest sport" at a time before any Jews reached similar status in "the national game" of baseball.[64] Friedman continued to play as a professional and then became a college coach.

By the late 1920s so many Jewish players starred on the gridiron that the media began selecting Jewish All-American squads. Ironically, a number of the Jewish all-stars played for Catholic Notre Dame. During 1929 and 1930 Marty Brill and Marchy Schwartz starred in the backfield with Carideo and Savoldi. They were supported by Clarence Kaplan and Sam Gellis, reserve halfbacks, and linemen Abie Zoss, Norm Herwit, and Sam Goldstein. Sam Horwitz captained the 1931 Chicago team, and Saul Sherman served as its quarterback from 1933–1936 before joining the professional Chicago Bears. Irv Kupcinet starred at North Dakota and played professionally before embarking on a media career that surpassed 50 years. Marshall Goldberg, another son of a Russian immigrant, made the All-America team as a Pitt halfback for three years, leading his team to a national championship in 1937. By the 1940s Sid Luckman became the reigning Jewish athletic hero as quarterback of the Chicago Bears. More than 150 Jews made it to the NFL, and most did so before 1950. Twenty-five played in 1936, a critical year for European Jews, highlighted by the Nazi Olympics in Berlin. For Jewish-Americans without a homeland football stood as a very visible reminder of acceptance and inclusion, albeit somewhat limited, as anti-Semitism reigned in other parts of the world.[65]

By the 1930s Jewish athletes in the United States had established themselves in boxing, basketball, and football. Though they may not yet have gained full acceptance for the Jewish people, they won distinction and a measure of respect that dispelled any notions of physical debility.

As Christians, Catholics may have found easier entry into American society, but as largely working class immigrants they found little common ground with the native, middle class mainstream. Catholic parishes both insulated their congregations from the outside world, and provided a comprehensive array of social services that limited the necessity for such contact. Communal cultures, such as the Catholics and Mormons, seemed suspicious to individualistic Protestants and nativists, engendering hostility and antagonism. Religious and even regional rivalries ensued in urban areas or locales where the ostracized gathered in large numbers, such as Chicago, Utah, or the Southwest.[66]

The Americanization of Catholicism, led by the prelates themselves, began in a gradual and uneven fashion by World War I; but anti-Catholic sentiments continued throughout the century. When Notre Dame traveled to Nebraska in 1915 the hometown fans taunted them as "fish eaters." In 1924 Notre Dame students fought with the Ku Klux Klan on the streets of South Bend, and such belligerence was not limited to the Midwest. Three years later Stanford severed athletic competition with St. Mary's after on-field fights in the latter's 16–0 win. In 1935 Ohio State fans greeted Notre Dame with chants of "Catholics go home." In the next decade Paul Blansard's anti-Catholic polemic, *American Freedom and Catholic Power*, reached the best-seller list. As late as 1995, when Northwestern upset Notre Dame, a winning fan responded that "We will always be intellectually superior to Notre Dame, and as far as their athletic relationship to God, now we've proven we are morally equal."[67]

Protestants considered Catholicism a residual culture, accustomed to rituals, symbolic ceremonies, and festivals mired in the past, and ruled by an undemocratic authoritarian figure in Rome. Such characteristics proved congruent with the football culture, however, and in that activity the adversaries found some common ground.[68]

Both Notre Dame and Georgetown students began playing football in 1887, and only two years later St. Vincent's College (now Loyola) played the University of Southern California on the West Coast. By 1903 Louis "Red" Salmon of Notre Dame gained All-America recognition during an unbeaten season.

Georgetown claimed the championship of the South Atlantic in 1910, suffering only one loss, when its players were kicked and punched in a game against Pittsburgh.[69]

Notre Dame found scheduling more difficult. The Western Conference (Big Ten) rejected its application for the third time in 1908. After it shocked Michigan with an 11–3 win in 1909 other teams refused to play. When Jesse Harper became athletic director at Notre Dame in 1912, the manager informed him that "A schedule for this school is indeed a tough proposition."[70] Anti-Catholic sentiments prevailed in the Midwest. Both Notre Dame and Marquette endured another Big Ten rejection in 1913. That same year in Chicago, the challenge of DePaul High School, the Catholic League champions, to Hyde Park, winners of the Public League, went unheeded, and left Catholics frustrated in their futility to confront their perceived oppressors.[71]

Notre Dame won national recognition, if not full acceptance, that same year in a stunning upset of Army as the passing attack of Gus Dorais to Knute Rockne fostered name recognition that soon served Notre Dame players well on the professional circuit. By 1914 Rockne and at least three other Notre Dame players earned pay from the Akron Indians team, and the Toledo Maroons gave Ray Eichenlaub more than $50 per game a year later. Dorais played for both the Fort Wayne Friars and the Massillon Tigers. Harry Costello, a Georgetown star, joined Canton in 1916. By 1920 so many Notre Dame players engaged in the practice that school authorities began expelling them from school.[72]

Nevertheless, Catholic players adopted the outlaw version of the game as a means to meet their needs. Between 1916 and 1919 workers had suffered a significant loss of purchasing power due to inflation. By 1918 prices rose 59 percent over the 1913 costs, and 20 percent of the workforce responded by striking the next year. Pro football players, however, might earn more than the average worker's weekly pay for a single game. Catholics, like George Halas, Chris O'Brien of the Chicago Cardinals, and Earl "Curly" Lambeau, an ex-Notre Damer who led the Green Bay Packers, took their entrepreneurial chances in the fledgling pro league, where ability counted more than religion or social class.[73]

Within the more established circles of the collegiate elites Catholics fared less well. In 1914 Notre Dame wanted to rent the University of Chicago field for a game against Carlisle, but encountered denial. Charles Comiskey, Catholic owner of the White Sox baseball team, offered his park "any time we want to use it"; thereby demonstrating the important self-help network that reinforced Catholic communalism.[74]

Notre Dame's Rose Bowl bid met similar denial in 1921. A committee member allegedly wanted "anyone but Notre Dame," and the home team, California, objected to the Catholics as pros. Another informant wrote Coach Rockne that "Pasadena is a terribly prejudiced place and they have little or no use for anything which they think Catholic ... they went out of their way to side track Notre Dame."[75]

Once again, the Big Ten rebuffed Notre Dame's application for admission in 1926; but the Catholic school no longer needed such recognition or inclusion. Its successes on the field made it a welcome attraction in the commercialized venue of intercollegiate athletics. Other teams from around the country clamored for a Notre Dame game that would fill the seats in its stadium. By 1929 Notre Dame games accounted for the three largest crowds ever to witness a football contest.[76]

In 1922 Notre Dame even traveled to Atlanta, Georgia, national headquarters of the Ku Klux Klan. It earned nearly $7,000; but had to endure anti-Catholic taunts and rebel yells in a 13–3 win over Georgia Tech. Between 1918 and 1923 the Catholic powerhouse had gone 49-4-3 and averaged 30 points per game, while giving up only five touchdowns in the latter year. It had become a national team, and the 1924 contingent assured its place in football mythology when sportswriter Grantland Rice glorified its "Four Horsemen." The team capped its national championship with a 27–10 rout of Stanford in the 1925 Rose Bowl, filling the stadium to capacity for the first time. By that time the bowl selection committee admitted that Notre Dame was the main attraction.[77]

Such success brought national recognition to the institution, its players, and Coach Rockne, who was courted by numerous schools. Iowa even offered to let him "name (his) own terms for a salary."[78] If schools could not get Rockne they settled for his famous players, sixty-eight of whom had college coaching positions by 1926. Others served the high schools in Chicago's Catholic League, sending Rockne a stream of star players and reinforcing the Catholic network and support system. Spearheaded by Notre Dame's success, other Catholic colleges and high schools adopted its coaches, strategies, and plays in a phenomenon known as "Catholic football," with which they challenged secular and implicitly Protestant foes. As early as 1915 Catholic Butte Central began a long rivalry with Butte High School in Montana. Between 1923 and 1941 Fordham met New York University in the annual "Battle of the Bronx." The 1931 contest drew 80,000 fans. Those series paled in comparison, however, to the Chicago high school championship which pitted the Catholic League champ against its counterpart from the Public Schools League. Started in 1927, the series continues in the 1990s. The 1937 game drew more than 120,000 to Soldier Field, the largest crowd to ever see any football game in the United States.[79]

On such occasions Catholics united in a religious crusade. Even as football drew Catholics closer to the dominant culture, it allowed them to revel in their alternative beliefs. They waved rosaries at football games and flaunted their success. Notre Dame went undefeated in 1929 and 1930, and after a 27–0 win over USC in Los Angeles, a Catholic fan chided, "Hey you—Methodists! You may beat Al Smith, but you can't beat Notre Dame."[80] The reference to the defeated Catholic presidential candidate of 1928 demonstrated Catholics' lingering perceptions of exclusion.

The Catholic colleges, however, proved more democratic and inclusive in their student bodies than the elite schools. Notre Dame drew few distinctions regarding football ability. Its teams included Protestants and Jews, and by 1929 its roster showed recruits from twenty-two states, though no African-Americans.[81]

The inclusion of Catholics continued sporadically over the succeeding years. The 1935 Notre Dame-Ohio State game engendered anti-Catholic sentiments once again; but in 1943 the U.S. military establishment invited Notre Dame to play in a game in North Africa to entertain the wartime troops. That offer preceded Blansard's diatribe by only three years, sending Catholics mixed messages. The controversial election of John F. Kennedy to the presidency and the continuing Chicago Prep Bowl still signify Catholics as "others." While football helped Catholics gain a measure of acceptance and bridge social distinctions, religion remains more divisive than class.[82]

Notre Dame still signifies difference within the American society. In 1998 Bishop Amat, a Catholic high school from California, traveled to Illinois to play Naperville Central, in a battle of national powers. With national rankings and regional prestige at stake, Amat's coach, Tom Salter, stated that

> the real highlight for the team is Saturday's excursion to Notre Dame. It just may be every Catholic high school football player's dream to play at Notre Dame or at least visit the place where Rockne coached and Montana led brilliant comebacks....That's the main reason we set up this trip.[83]

Football, however, helped to bridge class divisions, not only at the high school and college levels levels, but perhaps even more importantly, on the incipient professional and semipro circuits. Working class players found some validity in the American promise of opportunity through sport. More than 80 percent of the early professionals were noncollegians. Notre Dame alone sent sixty-five of its players to pro teams between 1920–1932; and half of its players still derived from the working class by 1965. Football promised social mobility, in the form of athletic scholarships or cash. John Brallier began playing for $10 per game as an 18-year-old in 1894. He stated that "The reason I took money to play football was because I wanted an education, and there was no money at home."[84] Haven Brigham, Ohio State center in 1910, quit school for the pros because "the money was too good to pass up."[85] Ralph Vince, an Italian immigrant and Ohio coal miner, also paid his way through school with his pro earnings from 1919–1923. R. T. Hallady, a University of Chicago player, continued to play for the Cardinals despite Stagg's threats to revoke his athletic letter and privileges, because, as Hallady stated, he wanted to own his own home.[86]

Even good high school players earned more playing football than they could in the factories each week. High schoolers in

Michigan got as much as $17 a game as early as 1919, and the team at St. Mary's Institute in Dayton evolved into the fully professional Dayton Triangles, charter members of the National Football League in 1922. More than a dozen such teams operated in the Chicago area alone during the World War I era. In a celebrated 1925 case, Ambrose McGuirk lost the rights to the Milwaukee franchise after the NFL discovered that he used high school players in a game against the Chicago Cardinals. Football thus provided easy access to money for many and at an early age reinforced a belief in opportunity and social mobility even as labor strikes, layoffs, and unemployment threatened otherwise.[87]

One need not be a player to share in such largesse either, as friends, family, and spectators often wagered on the outcomes. Gambling led to professionalism in the 1890s, and it soon infected the perceived amateurism of intercollegiate campuses as well. By 1920 Ohio State students bet thousands of dollars on games, and considered victories as "financial investments." Such practices permeated the Big Ten and other conferences, undaunted by the recent Black Sox scandal. Even town teams generated stakes of $50,000 or more for a single game. Working class patrons and the less wealthy thus found the means to supplement their wages, whereas losses only extended ongoing hardships, i.e., they had little to lose. Roy Rosenzweig has claimed that gambling served as a means to accommodate people into an unequal social order.[88]

If such wagers served as an investment for some, they also measured community pride. Townspeople supported their teams with subscriptions and businessmen funded operations as well. In 1905 Massillon found 122 subscribers, who raised $1,468 for their team. Boosterism fostered the town rivalries that spawned professionalism in Pennsylvania and Ohio; and such sustenance allowed small towns to compete with large city teams in the National Football League into the 1930s. Community pride still maintains the existence of Green Bay at that level, and nourishes the hopes of thousands of high schools against their local rivals throughout the country. In the process, isolated, secluded, or ethnocentric communities are engaged as part of the greater society.[89]

The physicality of football also held a natural appeal for the working class, who measured their prowess and earned their money with their bodies. Football allowed them to accept American capitalism on their own teams. Unlike the collegiate administrators, working class players saw no shame in accepting payment for their labors. To the contrary, they won even greater esteem among working class supporters for their ability to earn substantial sums congruent with working class norms. The elitism of the New England colleges which spawned the amateur ideology in the nineteenth century was upheld by the regulations of the National Collegiate Athletic Association. The Western and Missouri Valley Conferences banned all contact with professionalism in an attempt to destroy it. Major John L. Griffith, the Big Ten commissioner, denounced the pro version as "decadent," but working class players found in football an alternative cultural form that allowed them to participate in the mainstream without violating their own ideals or codes of conduct. Masculinity continued to be rooted in physicality for all classes, and Notre Dame even claimed that "manliness and ruggedness were inculcated in the entire student body" through intramural football. The school maintained its "rugged masculinity" by an absence of coeds, and symbolically portrayed it in the student uniform that consisted of corduroy pants, flannel shirts, and workmen's boots.[90]

But even as football allowed for the maintenance and even exaltation of class differences it also brought such groups closer together. On both the amateur collegiate and professional levels football merged the working class values of physicality with middle class commercialism and religious spectacle. Around 1910 the Toledo Maroons chose Arthur Gratop as their manager, not for any ostensible business acumen; but because his clerical position provided access to a typewriter. In similar fashion, Jack Cusack, a 21-year-old office worker for a gas company, became secretary-treasurer of the Canton team in 1912. But as the modernization and commercialization of pro football proceeded such neighborhood and town teams adopted entrepreneurial proficiencies or withered away. By the 1930s professional teams opted for middle class standards, collegiate players, and urban locations that promised the highest profits. The inclusion of African-Americans, ethnic immigrants, and the working class had already democratized the game as part of the popular culture and an alternative to the elitist ideology of amateurism. Such perceptions of equality may have alleviated labor strife and diminished any radical class consciousness when class struggles could be settled on the football field.[91]

Despite increasing commercialization and rising costs, the physicality of the game endeared it to working class players and fans in the succeeding years. Just as Green Bay remains a residual element of premodern football, the game retains residual, human characteristics in an increasingly technological age. Ed Sprinkle, a Chicago Bears player, recalled the community rivalry that continues today

> The Packers' fans would raise cane (sic) trying to keep you up at night...Fans would be right behind you when you were on the bench. They'd be cussing you out and throw a bottle at you once in a while....You'd walk down the street and kids would spit at you.

Sid Luckman charged that "They would bite you and put their fingers in your eyes...a Packer kicked me in the nose with his cleats," and broke it. When a Bear player got ejected from a 1950 game for slugging a Packer and knocking him unconscious, owner-coach George Halas gladly paid the $50 league fine for him. Bart Starr later claimed that "it was a great David and Goliath type of happening: a small-town team playing another from one of the country's largest cities."[92] Football allowed room for such dissimilarity.

The growth of football, particularly after the turn of the century, also allowed subordinate groups to challenge the Social Darwinian beliefs and stereotypes that characterized them as "others." To a greater degree, football bridged some racial, religious, class, and ethnic divisions. The Notre Dame team of 1929 included Italians, Irish, Eastern Europeans, Germans, and Jews recruited from twenty-two different states, with which it played both secular and religious opponents across the country. Similar social evolutions took place on the high school teams of every cosmopolitan city in America as disparate groups found some common ground in the popular culture of football.[93] Both civic education in the public schools and sport outside of that environment dissipated, to a great degree, lingering class consciousness and ethnic tensions. Immigrant offspring learned to transfer communal family, clan, and ethnic loyalties to the larger community of country with patriotic fervor.

The incorporation of alternative customs, classes, peoples, and places eventually produced a national football culture more inclusive and democratic than that envisioned by Walter Camp or Caspar Whitney. Football, however, held different meanings for the different geographical regions of the country and their amalgamation within that value system proceeded unevenly and not without cultural tensions.

Notes

1. Several case studies analyze the role of sport in the Americanization process. See Stephen Hardy, *How Boston Played*; Dale Somers, *The Rise of Sport in New Orleans, 1850–1900* (Baton Rouge: Louisiana State University Press, 1972); Roy Rosenzweig, *Eight Hours for What We Will: Workers and Leisure in an Industrial City, 1870–1920* (New York: Cambridge University Press, 1983); Rob Ruck, *Sandlot Seasons: Sport in Black Pittsburgh* (Urbana: University of Illinois Press, 1987); Steven Riess, *City Games: The Evolution of American Society and the Rise of Sports* (Urbana: University of Illinois, 1989); Dominick Cavallo, *Muscles and Morals: Organized Playgrounds and Urban Reform, 1880–1920* (Philadelphia; University of Pennsylvania Press, 1981); Cary Goodman, *Choosing Sides: Playgrounds and Street Life on the Lower East Side* (New York: Schocken Books, 1979); and Gerald R. Gems, *Windy City Wars*.

2. Townsend, *Manhood at Harvard*, 192.

3. Steven J. Overman, *The Influence of the Protestant Ethic on Sport and Recreation* (Brookfield, VT: Avebury, 1997), 161.

4. *Yale News*, Feb. 5, 1885, in Box 24, folder 1, Stagg Papers.

5. Caspar Whitney to Walter Camp, Sept. 10, 1891, Camp Papers, Reel 9.

6. J. Kinzer Shell, M.D., to Walter Camp, Apr. 21, 1894, Camp Papers, Reel 15.

7. Rockne, cited in Lester, *Stagg's University*, 121.

8. See David W. Zang, *Fleet Walker's Divided Heart: The Life of Baseball's First Black Major Leaguer* (Lincoln: University of Nebraska Press, 1995), 26–47. See New Orleans *Times-Democrat*, Sept. 7, 1892, 1, 4, for coverage of the Dixon-Skelly fight. See Randy Roberts, *Papa Jack: Jack Johnson and the Era of White Hopes* (Riverside, NY: The Free Press, 1983) on Johnson's eventful life. Horseracing and cycling provided African-Americans with opportunities and visibility through the 1890s but excluded them thereafter.

9. John Hoberman, *Darwin's Athletes: How Sport Has Damaged Black America and Preserved the Myth of Race* (Boston: Houghton Mifflin, 1997), 61–75.

10. Ralph Stone to T. Hawley Tapping, Jan. 10, 1955, and Roger Sherman to T. Hawley Tapping, Jan. 19, 1955, in Jewett file, Box 35, University of Michigan Archives. Roberts, *The Big Nine*, 88, lists Jewett's appearance at Northwestern in 1894. The Northwestern University archives indicate that Jewett entered the medical school in 1893 and played football both years.

11. Edna and Art Rust, Jr., *Art Rust's Illustrated History of the Black Athlete* (Garden City, NY: Doubleday & Co., 1985), 226; Bealle, *The History of Football at Harvard*, 534–536.

12. Townsend, *Manhood at Harvard*, 234, 247.

13. Hurd, *Black College Football*, 13, 28, 32; John Heisman, "Signals," *Collier's* (Oct. 6, 1928), 32.

14. Weyand, *Saga of American Football*, 78; Carroll, *Fritz Pollard*, 18–20; *Chicago Tribune*, Nov. 24, 1902, 6; Dec. 7, 1902, 9 (quote).

15. W. J. Davis to Keene Fitzpatrick, Aug. 17, 1904, Box 1, Board in Control of Intercollegiate Athletics, University of Michigan.

16. Stagg-McGugin correspondence, Nov. 16, 1916; Dec. 11, 1916; Dec. 14, 1916 (quote), in Box 42, folder 13, Stagg Papers.

17. Oriard, *Reading Football*, 232–233; Bob Royce, "Bridge Builder," *College Football Historical Society*, 5:2 (Feb. 1992), 5–6; Jack W. Berryman, "Early Black Leadership in Collegiate Football," *Historical Journal of Massachusetts*, 9 (June 1981), 17–28, 85 fn. 51; Carroll, *Fritz Pollard*, 109–112; Martin Bauml Duberman, *Paul Robeson* (New York: Alfred A. Knopf, 1988), 19–24.

18. *Chicago Defender*, Jan. 22, 1910, 1.

19. Scott Dominiak, "The honor of my race, family, and self is at stake," *College Football Historical Society*, 3:2 (Feb. 1990), 12–13.

20. Hurd, *Black College Football*, 13, 163–165; Wakefield, *Playing to Win*, 126. Arthur R. Ashe, *A Hard Road to Glory: Football* (New York: Armistad, 1988), 9, indicates a black All-American selection as early as 1911.

21. Bob Braunwart and Bob Carroll, "The Ohio League," *Coffin Corner*, 3:7 (July 1981), 1–3; Robert W. Peterson, *Pigskin: The Early Years of Pro Football* (New York: Oxford University Press, 1997), 173.

22. Peterson, *Pigskin*, 173–180; (Carroll, *Fritz Pollard*, 133, lists Baker as "Young"); Carroll, *Fritz Pollard*, 81, 128–183; see Ocania Chalk, *Pioneers of Black Sport* (New York: Dodd, Mead & Co., 1975), 222–233, for the few African-American players of the 1930s.

23. Gerald R. Gems, "The Construction, Negotiation, and Transformation of Racial Identity in American Football," *American Indian Culture and Research Journal*; 22:2 (July 1998), 131–150.

24. Frederick E. Hoxie, *A Final Promise: The Campaign to Assimilate the Indians, 1880–1920* (New York: Cambridge University Press, 1989); John S. Steckbeck, *Fabulous Redmen: The Carlisle Indians and Their Famous Football Teams* (Harrisburg, PA: J. Horace McFarland Co., 1951), 3–17. For a more critical analysis of the Carlisle program see Jack Newcombe, *The Best of the Athletic Boys*.

25. Glenn S. Warner, "The Indian Massacres," *Collier's*, Oct. 17, 1931, 8, 63; Steckbeck, *Fabulous Redmen*, 31, 34, 45–47, 53, 57, 62, 96; Weyand, *Saga of American Football*, 124–125.

26. Glenn S. Warner to A. A. Stagg, Mar. 5, 1900; Stagg to Warner, Mar. 10, 1900, Stagg Papers, Box 41, folder 9.

27. Michigan—Carlisle game contract, Nov. 2, 1901, Board in Control of Intercollegiate Athletics, University of Michigan Archives; Warner, "Indian Massacres," 62.

28. Bealle, *The History of Football at Harvard*, 147.

29. K. E. Davis to Walter Camp, Feb. 16, 1914, Camp Papers, Reel 7.

30. Oriard, *Reading Football*, 233–247; Glenn S. Warner, "Heap Big Run—Most—Fast," *Collier's*, Oct. 24, 1931, 19 (quote).

31. Warner, "The Indian Massacres," 7, 8 (quotes); Steckbeck, *Fabulous Redmen*, 54–55, 107.

32. The only Carlisle loss came in 1917, a year before the school's closing when the football team was no longer prominent. Steckbeck, *Fabulous Redmen*, 61, 95 (quote).

33. Weyand, *Saga of American Football*, 101.

34. Steckbeck, *Fabulous Redmen*, 110; Marc S. Maltby, *The Origins and Early Development of Professional Football* (New York: Garland Pub., 1997), 130; Warner, "Heap Big Run—Most—Fast," 19, 46 (quotes).

35. Maltby, *The Origins and Early Development of Professional Football*, 60, 71–77, 90–92; Peterson, *Pigskin*, 38–39.

36. Peterson, *Pigskin*, 54–56; Maltby, *The Origins and Early Development of Professional Football*, 130–133; Bob Braunwart, Bob Carroll, and Joe Horrigan, "Oorang Indians," *Coffin Corner*, 3:1 (Jan. 1981), 1–8.

37. David L. Porter, ed., *Biographical Dictionary of American Sports: 1989–1992 Supplement for Baseball, Football, Basketball and Other Sports* (Westport, CT: Greenwood Press, 1992), 396–397, 469–470; John C. Hibner, "Lone Star Dietz," *College Football Historical Society*, 1:5 (August 1988), 1–4.

38. Ray Schmidt, "Princes of the Prairies," *College Football Historical Society*, 2:2 (Feb. 1989), 1–8, on McLain and the 1926 Haskell team; William Peterson to Amos Alonzo Stagg, Dec. 6, 1900, (quote), Stagg Papers, Box 41, folder 9; W. M. Peterson to Football team manager, Jan. 9, 1901, Board in Control of Intercollegiate Athletics, University of Michigan Archives. The NCAA does not recognize statistics prior to 1937 as official records.

39. Schmidt, "Princes of the Prairies," 5, 6 (quotes), 8. Schmidt, editor of the College Football Historical Society publication, has confirmed that none of the eastern Big Three offered a game. Brown and Haskell played in 1924. In the Big Ten only Minnesota competed with Haskell after 1916, Ray Schmidt to author, Sept. 9, 1997.

40. Oscar Handlin, *The Uprooted* (New York: Grosset & Dunlap, 1951), 35; see George B. Kirsch, *Sports in North America: A Documentary History, vol. 3: The Rise of Modern Sports, 1840–1860* (Gulf Breeze, FL: Academic International Press, 1992), 133–154, on Morrissey and Heenan.

41. Maltby, *The Origins and Early Development of Professional Football*, 49; Riess, *Sport in Industrial America*, 127; Porter, ed., *Biographical Dictionary of American Sports: Football* (Westport, CT: Greenwood Press, 1987), 269–270.

42. Bolton, *War Eagle*, 74–76; Maltby, *The Origins and Early Development of Professional Football*, 71–78.

43. Maltby, *Origins and Early Development of Professional Football*, 73, 164, 169; Bob Carroll, *The Ohio League: 1910–1919* (N. Huntingdon, PA: Pro Football Researchers Assn., 1997), 82, 88–90, 93.

44. Handlin, *The Uprooted*, 36; David L. Porter, ed., *Biographical Dictionary of American Sports: 1992–1995 Supplement*, 442–443; Bob Carroll, *The Ohio League, 1910–1919*, 7, 30; Peterson, *Pigskin*, 60–62; Hans Helland Scrapbook, University of Texas, Barker Texas History Center Collection; Sugar, *The SEC*, 98; David L. Porter, ed., *Biographical Dictionary of American Sports: Football*, 265–267, 673–674.

45. Porter, *Biographical Dictionary of American Sports: Football*, 44–45, 645; Gene Schoor, *100 Years of Army–Navy Football* (New York: Henry Holt & Co., 1989), 104–105.

46. Porter, *Biographical Dictionary of American Sports: Football*, 45–46; *The Penn Stater*, (Nov. 1952), 3 (provided by Ron Smith); *New York Times*, Oct. 4, 1936, Sec. 5:11.

47. George Halas, with Gwen Morgan and Arthur Veysey, *Halas by Halas* (New York: McGraw-Hill Co., 1979).

48. Porter, *Biographical Dictionary of American Sports: Football*, 32–33. Bednarik was selected as an All-Pro in 1950–56, and again in 1960.

49. The game is not listed in Stagg's records, as he considered such encounters practice scrimmages. See D. M. Krzywonos, ed., *The Poles of Chicago, 1837–1937* (Chicago: Polish Pageant, Inc., 1937), 145–148. For Polish football in Chicago, see *Dziennik Chicagoski*, Oct. 8, 1904; Oct. 19, 1906; translated in Works Progress Administration, Foreign Language Press Survey (FLPS), 1942.

50. Davis, *Football*, 89; Weyand, *Saga of American Football*, 75, 150; Presbrey and Moffat, eds., *Athletics at Princeton*, 392, 396; Peterson, *Pigskin*, 52–53, 113, 122; Maltby, *The Origins and Early Development of Professional Football*, 164; Carroll, *The Ohio League*, 89–90; Dziennik *Zwiazkowy*, Nov. 26, 1927 (FLPS); Carl Becker, "The Tom Thumb Game: Bears vs. Spartans, 1932," *Journal of Sport History*, 22:3 (Fall 1995), 216–227; Porter, *Biographical Dictionary of American Sports: Football*, 415–418; Kevin Britz, "Of Football and Frontiers," *Journal of Sport History*, 20:2 (Summer 1993), 110, claims that Nagurski favored his Ukrainian ancestry.

51. *Aurora Beacon News*, Oct. 23, 1971 (clipping); Porter, *Biographical Dictionary of American Sports: 1992–1995 Supplement*, 423–424; Porter, *Biographical Dictionary of American Sports: Football*, 613–615, 660–661.

52. Eric Foner and John Garraty, eds., *The Reader's Companion to American History*, 534; *Ole Miss Rebels*, 28; Board in Control of Intercollegiate Athletics, Box 39, Michigan Archives; Maltby, *The Origins and Early Development of Professional Football*, 53; Nelson, *Anatomy of a Game*, 202; Jerre Mangione and Ben Morreale, *La Storia: Five Centuries of the Italian-American Experience* (New York: Harper Collins, 1992), 382–384.

53. W. J. Flynn to J. M. Byrne, Feb. 26, 1923, UADR, Box 9, file 17, University of Notre Dame Archives.

54. Porter, *Biographical Dictionary of American Sports: Football*, 37, 43, 88, 94–95; Sperber, *Shake Down the Thunder*, 315–318, 335–339; Schoor, *100 Years of Army–Navy Football*, 104–105; Peterson, *Pigskin*, 111–112, 121–122, 137.

55. Porter, *Biographical Dictionary of American Sports: Football*, 382, 433–434.

56. Evans, *Fifty Years of Football at Syracuse University*, 187; Mario Longoria, *Athletes Remembered: Mexicano/Latino Professional Football Players, 1929–1970* (Tempe, AZ: Bilingual Press, 1970), 3–13.

57. Evans, *Fifty Years of Football at Syracuse University*, 99.

58. *Northtown Economist*, Oct. 31, 1928, 10, lists rosters and stories of Chicago neighborhood teams; Austin High School, *Maroon and White*, 1937 (yearbook), 95. See Gerald R. Gems, "The Neighborhood Athletic Club: An Ethnographic Study of a Working Class Athletic Fraternity in Chicago, 1917–1984," *Colby Quarterly*, 32:1 (March 1996), 36–44, for a case study of a typical multiethnic, multiracial football team.

59. Newspaper clipping, Nov. 30, 1910; *The Texan*, Oct. 14, 1911, 1; Oct. 21, 1911, 1, all in Hans Helland Scrapbook, Barker Texas History Center; *Chicago Sun-Times*, Oct. 6, 1991, 1, 30–31.

60. Maltby, *The Origins and Early Development of Professional Football*, 100; Chicago Hebrew Institute, *Observer*, 1:3 (Feb. 1913), 5–6 (quote).

61. Sander L. Gilman, "Damaged Men: Thoughts on Kafka's Body," in Maurice Berger, Brian Wallis, and Simon Watson, eds., *Constructing Masculinity* (New York: Routledge, 1995), 176–189.

62. *Observer*, 1:1 (Nov. 1912), 14–15; Jim Quirk, "The Minneapolis Marines: Minnesota's Forgotten NFL Team," *Coffin Corner*, 20: 1 (1998), 10–12.

63. Hibner, *The Rose Bowl*, 70–74; no author, "A Ralph by Any Other Name," *Coffin Corner*, 18:6 (1997), 21.

64. Peter Levine, *Ellis Island to Ebbets Field: Sport and the American Jewish Experience* (New York: Oxford University Press, 1992), 212.

65. Ibid., 203, 209–210, 212–215; Sperber, *Shake Down the Thunder*, 298–299; Lester, *Stagg's University*, 144, 155; Kenan Heise and Mark Frazel, *Hands on Chicago: Getting Hold of the City* (Chicago: Bonus Books, 1987), 89. Steven A. Riess, "Sport and the American Jew: A Second Look," *American Jewish History*, 83:1 (March 1995), 6, on NFL figures.

66. Witold Rybczynski, *City Life: Urban Expectations in a New World* (New York: Harper Collins, 1995), 82–83; Phyllis Rose, "Pioneers on a Mission," *Civilization* (Feb./Mar. 1997), 56–63.

67. James Hennesey, *American Catholics: A History of the Roman Catholic Community in the United States* (New York: Oxford University Press, 1981); John D. McCallum, *Big Eight Football* (New York: Charles Scribner's Sons, 1979), 33–34 (quote); Sperber, *Shake Down the Thunder*, 157–162, 435 (quote); Hibner, *The Rose Bowl*, 166; John T. McGreevy, "Thinking on One's Own: Catholicism in the American Intellectual Imagination, 1928–1960," *Journal of American History*, 84:1 (June 1997), 97; Cindy Kintigh quoted in *Chicago Sun-Times*, Sept. 3, 1995, 21.

68. Alan G. Ingham and Stephen Hardy, "Introduction: Sport Studies Through the Lens of Raymond Williams," in Alan G. Ingham and John Loy, eds., *Sport in Social Development* (Champaign, IL: Human Kinetics, 1993), 1–19; Kammen, *Mystic Chords of Memory*, 205; Overman, *The Influence of the Protestant Work Ethic on Sport and Recreation*, 152.

69. Sperber, *Shake Down the Thunder*, 11; Weyand, *Saga of American Football*, 79, 123; Ray Schmidt, "The Blue and Gray," *College Football Historical Society*, 6:3 (May 1993), 4–6.

70. Sperber, *Shake Down the Thunder*, 18–20; Weyand, *Saga of American Football*, 92–93; William C. Cotter to Jessie (sic) Harper, Dec. 16, 1912, UADR, Box 2, file 122, Notre Dame Archives.

71. James Orin Murfin Papers, Box 8, folder 2, University of Michigan Archives, and Dec. 6, 1913 Conference Minutes, 4, in Box 84, folder 2, Stagg Papers, University of Chicago, on Notre Dame, Marquette rejection to the then Big 9.

Chicago Record-Herald, Nov. 24, 1913, 11, on DePaul and Catholic frustrations.

72. Maltby, *The Origins and Early Development of Professional Football*, 94, 125–129, 135, 139–140; Emil Klosinski, "Inflation of 1920: A Tale of Two Cities," *Coffin Corner,* 14:3 (July 1992), 15–19, states that Rockne played professionally with Fort Wayne as early as 1913. Salmon turned pro even earlier, in 1905.

Emil Klosinski, "When Notre Dame Won the Rockford City Championship," *Coffin Corner,* 7:11–12 (Nov./Dec. 1985), 3–5. See Emil Klosinski, *Pro Football in the Days of Rockne* (New York: Carlton Press, 1970), for a full treatment of the era.

73. Blum, et al., *The National Experience,* 603; Foner and Garraty, eds., *Reader's Companion to American History,* 633.

74. Jesse Harper to Amos Alonzo Stagg, Jan. 19, 1914 (quote); Stagg to Harper, Jan. 29, 1914; Harper to Lambert G. Sullivan, Feb. 23, 1914, in UADR, Box 3, file 91, Notre Dame Archives.

75. Leo "Red" Ward to Knute Rockne, Dec. 7, 1921, UADR, Box 21, file 63 (quote); Seward A. Simons to William (sic) Rockne, Dec. 14, 1921, UADR, Box 6, file 96, Notre Dame Archives. Paul Shoup to Rockne, Nov. 16, 1921, Box 6, file 81, agrees with Ward's assessment.

76. Sperber, *Shake Down the Thunder*, 207–212; see UADR, Box 6, files 61, 79, 96–97, Notre Dame Archives, for game solicitations. Attendance figures gleaned from *NCAA Football* (Overland, KS: NCAA, 1991), 415.

77. Sperber, *Shake Down the Thunder*, 134–135; Charles Fountain, *Sportswriter: The Life and Times of Grantland Rice* (New York: Oxford University Press, 1993), 11–30; Weyand, *Saga of American Football*, 140; Leo B. Ward to Knute Rockne, Dec. 8, 1924, UADR, Box 21, file 63, Notre Dame Archives.

78. See UADR, Box 6, files 61–62, 81, Notre Dame Archives, on coaching offers to Rockne. C. W. Mayser to Rockne, Dec. 8, 1921 (quote), file 81.

79. Sperber, *Shake Down the Thunder*, 228–229; McCallum, *Big Ten Football*, 25, states that all 11 starters and some substitutes from the 1924 team took coaching jobs.

Stan Cofall to Rockne, Aug. 2, 1922, UADR, Box 6, file 62; and E. L. Lambeau to Rockne, May 4, 1921, UADR, Box 6, file 80, for examples of mutual support.

1919 newspaper clipping, football file, Butte-Silver Bow Archives; Pat Kearney, *Butte's Big Game: Butte Central vs. Butte High* (Butte: Artcraft, 1989).

Ed Gilleran, "The Battle of the Bronx," *College Football Historical Society*, 6:2 (Feb. 1993), 1–5; Gerald R. Gems, "The Prep Bowl."

80. Sperber, *Shake Down the Thunder*, 344.

81. Lester, *Stagg's University*, 120–121; 1929 roster in UADR, Box 6, file 193 in Notre Dame Archives.

82. Wakefield, *Playing to Win*, 89.

83. *Naperville Sun*, Sept. 2, 1998, 67.

84. 78. Steven A. Riess, "A Social Profile of the Professional Football Player, 1920–1982," in Paul A. Staudohar and James A. Mangan, eds., *The Business of Professional Sports* (Urbana: University of Illinois Press, 1991), 222–246; Maltby, *The Origins and Early Development of Professional Football*, 51–52 (quote).

85. Ibid., 128.

86. No author, "Ralph Vince," *Coffin Corner*, 19:1 (Jan. 1997), 17; "The Visit of R.T. Hallady, Nov. 12, 1922," Box 24, folder 9, Stagg Papers.

87. "Meff" to Stagg, Jan. 17, 1917; Pro Football, 1919, Box 24, folder 9, Stagg Papers; Carroll, *The Ohio League*, 26, 52; Klosinski, *Pro Football in the Days of Rockne*; Al F. Gorman, city clerk, Resolution of the City Council, Jan. 16, 1926; Report of the Committee on Relation of Professional Athletics as it Concerns High School Athletics, Coaches, and Officials, Jan. 20, 1926, in the football file, 1924–1930, Chicago Public Schools Athletic League Archives. It is not certain that McGuirk's high schoolers were paid for the impromptu game.

See Allen L. Sack and Robert Thiel, "College Football and Social Mobility: A Case Study of Notre Dame Football Players," *Sociology of Education*, 52 (Jan. 1979), 60–66; and Donald W. Calhoun, *Sport, Culture, and Personality* (Champaign: Human Kinetics, 1987), 208–209, for mobility patterns and working class testimonials to football.

88. Charles Smith to Stagg, Nov. 4, 1903, Box 42, folder 15, offers a $300 bet; David Kinley to John L. Griffith, Oct. 19, 1923, on Ohio State betting, Box 2, folder 22, and Fielding H. Yost, "Loyalty and Betting," Box 2, folder 22, all in Stagg Papers; *Bulldogs on Sunday, 1922,* 5–9; Roy Rosenzweig, book review of Ann Fabian, *Card Sharps, Dream Books, and Bucket Shops: Gambling in Nineteenth Century America,* in *Journal of Sport History,* 19:2 (Summer 1992), 172–174.

89. Maltby, *The Origins and Early Development of Professional Football,* 108–110; Paul J. Zbiek, "Coal Towns and Gridiron: The Development of Community Consciousness and Scholastic Football in Pennsylvania's Anthracite Region," *North American Society for Sport History Proceedings,* 1991, 40–41; Phil Payne, "Boosterism and the Heroic Vision: Football Players as Symbol of Community Virtue," presented at the North American Society for Sport History Convention, May 25, 1992, Halifax, Nova Scotia; Bissinger, *Friday Night Lights.*

90. Peterson, *Pigskin,* 92; no author, "Rockne's Wonder Teams Built on Notre Dame's Virility," *The Notre Dame Scholastic* (Nov. 21, 1924), 222, 224.

91. Maltby, *The Origins and Early Development of Professional Football,* 103, 119–121; Peterson, *Pigskin,* 54–56, 136–137; see Bob Carroll, *The Ohio League, 1910–1919,* for a narrative history of the modernization process.

92. Phil Barber and Ray Didinger, *Football America: Celebrating Our National Passion* (Atlanta: Turner Pub., 1996), 193, 210–223; *Chicago Sun-Times,* Aug. 31, 1997, 11A–13A (quotes).

93. UADR, Box 6, file 193, Notre Dame Archives; Sperber, *Shake Down the Thunder,* 296–322.

Chapter 5

Gridiron Wars: Negotiating a National Sporting Culture

As the Americans struggled to assimilate the throngs of immigrants, they also labored over the discord between themselves. In addition to its multicultural population each region of the country had developed its own characteristics, and not all of its differences were settled by the Civil War. By the 1890s the growing Midwest vied with the East for leadership. Chicago began to challenge New York as the cultural leader, and it won the right over its rival to host the 1893 World's Fair. Chicago, and then St. Louis, claimed the right to host the 1904 Olympics, eventually held in conjunction with the latter's world's fair. The South persisted in the retention of its Lost Cause ideology, hampering any reunification efforts. Still largely rural and agricultural it seemed out of step with the pace of modern America. The West, no longer a frontier, but with vast stretches of open land and newer cities, pondered an uncertain future; but wanted a fuller partnership with the whole.[1]

In 1892 forty percent of Americans lived in cities, and that figure surpassed 50 percent in 1920. With the transition to city life a greater homogenization of culture took place, emphasizing urban, commercial values. Railroads and technology brought goods and ideas to the hinterlands, producing urban-rural tensions, civic boosterism, and regionalism; all of which were, and still are, played out on the football field. Unlike the professional baseball leagues, which restricted play to the northeast quadrant of the country, or constrained teams in regional associations, most college football teams were free to roam far and wide in search of glory. Civic boosters fostered pride and profit by attracting top teams to their area.[2]

Cultural homogenization proceeded at a slow and uneven pace, however, as the various regions clung to their social, political, and economic distinctions. Virginia originally chose uniform colors of gray and red to signify allegiance to the Confederacy. At Trinity College (Duke) in North Carolina, brothers aptly named Stonewall Jackson Durham and Robert E. Lee Durham upheld southern pride in 1891. Four years later Wyoming chose brown and yellow as its school colors to commemorate its brown-eyed Susan flowers, and Texas players became the "longhorns" in 1904. In Illinois, supporters declared "We are different, somehow, we of the middle west—not particularly better, but different. We are uniquely ourselves."[3]

The elites of the Northeast also considered themselves to be different, but not in any democratic sense. If they could not limit the growth of football they intended to reserve power and status for themselves. They made the rules and refused to travel outside New England, restricting challenge matches to their home fields and limiting "championships" to a select few. Michigan traveled to the East in 1881 to test itself against the Big Three. The *Boston Herald* dismissed Harvard's opponents as "crude blacksmiths, miners and backwoodsmen."[4] Such indignities and defeats relegated upstarts and aspirants, at least temporarily, to intraregional honors.

Minnesota declared itself "champions of the Northwest" as early as 1890, and gloried in a 63–0 win over the "aloof" Wisconsin team. Wisconsin viewed the new University of Chicago as an "academic interloper," who "deserved a good beating," which the more established institution delivered in a 30–0 win in 1894. Indiana claimed the state championship when it beat Purdue, Notre Dame, Vincennes, and Earlham in 1900. Kansas and Missouri had already been playing for the "championship of the Missouri Valley" since 1892, and both sought competition with Chicago. Missouri got a match with Illinois in 1896 and despite several injuries in a 10–0 win, the victorious Illini claimed to give the "tigers a good beating" and that "those fellows from Missouri don't know any real football."[5]

In the South, Trinity (Duke) became one of the first schools to adopt the game, encouraged by its new president, J. F. Crowell, in 1887. Crowell even coached intramural play, which began in November of that year. Challenges from and to Chapel Hill occurred within a year, with a resultant Thanksgiving Day game against North Carolina in Raleigh in 1888. The Trinity win alleviated their rivals' condescending attitudes, enhanced the school's reputation, and "gave...an indefinable prestige."[6] When Trinity defeated Virginia only three years later it claimed the championship of the South.

By the 1890s North Carolina also challenged Virginia for southern honors, while Mississippi traveled north to Memphis and south to New Orleans for interstate contests in 1893. Within a decade Mississippi and Mississippi A&M (now Mississippi State) began a long rivalry that exemplified the emerging urban-rural tensions, with Ole Miss declared the "aristocrats'" school and A&M relegated to "farmers, rednecks, and cowpunchers."[7] When Auburn traveled to Atlanta for a match with Georgia in 1892 fans stood in the rain two hours before gametime to witness the Auburn victory. Leonard Wood refereed the Tennessee State-Auburn game of 1893 and reported to Walter Camp that "Foot ball is all the rage down here...."[8] North Carolina invaded New York City that same year for a game with Lehigh, and Centre College tried to induce Chicago into a game in Louisville or Lexington with a financial guarantee and the conviction that "Kentucky people think foot-ball better than horseracing."[9] Vanderbilt offered similar assurances to Chicago in 1894, and embarked on national pretensions of its own within a decade. Sewanee, however, laid greater claim to southern laurels when it traveled 2,500 miles from Tennessee to Texas and returned undefeated in 1899. With five victories in six days, and twelve overall, the school paper proclaimed that "The Varsity's achievements are unparalleled, and...will remain unequaled for many generations. No other eleven, east, west, north, or south can boast of ten successive victories with a goal line uncrossed by an opponent."[10] While baseball, the "national" game, was played even more widely at the time, the National League centered in the East. Territorial associations and media focus on teams east of the Mississippi River limited any opportunities for greater glory and renown.[11]

In the southwest, the Dallas Foot Ball Club claimed to be "the champions of Texas," as early as 1893; but were soon challenged by the state university. Texas A&M joined the fray in 1894, a year after New Mexico State entered the football wars. Baylor and Texas Christian contended for local honors in Waco by 1899, as the Arizona schools fielded their first teams. The intrasectional Texas-Oklahoma rivalry began a year later. The Oklahoma-Kansas series began in 1903, and virtually every state emphasized a regional rivalry as Florida met Florida State, Auburn encountered Alabama, Georgia matched Georgia Tech, and Indiana opposed Purdue.[12]

Easterners introduced football to the Far West in the 1880s, as athletic clubs and high schools engaged in rugby in and around San Francisco. Five teams constituted the California Football League in 1886 as the game evolved toward the style played in the East. In 1891 the Olympic Club of San Francisco defeated a Los Angeles team, and a rivalry between the new Stanford University and the University of California began with their first game in the spring of 1892. That fall the two schools brought Walter Camp and Thomas McClung from Yale as tutors, and drew 15,000 to a 10–10 tie in December. Stanford then toured the state, defeating all other opponents. California then secured Pudge Heffelfinger as its coach for 1893. Locals predicted that "the future will see teams on the coast that will rival those of the Eastern universities."[13] The next year Chicago traveled cross country to play the California teams, and the Salt Lake City YMCA, which claimed to be "champion of the territory."[14]

Football appeared in the mountain states during the 1880s. Colorado College took up the rugby game in 1882; and it defeated Denver three years later in the Americanized version of the sport. Washington fielded its first team in 1889 and Washington State began playing soon after the school's founding in 1891. Both it and Idaho claim the victory in their initial 1893 game. Oregon State began play the same year and reveled as its " 'farmers' took care of the 'dudes' without much trouble" in the ensuing battles between rural and urban representatives.[15] The Aggies took particular pride in shutting out all opponents on their home field in their initial season, stating that "Americans fight best when defending their own soil."[16]

Wyoming played Colorado teams by 1895 and even the cowboys and miners of Butte, Montana engaged in the game as a measure of community pride and an extension of their gambling activities. Butte played Omaha in 1894 and when the Reliance Club of Oakland hosted Butte in 1895, "...the game was regarded as a contest between California and Montana, rather than a game between Reliance and Butte...."[17] Reliance drafted star players from the Olympic Club in San Francisco and another from Stanford to augment its squad, and 1,000 spectators showed up to watch in the mud. The newspaper stated that "A large sum of money changed hands on the game, as the Montana men brought with them plenty of coin and bet it freely."[18] Reliance needed the help of R. E. Ransome, a club member, who acted as umpire. His egregious calls gave his team a 10–4 win amidst protests. Butte offered $1,000 for a rematch and the Southern Pacific Railroad offered free transport to a neutral site in Santa Monica; but Reliance declined. Butte avenged itself with a Christmas day win over the Olympic Club, which had bolstered its team with Reliance players and another from Stanford.[19]

Butte offered the University of Chicago $1,000 for a contest in Montana. Butte had already beaten Nebraska and tried to get Michigan to come westward. It did entice Iowa State, coached by Pop Warner, for an 1895 game. Warner reputedly lost more than the game, betting a month's salary that his team could beat the unknown westerners. In a rematch the next year, Butte added insult to injury after a 32–6 win as the *Butte Miner* declared that "The visitors came on sedately huddled in blankets and quilts, resembling so many squaws ...good, husky sons of farmers, but not owning the matured muscles of Butte's full grown men."[20] Butte and other western communities continued to challenge and beat, on a regular basis, the high schools and college teams of the urban centers. Such victories meant more than just a game. Commercialized athletic contests eased the hinterlands into the mainstream popular culture, while allowing expressions of regional pride and rural values in an urbanizing world.[21]

Regional pride resurfaced in the Midwest when an eastern team, Cornell, deigned to travel from its home base for an 1890 game with Michigan in Detroit and another in Chicago. Though the easterners won Cornell returned to Chicago the next year for rematches, including a game against a Chicago all-star team, composed of former Ivy leaguers. This time the Chicago team prevailed, 12–4, in a brutal game. Yale had beaten Cornell only 6–0; but the Chicagoans' challenge to Yale went unheeded.[22]

The rivalry between the East and Midwest began with the Michigan tour of 1881 and intensified with the Michigan-Cornell series of the 1890s. When Purdue scored 486 points to its opponents' 12 in 1892, the media declared that "Purdue…is the strongest in the West, and it is only to be regretted that no opportunity was offered by which its strength could have been tested against the more widly (sic) advertised teams of the great Eastern universities."[23] In 1894 Michigan earned its first win over the East by defeating Cornell 12–4. By 1895 both Michigan and Wisconsin came within a score of beating Harvard and Yale respectively.

The University of Chicago proposed a home-and-home series with Penn in 1898 by stating that "our agreement to join in football will be the first attempt to bring East and West together and to make what might be termed a national championship."[24] Penn won a narrow victory and the teams tied the following year, thus ending Penn's 24-game win streak and prolonging the quest for superiority. Such contests signified an ongoing demand for both regional identity and commercial dominance in the larger cultural power struggle.

Both Michigan and Chicago aspired to national leadership and their football teams presented a highly visible symbol of community pride and strength. Chicagoans perceived themselves as heir apparent to the cultural leadership of the East, an assumption reinforced by its wresting of the 1893 World's Fair from New York. The loud and frequent pronouncements of arrival on the national scene earned Chicago the sobriquet of "the Windy City." In the regional competition for business and profit, Michigan, too, felt that it "is destined to be the connecting link between the east and west."[25] Football games provided one means to demonstrate easy rail access to urban centers and gain greater national attention. Michigan boosters proclaimed an 1897 high school game between Tonawanda, New York and Madison, Wisconsin a "national championship" to be played in Detroit, the agreed upon halfway point between the opponents.[26]

When Chicago defeated Cornell 17–6 in 1899 an Ann Arbor resident wrote Stagg that Michigan was "sore that *Chicago* beat an eastern team; but all agreed that it was a mighty good lesson for the east."[27] Michigan preferred that it, rather than its rival, carry the regional laurels. Three weeks later the eastern media still claimed that Cornell was the better team.[28]

Disagreements over the rules exacerbated the regional competition. The eastern oligarchy that created and revised the rules annually had little sympathy for western concerns until coaches from the Midwest threatened the eastern hegemony with their own sectional committee in 1895. The rebellion led to separate committees after 1896; and the Chicago-Penn series occurred under alternate sets of rules. An eastern official assailed the "impertinence" of western rule revisions, and Wisconsin withdrew from the western group for fear of losing its important eastern matchups. Southern schools, however, favored the western rules. Such allegiance forced acquiescence by the East, and led to Stagg's inclusion on the eastern rules committee. Interregional contests necessitated greater uniformity; but quarrels persisted for years, particularly over the forward pass, contrasting styles of play, and the selection of All-American teams.[29]

Noneasterners bristled over the seemingly endless honors bestowed on eastern players, particularly those of the Big Three, who monopolized Camp and Whitney's awards for decades. Sportswriters from other regions railed against the elitist bias and the failure to acknowledge the worth of their own players. In reaction they began selecting and publishing their own All-Western and All-Southern teams. The eastern selectors simply chose the players whom they had seen perform; so noneastern teams had to travel eastward to prove themselves. In 1898 Chicago's Clarence Hershberger and Wisconsin's Pat O'Dea became the first noneasterners elected to the All-America team. O'Dea, an Australian, set the Amateur Athletic Union records for both a punt (87 yards, 10 inches) and a drop kick (63 yards, 11 inches). Nevertheless, eastern players dominated the honorary team for another two decades, and at least 100 such all-star teams proliferated by 1910 as the various regions contended for recognition and the media capitalized on such interest by publishing their own choices. When Walter Camp published his all-time All-America team in 1910, Ivy Leaguers still held eight of the eleven spots.[30]

The Midwestern fans asked "How can western universities with 5,000 students not have as many athletes as eastern colleges with only hundreds of students?"[31] A few years later, the Far West also complained. The University of Washington had been undefeated for eight years, and a fan expressed both his regional and class consciousness directly to Walter Camp.

> The University of Washington is as good as any in the East. Man for man those boys from the Rocky mountains (sic) and points west are more fit. True they haven't the prep school training, but their aptitude both for fight, and physique is greater....The sacred confines of Yale and Harvard may contain a good deal of football knowledge, but not all of the football ability—not by a damn sight.[32]

Midwestern schools began forming their own athletic conferences as early as 1886, with the formation of the Indiana Football League. The Western Conference (Big Ten), formed in 1895, soon led the independence movement against the East. Stagg informed George Woodruff of Penn that "We have gone ahead (and changed the rules) because we felt that the Eastern Committee was not doing its duty in this matter."[33]

The various regions of the country had developed alternative football cultures, evident not only in their dissension over the rules, but in their styles of play. While the eastern teams favored ball control, mass formations, and a conservative kicking game, the West and South practiced an "open" style of end runs, fakes, passes, innovative strategies and trick plays. The difference in styles transcended the field of play, for by the turn of the century, the Midwest perceived itself as more progressive than the stodgy East, and ready to assume the cultural mantle.[34]

During the 1899 season Chicago went undefeated, tying Penn; but beating both Cornell and Brown. Michigan intensified western claims to superiority by outscoring its opponents 501 to 0 in 1901 and claiming the "national championship." It concluded its season with a 49–0 romp over Stanford in the first Rose Bowl; but only one of its victories came at the expense of an eastern team, a 128–0 rout over the University of Buffalo. On that occasion the Buffalo coach, confident after his team had beaten Dartmouth, bet a Michigan student that his team would not score. Yost refused the coach's plea to suspend the game at halftime, though he already led 55–0. Harvard asserted its own claim to national honors based on its conquest of Yale and dominance of the East.[35]

While the eastern teams still emphasized mass plays as a measure of their masculinity, the Midwesterners won by attrition, wearing down their opponents and demonstrating their superior fitness. In the Rose Bowl game against Stanford, Michigan ran off 142 plays, gaining 1,463 yards. When Yost again refused his counterpart's pleas to end the debacle, the more sportsmanlike team captains agreed to quit with eight minutes still left on the clock. During the following season, Chicago and Michigan featured 100 plays during each of the 45-minute halves, and the Chicago-Wisconsin contest managed 112 snaps in the first half alone.[36]

High school coaches developed some of the tactical innovations, such as shifts and, later, the screen pass. In 1902 a high school team finally established the ascendance of the Midwest. A post-season matchup between Chicago's Hyde Park High School and Brooklyn Polytechnic featured the contrasting styles of play. Both Amos Alonzo Stagg and his rival, Fielding Yost of Michigan, tutored the Chicagoans in their practices to assure a respectable showing. Hyde Park proved more than respectable, allowing Brooklyn only one first down in overwhelming their visitors 105–0. New Yorkers complained that Poly was not their best team, and Charles H. Ebbets, owner of the Brooklyn baseball team, guaranteed expenses for a rematch of top teams the next year. The attempt to salvage eastern pride and football status failed once again, as Chicago's North Division High School led Brooklyn Boys' High 75–0 before darkness brought a cessation to the fiasco.

Easterners reluctantly admitted the superiority of the western style of play.[37]

By that time Yost had already thrown down the gauntlet to the eastern colleges, when he challenged that

> The East will need to look to her laurels, for no longer do the leading western teams consider themselves inferior in any way to the best 11 the East can produce...and one finds that the public generally west of the Ohio River believes that a game between the champion team of the West and East would result in favor of the former. They are willing to be shown if our Eastern friends are willing to undertake the task.[38]

Chicago temporarily derailed Michigan's grandiose aspirations in a 1905 regional showdown. Even Walter Camp attended the "western championship" game to witness Chicago's 2–0 victory. The importance of the contest caused the Michigan player who gave up the safety years of anguish and resulted in his suicide.[39]

Circumstances interceded, however, as rising deaths, serious injuries, professionalism, and eligibility issues led to a national reform movement that disrupted the quest for national supremacy. College presidents and faculty assumed greater control over students' athletic activities. After the 1905 season a New York meeting of sixty-eight schools initiated the campaign which eventually resulted in a national governing body, the National Collegiate Athletic Association, with greater representation of schools from the Midwest and South. Some schools banned football altogether in favor of rugby, and even regional powers like the Western Conference (then the Big 9), prohibited interregional contests, and limited teams to five games per season. Michigan promptly quit the conference and its hiatus lasted until 1917. The interregional quarrels continued off the field, however. Eastern and western schools agreed on a centralized board of approved officials but separate rules committees made their own assignments. Eastern schools still seemed reluctant to approve of the forward pass, a strategy employed by the West as part of the "open" game, that might also alleviate the rising injury toll. The eastern group maintained that "brutality is more dependent

upon the character of the players than the rules of the game,"
and favored individual institutional responsibility in the approval of team rosters.[40]

The worth of the "open" style of play became apparent once
again in 1906. The previous year St. Louis University had lost
to Iowa, 31–10. Iowa adhered to the old running attack in the
rematch, while St. Louis, under Coach Eddie Cochems, featured the innovative forward pass. Four of the passes accounted for touchdowns in a 39–0 rout, as St. Louis led the
nation in scoring during an undefeated season. That same
year Chicago employed sixty-four different pass patterns,
including flankers, a pass to a guard, and the trick, "sleeper"
play, in which an end hid among teammates on the sideline.
Such diversity resulted in a 63–0 win over Illinois. In 1907
Illinois completed thirty passes of its own against Northwestern, and Carlisle defeated Penn, 26–6, with the pass. Such
tactics proved successful and entertaining. Midwestern teams
began drawing crowds of 10–15,000; and small schools found
that they could humble larger institutions by relying on fi-
nesse rather than brawn.[41]

The "open" game proved safer as well, at least temporarily.
The 1905 season resulted in twenty-four deaths overall, a
figure reduced to ten by 1908. The decline in deaths did not
mean any diminution in intent, however. In a 1908 game
between Union and Wesleyan seventeen players were
knocked unconscious, and five required hospitalization. A
return to mass play during the 1909 season brought a resur-
gent death toll as well. The thirty-three casualties that year
engendered renewed opposition to the game and rule revisions
to allow more passing.[42]

After Arkansas lost to St. Louis it hired Hugo Bezdek from
the University of Chicago to teach its team the passing game.
Other colleges in the South and West also began to hire
players from such pioneering teams as coaches. By 1907 at
least fourteen former Chicago players held such jobs, and
Stagg's influence only increased after he beat both eastern
(Penn) and western champions (Brigham Young University)
in 1908. That year he also won appointment to the American
Olympic Committee. Northwestern had already wooed Horace Butterworth, manager of the Chicago teams, to its campus

in 1902 with a tenured faculty position as athletic director. As did his mentor, he soon centralized power and produced a profitable athletic enterprise. Even Princeton hired Stagg's assistant, Joseph Raycroft, as its athletic director in 1911. Raycroft soon wrote to Stagg derisively about the eastern powers. "I am not sure whether it would make you weep or laugh to watch a couple of these 'big teams' play football. Some day one of these three institutions is going to turn out a team which is going to play modern football."[43] The remark characterized perceptions of cultural transition well beyond the football field.

Midwesterners perceived both their football style and their civic affairs as more progressive approaches to a modernizing world. Architect Daniel Burnham's Chicago Plan envisioned a magnificent lakefront, and other municipalities emulated its skyscrapers, parks, and playground system. Jane Addams, head of the Hull House settlement, became the most famous woman in America. The shift in leadership became apparent on the football field as well. Whereas St. Louis University threw its passes to roving receivers who maneuvered across the field, Yale and Harvard still sought the security of conservatism by surrounding a receiver with protection. After William Sprackling, Brown's quarterback, won All-America honors in 1910, he admitted that he had learned his passing skills at his Cleveland high school from a former Wisconsin player, and that "the Middle West was away (sic) ahead of the east in developing the forward pass."[44] Yale admitted as much when it adopted the Minnesota shift that same year; but the Western Conference reforms eliminated interregional showdowns. Only the renegade Michigan team continued to compete against the East.[45]

So when a small Catholic school traveled to West Point to face the symbol of eastern power in 1913, Notre Dame's Knute Rockne stated "We went out to play the Army...believing that we represented not only our school but the whole aspiring Middle West."[46] The stunning 35–13 Notre Dame victory catapulted Rockne to fame, insured the validity of the passing attack, and enhanced a national reputation for "Catholic" football.

The Notre Dame win had a major impact. Newspapers drew attention to the "Catholic" triumph. The *Chicago Daily News* called it "especially important," noting that Notre Dame even outplayed Army in the eastern mainstay, "straight (power) football" in an "overwhelming victory."[47] The *Inter Ocean* agreed that "The Cadets were outclassed in every department of the game...they looked like novices beside the Westerners."[48] The *Chicago Evening Post* termed it a "crushing defeat of Army," and that the "Catholic victory over Army (was the) most notable in years," and that it put Notre Dame "on par with the most formidable (teams) in the country."[49]

Combined with Michigan's 43–7 rout of Syracuse on the same day, the Midwesterners gloried in a renewed prominence. The *Evening Post* simply claimed that "the West Gains Much Prestige by Football Victories over the East"; while the *Daily News* stated that the dual victories "precludes the suggestion of eastern superiority." The latter called attention to the fact that Army had already beaten Colgate (3–0), which had previously defeated Yale (16–6).[50]

While Notre Dame had been fielding winning football teams for years, the media attention propelled its evolution into a national phenomenon even before Knute Rockne's national championships. In retrospect, one historian even claimed that the 1913 game provided "the greatest single miracle in the history of Catholic higher education."[51] The next year Notre Dame began playing in Chicago to larger crowds and greater national attention.[52]

Notre Dame had already found it difficult to schedule games after defeating Michigan in 1909, due to anti-Catholicism and its growing reputation as a football force. By 1913 it hosted South Dakota and traveled as far as Texas, where the Catholics delivered a 30–7 victory on Thanksgiving. By 1914 it had a 27-game undefeated streak before succumbing to Yale. Notre Dame players brought their expertise to other Catholic colleges and parochial schools as coaches, who soon adopted the Notre Dame style. Catholic coaches felt it a duty if not an obligation to send their best players to the South Bend campus in succeeding years as football spearheaded the Catholic drive for greater inclusion in American society; but on its own terms. After an undefeated 1920 season and the number one ranking in one poll a Notre Dame fan penned his class-conscious scorn. "None a you (sic) eastern cake eaters have anything on the raw boned sons of the prairies."[53]

The waning of eastern dominance won greater representation in the power structure for other previously excluded groups as well. By 1913 the NCAA included representatives from the Northeast, Midwest, South, and East. Within three years Oregon Agricultural College (now Oregon State) became the western representative as the governing body slowly began to approximate a democracy.[54]

Football greatly assisted the marginalized regions in their quest for acceptance. Before the Midwest could fully enjoy its emerging preeminence, teams from the Far West and South began to contend for national recognition. As early as the 1890s Stanford, California, Salt Lake City, and Butte, Montana, were quick to challenge the Midwest and East with mixed results. Carlisle made two western tours, in 1899 and again in 1903, and returned undefeated and unscored upon each time. Oregon teams entered intraregional play against California and Stanford in 1905; and in 1909 Denver nearly defeated Carlisle, 8–4. The *Denver Post* remarked that "In one bound the Denver team soared from mere local representatives to a rank with the country's fastest teams."[55]

Entrepreneurs, often alumni relocated in the West or South who were eager to see their alma mater play, promoted interregional contests for personal and civic pride. Pasadena resurrected the Rose Bowl despite the original debacle to attract attention to the area. When Washington State defeated Brown in 1916, and Oregon beat Penn the following year, the West proclaimed its arrival on the national scene. The organizing committee declared the Rose Bowl "the greatest thing in sport that has ever reached the Pacific Coast...and that the East, as well as the West, has recognized the important place which the Tournament game now occupies in the foot ball world."[56] Eastern schools began applying for the 1918 game within a week after the 1917 loss.

The World War I years featured military service teams in the Rose Bowl; but westerners gained additional respect thereafter. In 1920 Harold "Brick" Muller gained All-American recognition as he led the California "wonder team" to the first of four undefeated seasons. Harvard won a narrow 7–6 victory over Oregon in the 1920 Rose Bowl; but California demoralized the Big Ten with a 28–0 defeat of previously unbeaten Ohio State in the 1921 contest. Stanford and the University of Southern California also produced top teams throughout the remainder of the decade, with USC claiming the national championship in 1928.[57]

Football provided even greater opportunity for the South, eventually incorporating the region into the mainstream American culture. The South had followed a separate historical experience, with fewer immigrants, an agricultural tradition, an emphasis on evangelical Protestantism, and a clearly established social and gender hierarchy. In its language, music, and food the South stood apart; yet saw itself as the bastion of true Americanism. Lacking any major commercial or industrial center, still grieving over its lost honor in the Lost Cause, and left behind in a modernizing America, football accorded the South a measure of recognition, respect, and a renewed sense of self-worth, and satisfied both its sense of honor and martial spirit, just as the duel had previously done. In its rituals and meanings football assumed the status of a civil religion in the South. A recent history of the region has charged that "one of the most violent sports played in the United States enjoys its greatest success and has its greatest following in the one region that has historically embraced violence as an accepted means of self-expression."[58]

Football brought greater commercialization and an urban culture to the South, a movement fostered by middle class businessmen; yet it did so while still upholding, in fact reinforcing, the region's traditional values. The appeal to southern honor appeared soon after southern schools adopted the game. The Baton Rouge *Daily Advocate* appealed to the Louisiana State players to "uphold the honor of the city" in their 1893 game against Tulane in New Orleans.[59] That same year North Carolina ventured north, absorbing a 34–0 loss to Lehigh in New York; but gaining the approval of one sportswriter, who claimed that it "spoke volumes for the progressive spirit of the athletic management at Chapel Hill."[60]

By 1897 Vanderbilt's school paper admonished that "freshmen would be shirking their duty...if they did not do their part in bringing Vanderbilt greater glory through football."[61] In 1899 North Carolina traveled to Princeton and Virginia met Michigan at Detroit, but neither could uphold southern honor. Sewanee, the bastion of the southern aristocracy and Lost Cause ideology, won recognition for the South in 1899; but beat only regional teams. Vanderbilt, however, beat Cincinnati, 6–0, though it also lost to Indiana, 20–0 in 1899. Fifteen thousand witnessed the southern championship game between rivals Virginia and North Carolina in 1900, won by the former, 17–0. Virginia's confidence, and that of the South, was further buoyed in 1902 when it narrowly defeated the nationally prominent Carlisle Indians, 6–5.[62]

Vanderbilt, too, challenged the North. Unbeaten by any southern teams from 1903–1908, it played a series against Michigan, and games against Ohio State, and Navy. In 1906 Vanderbilt defeated Carlisle when the latter enjoyed the number five ranking. The *Nashville Banner* quickly proclaimed that "The Commodores have put themselves in a class with the leaders of both East and West."[63] Vanderbilt buttressed its claim in a scoreless tie with Yale in 1910 at New Haven. Vanderbilt's coach, Dan McGugin, ironically the son of a Union army veteran and a former Michigan player, exhorted his charges to vindicate southern pride and their mothers' honor whenever they confronted northern teams. Before the Yale contest he told them "It was South versus North, Confederate against Yankee. Remember the campfires of your fathers and forefathers...."[64] Other southern teams soon challenged the North thereafter.

Southerners began to flex their muscles off the field as well. At the 1911 rules meeting northeastern schools voted to eliminate the forward pass; but southerners allied with the Midwest and threatened secession, forcing the northerners to reverse their decision. Southerners considered the pass to be the "cavalry" of their offense, and as in the Civil War, it could turn the tide of battle. In 1914 Oklahoma led the major colleges in scoring by throwing 30–35 passes a game, 25 accounting for touchdowns en route to a 9-1-1 season. The following year it went undefeated. In 1915 Virginia defeated Yale, 10–0, gaining one of the South's greatest victories over a major northern team.[65]

Two years later the Western Conference champion, Ohio State, traveled to Montgomery, Alabama to play Auburn. The *Birmingham News* remarked that

> the game will be fought in the proud shadow of the capitol of the Confederacy, and the grandfathers of these southern boys...were the men that hurled back those Yankee invaders as gamely for four long years in the '60s...the feeling still lingers way down deep in the heart of every Southerner that one fellow from Alabama can lick four Yankees.[66]

An overmatched but inspired Auburn team battled to a scoreless tie. That same year Georgia Tech went undefeated and garnered the national championship after a convincing 41–0 rout of Penn. In 1920 the Virginia Military Institute also defeated Penn, 27–7, as the band played "Dixie" after each score in Philadelphia. VMI finished the season undefeated and ranked in the top ten by Walter Camp. Its star player, Jim Leech, who had been a marine in World War I, led the nation in scoring with 210 points. Tiny Centre College of Kentucky had only about 250 students, and only 16 football players; but defeated Harvard, 6–0, in 1921. Harvard had been undefeated in the two previous seasons. Centre, which featured seven Texans on its team, then lost to Texas Christian, 22–14, and even Walter Camp was forced to admit that the brand of football in the Southwest was equal to that played anywhere and that "a winning team might be developed in any section of the country."[67]

Despite the subsequent loss, Centre's upset of Harvard brought immediate redemption for the South. The game was still hailed 75 years later, as the academic *Chronicle of Higher Education* portrayed Harvard as symbolic of the dominant East, aristocrat versus commoner, capitalist against agrarian. Centre's jerseys had allegedly been bought at a rummage sale, and its victory was "portrayed as a triumph of simple virtues and a harbinger of a new and more robust American masculinity."[68]

The Midwest made its own claims to supremacy in 1921, as Notre Dame defeated Army, Nebraska beat Pittsburgh, and Chicago overcame Princeton, prompting Amos Alonzo Stagg to write Knute Rockne that such victories "certainly should establish the West's football prestige firmly throughout the country."[69]

The South continued its emergence as well. In 1922 Alabama defeated Penn in Philadelphia, 9–7; and Vanderbilt reasserted itself against Minnesota in 1924. Once again, McGugin rallied his team by stating

> Men, those people in the stands out there haven't heard of Southern football. When they think about the South, they think about the Civil War—pain, suffering and death. Many people have no idea of what Southern manhood is all about. Today we can show them...your mothers...wondered when the time would come when you could bring honor to the South. That time has arrived.[70]

Vanderbilt triumphed 16–0.

As the various teams contended for regional and national honor they drew immense crowds. Traditional bleachers and grandstands could no longer accommodate the swelling numbers and colleges began building permanent, concrete stadiums. In 1903 Harvard constructed a steel-reinforced stadium that seated 40,000; but even that proved inadequate. By 1922 the Yale Bowl and the new edifice at Ohio State allowed for more than 70,000, and writers praised both the classical architecture and the gargantuan dimensions of the arenas which even surpassed the Roman Colosseum. Los Angeles soon constructed its own Coliseum and Chicago's Soldier Field, opened in 1924, eventually held more than 120,000. The general public more so than alumni filled the seats, incorporating the masses in a popular sporting culture of national dimensions and reminiscent of the Roman Empire, not only in its classical architecture; but in its gladiatorial spectacles as well.[71]

For those who could not attend, radio stations began broadcasting play-by-play accounts in 1920, when Texas faced Texas A&M. The Chicago-Princeton series of 1921–1922 prompted a national broadcast by linking stations across the country. Chicago won the East-West encounter 9–0 at Princeton, and had more than 120,000 ticket requests for the rematch in Chicago. Princeton's first trip westward resulted in a thrilling

21–18 comeback; ironically, by employing the passing strategy favored by the West.[72]

In 1923 Southern Methodist went undefeated with an offense described as an aerial circus, and Alabama gave further credence to southern claims when it met heavily favored Washington in the 1926 Rose Bowl. Coach Wallace Wade reminded the players that they had the chance to establish national recognition for southern football. Charlie Paddock, the Olympic track star, provided a radio broadcast as Alabama prevailed, 20–19. Its stars, Johnny Mack Brown and Herman Brix, soon became Hollywood movie stars.[73]

Alabama returned to the Rose Bowl in 1927, and was greeted by the Daughters of the Confederacy in Pasadena. Alabama managed a 7–7 tie with Stanford, which had been ranked number one. Alabama, Southern Methodist, and Tennessee all went undefeated in 1927, with the latter starting a 27-game win streak. Georgia Tech and Tulane went without a loss in 1928 and 1929 respectively, and by 1930 the South could recite a litany of conquests over other regions. Southern successes engendered wild celebrations, Confederate flag waving, rebel yells, and the playing of "Dixie." Reporters praised the reckless bravado, "enthusiastic abandon and dogged determination" of their heroes, "who don't know the war is over." After Georgia defeated Yale a writer impugned the northerners' masculinity by stating that "The Elis shriveled like the violets worn by their feminine sympathizers, but the heat-hardened youngsters from Georgia's red clay hills seemed to revel in the humidity."[74]

In 1931 Tennessee won an invitation to a post-season charity game against New York University, which drew more than 40,000 at the height of the Depression. The 13–0 Tennessee win brought a measure of national prominence years before the Tennessee Valley Authority project or the Great Smoky Mountains National Park lent prestige to the state. Alabama repeated as Rose Bowl victors in 1931 and 1935 with convincing wins, and 85,000 witnessed the latter game. Football, in fact, became so integral to southern pride and self-esteem that Governor Huey Long personally led the Louisiana State cheering section and assured a following for away games by forcing railroads to reduce their rates for students' excur-

sions and more than quadrupling the size of the school band.
His "refusal to associate with losers" led to personal recruiting, coaching interventions, and care for injured players at the
governor's mansion. Long's lofty aspirations for the team
coincided with his own national ambitions, and he intended
to ride the wave of football to the top.[75]

Texas Christian University thrilled its fans and won national recognition with the aerial artistry of Sammy Baugh,
who accounted for forty touchdowns by 1936. Two years later
it won the national championship. In 1943 southern teams
appeared in each of the four major bowl games. Confederate
warriors continued to uphold the particular southern cultural
values until teams became integrated as late as the 1970s.
Georgia Tech still retains as its fight song the tune to "the
Bonnie Blue Flag," the original symbol of southern secession,
and both Mississippi and the Citadel still wave the banner.[76]

The South found another means to promote the region
through football. By the 1930s bowl games proliferated
throughout the area and remain major spectacles today. While
the Dixie Classic and Palm Bowl proved short-lived, the Gator,
Sugar, Cotton, Orange, Citrus, and Peach Bowls (though
renamed for corporate sponsors), along with the Blue-Gray
game are still post-season fixtures, fully incorporated in the
commercialized structure and touting regionalism. The promotion of such urban spectacles signaled a transition in southern culture. While football still upheld traditional values of
gallantry, honor, and racial segregation; it also brought a
greater inclusion in a more modern, homogeneous, and national culture.[77]

Political, cultural, and even intraregional differences were
projected to national audiences when southern teams traveled
outside the region or entertained northern opponents. Within
the states class divisions found catharsis on the football field,
particularly in games between the state universities and their
agricultural counterparts. While Mississippi students deni-
grated Mississippi State fans as social inferiors, the latter
continued to ring their cow bells with each score, to demonstrate their plebeian pride. For southerners football served
the surrogate function previously accorded to dueling as a
means to avenge perceived insults.[78] The merger of politics,

ideology, and culture on the national arena of the football field gradually diluted southern separatism however.

Football, in fact, greatly aided in the breakdown of the South's most visible regional distinction, its entrenched and systematic separation of the races. After the exclusion of African-American players from the ranks of professional football in 1934, blacks continued to play for colleges in the North and West with distinction. Blacks reappeared in professional football in 1946 when the Los Angeles Rams signed Kenny Washington and Woody Strode to contracts, and the Cleveland Browns of the rival All-American Football Conference acquired Bill Willis and Marion Motley that same season, a year before Jackie Robinson made baseball history. The next year Mississippi adopted the southern plantation owner as its mascot. Its supporters began effecting antebellum hats and ties at its games, and waving the Confederate flag in lieu of pennants. "Dixie" became the official fight song as the state countered with an attempt to retain its regressive racial stance. Other southern college teams adhered to their segregation policies at home; but gradually relented outside of the region.[79]

The "gentlemen's agreements," whereby coaches of northern teams agreed not to play their black athletes in games against southern schools, began to erode by the 1920s as a few brave schools refused to honor such requests. When Washington and Lee left Virginia to play at Washington and Jefferson in a 1923 game in Pennsylvania, they expected their opponents to bench their African-American quarterback. When Washington and Jefferson refused the southerners returned home. By the 1930s northern coaches sometimes used their black players for interregional home games; though they remained banned from southern campuses. The disadvantages of such arrangements proved readily apparent in the Syracuse-Maryland series of 1937–1938. In the first game, played at Maryland, Syracuse could not use its star, Wilmeth Sidat-Singh, an African-American who had been adopted by a Hindu doctor. Maryland won the game 14–0. In the return match at Syracuse Sidat-Singh led his team to a 51–0 rout.[80]

World War II, the integration of baseball, the *Brown v. Board of Education* decision, and the South's increasing inability to attract top northern teams for contests under such conditions hastened the downfall of segregation. Virginia students voted to allow Harvard's Chester Pierce to play in their 1947 game at Charlottesville, and even gave him a standing ovation when he left the field in the fourth quarter. Penn State brought two black players to compete against Southern Methodist in the 1948 Cotton Bowl. In 1950 Georgia began playing against integrated teams; but only outside the South. Georgia Tech did so in 1952, losing its national championship title of the previous year and a 31-game unbeaten streak to Notre Dame, which had two African-Americans on its team. By the mid-1950s the Cotton, Orange, and Sugar Bowl committees accepted integrated teams, and southern teams who refused to play against the northerners could hardly claim any "national" honors. When Governor Marvin Griffin tried to place southern ideology above pride and profit by barring Georgia Tech from the 1956 Sugar Bowl, students burned him in effigy and marched on the state capitol and his governor's mansion. The Georgia Board of Regents approved the trip to New Orleans.[81]

That fall North Texas State became the first southern college to desegregate its team, and it earned a Sun Bowl berth in 1959. Despite the success of North Texas State, court-ordered integration produced a backlash throughout most of the South, and white football teams symbolized the defiant adherence to tradition. One such team, Alabama, won the national championship in 1961, 1964, and 1965; and its coach, Paul "Bear" Bryant, became a southern icon. But Coach Bryant realized that his proud state could not continue to hold such honors without the best athletes, some of whom were African-Americans. Alabama won eight Southeastern Conference titles and three more national championships in the 1970s; but with integrated teams, as the South became a full partner in the national sporting culture.[82]

Although WASPs perceived the United States as a democratic and favored nation, that image reflected their own experiences and opportunities. Non-whites, immigrants, and non-Protestants often held conflicting views. The greater inclusion of such groups, visibly enhanced by their participation in football, gave members of both the dominant and subordinate groups some sense of hope and a degree of gratification in the perception of the American promise fulfilled. Whites and some blacks felt that racial progress was being made.

As football won over supporters and adherents to the Americanization process the evolution of the game both assuaged and engendered regional rivalries. Rules, scheduling, and regulation required almost all teams to become part of a unified bureaucracy at professional, collegiate, and interscholastic levels. Political, socioeconomic, religious, and regional differences became a part of the game, eventually integrating pluralistic values within a common framework of commercialized competition. Rivalries became intrinsic to the game, traditions fostered interest, excitement, and the historical construction of a national identity. As various groups and regions won representation on the governance bodies and achieved successes on the field they became a greater part of the whole, while still maintaining their particular characteristics.

Notes

1. Badger, *The Great American Fair;* Robert K. Barney, "Born from Dilemma: American Awakens to the Modern Olympic Games, 1901–1903," *Olympika* (1992), 92–135; *The Greatest of Expositions* (St. Louis: Louisiana Purchase Exposition, 1904); Grantham, *The South in Modern America;* Foster, *Ghosts of the Confederacy.*

2. Rybczynski, *City Life,* 111–113; Olivia Mahoney, "Expanding Empire: Chicago and the West," *Chicago History,* 27:1 (Spring 1997), 4–21; see R. B. Watrous, president of the Milwaukee Citizens Business League to Charles Baird, Dec. 3, 1902; and C. D. Daggett to Football Manager, Dec. 2, 1903, Board in Control of Intercollegiate Athletics, Bentley Library, University of Michigan Archives, for examples of solicitations.

3. Nora Campbell Chaffin, *Trinity College, 1839–1892,* 445; Patrick B. Miller, "The Manly, the Moral, and the Proficient," 285–316; *1996 Wyoming Football Media Guide,* 99; *The Story of the Stadium,* n.p. (quote), Box 1, Robert C. Zuppke Papers, University of Illinois Archives. See Bogue, *Frederick Jackson Turner,* on the greatest proponent of sectionalism. Turner perceived the Midwest to be the "most democratic" (p. 244).

4. Richard Dott Papers, and Ralph Stone to H. G. Salsinger, Oct. 19, 1949, in Ralph Stone Papers, Box 1; both at Bentley Library, University of Michigan. *Boston Herald,* cited in Weyand, *Saga of American Football,* 56.

5. Roberts, *The Big Nine,* 28 (quote), 139, 180; Arthur Mosse to Walter Camp, Nov. 15, 1909, Reel 13, Camp Papers; F. D. Cornell to A. A. Stagg, Aug. 27, 1893, and Samuel A. Smoke to Stagg, Sept. 9, 1893, Box 41, folder 3, Stagg Papers; *Chicago Times Herald,* Oct. 31, 1896, 11, in George Huff Papers, series 16/1/21, University of Illinois Archives. See Bogue, *Frederick Jackson Turner,* 71, 126, 156, 453, on the academic, as well as athletic rivalry between Wisconsin and Chicago.

6. Chaffin, *Trinity College, 1839–1892,* 443–444.

7. Mike Butler, "Confederate Flags, Class Conflict, a Golden Egg, and Castrated Bulls: A Historical Examination of the Ole Miss-Mississippi State Football Rivalry," *Journal of Mississippi History,* 59 (Summer 1997), 123–139.

8. Battle, *History of the University of North Carolina,* 477; Louis R. Wilson, *The University of North Carolina, 1900–1930* (Chapel Hill: University of North Carolina Press, 1957), 146–151; *Ole Miss Rebels,* 23.

Bolton, *War Eagle,* 23, 36; Leonard Wood to Camp, Nov. 19, 1893, Reel 18, Camp Papers (quote).

9. Miles, "Football in the South;" W. D. Berry to Stagg, Oct. 27, 1893, Box 41, Stagg Papers, (quote).

10. J. Granberry Jackson to A. A. Stagg, July 6, 1894, Box 41, Stagg Papers; Wendell Givens, *Ninety-Nine Iron: The Season Sewanee Won 5 Games in 6 Days* (Birmingham, AL: Seacoast Pub., 1992), 23 (quote). Sewanee won two more games that year against Auburn and North Carolina; but the former managed to score.

11. Henry Chadwick, ed., *Spalding's Base Ball Guide and Official League Book* (New York: American Sports Pub. Co.), published annually, provided little or no coverage of Southern or Western teams. The 1901 issue included a photo of the Denver team and brief mention of the California league, p. 107.

12. Maysel, *Here Come the Longhorns,* 1; Kent Keeth, "Looking Back at Baylor," in *The Baylor Line* (Oct. 1975), 65. Brad Fugua, *Glory of the Gridiron* (1994), (6); (7), 6; (12), 7–8; (13), 7, College

Football Hall of Fame Archives; "Football Notes," *NCAA News,* Nov. 12, 1990, 5.

13. Craig, "Football on the Pacific Slope," (quote); Walter Heffelfinger to Walter Camp, Sept. 10, 1893, Reel 9, Camp Papers.

14. H. S. Hicks to A. A. Stagg, Dec. 10, 1894; Dec. 13, 1894; J. O. Cross to Stagg, Dec. 29, 1894, Box 41, folder 4, Stagg Papers. For trip details, see Lester, *Stagg's University,* 28–31, and Box 18, folder 6, Stagg Papers.

15. Weyand, *Saga of American Football,* 123; Lawrence R. Stark to author, Nov. 26, 1996: Richard Fry, *The Crimson and the Grey* (Pullman, WA: Washington State University, 1989), 10–11. *The Oregon Stater; Football Centennial,* 1993, 10 (quote).

16. *The Hayseed, 1894,* 42 (yearbook), Oregon State University Archives, PUB 2-11c.

17. Patrick F. Morris, "Early Days of Football in Anaconda," uncited manuscript, 10–11, Butte-Silver Bow Archives, *Anaconda Standard,* Dec. 25, 1895 (clipping in Butte-Silver Bow Archives).

18. *Anaconda Standard,* Dec. 25, 1895 (clipping in Butte-Silver Bow Archives).

19. *Anaconda Standard,* Dec. 25, 1895 (clipping), referee George B. Diggert admitted that two of Ransome's calls were "unquestionably unfair and greatly against Butte." Three of his decisions resulted in Butte turnovers, one occurring within the 10-yard line. *Anaconda Standard,* Dec. 26, 1895 (clipping), *Butte Miner,* Dec. 27, 1896, 1.

20. *Butte Miner,* Nov. 23, 1896, 5.

21. *Wyoming Football Media Guide, 1996,* 89; Maltby, *The Origins and Early Development of Professional Football,* 61; D'Gay Stivers to A. A. Stagg, Apr. 24, 1895; July 10, 1895; Box 41, folder 5, Stagg Papers; Bob Royce, "Warner's Debut," *College Football Historical Society,* 8:2 (Feb. 1995), 1-2; *Butte-Miner,* Nov. 15, 1896, 8; Nov. 21, 1896, 5; Nov. 22, 1896, 5; Nov. 23, 1896, 5; Bob Pruter, "Intersectional Football Contests, 1900–1995," unpublished study.

22. *Chicago Tribune,* Nov. 27, 1891, 7; Ralph Stone Papers, Box 1, University of Michigan Archives; *Chicago Tribune,* Nov. 28, 1890, 1; Nov. 27, 1891, 7; Nov. 29, 1891, 6.

23. *The Graphic,* Dec. 3, 1892, 409, in Box 24, folder 2, Stagg Papers; Henry L. Williams, "Middle Western Football," *Outing,* 39, (Nov. 1901), 206–208.

24. *Times-Herald,* Nov. 14, 1897, clipping in Box 24, folder 2; A. A. Stagg to George W. Woodruff, Mar. 22, 1898, Box 42, folder 6, Stagg Papers (quote).

25. A. L. Shepard to Ward Hughes, Nov. 8, 1897, folder 5, Board in Control of Intercollegiate Athletics, University of Michigan Archives.

26. Joseph Jackson to Ward Hughes, Dec. 9, 1897, folder 5, Board in Control of Intercollegiate Athletics, University of Michigan Archives.

27. Davy to Stagg, Oct. 17, 1899, Box 41, folder 9, Stagg Papers.

28. John Coulter to Stagg, Nov. 9, 1899, Box 41, folder 9, Stagg Papers.

29. Nelson, *Anatomy of a Game,* 33, 42, 70–79, 86–87, 533–551; Davis, *Football,* 101; Walter Camp to A. A. Stagg, Apr. 6, 1895, Box 41, folder 5; Stagg to George Woodruff, June 20, 1898, Box 42, folder 6, Stagg Papers; A. A Stagg to Walter Camp, Jan. 11, 1896, Reel 16, Camp Papers. See Box 50, folder 21, Stagg Papers, and *Proceedings of Intercollegiate Conference of Faculty Representatives* (Minneapolis: University Press, 1901) in 28/1/805, University of Illinois Archives, on the ongoing rules controversy.

30. See Camp Papers, Reels 1, 6, 9, 14, 15, for continuing sectional pleas for inclusion; Box 38, folder 87, on the 1903 All-Western team; Weyand, *Saga of American Football,* 59; Lester, *Stagg's University,* 119; Camp, *The Book of Foot-ball,* 342–356.

31. R. S. Crowl, "A Justification for the Grudge of the West Against Walter Camp," *The Wisconsin Athletic Bulletin,* Dec. 14, 1912, 23–24, in Box 25, folder 3, Stagg Papers.

32. Washington went 58-0-3 between 1908–1916; R. C. Sackett to Walter Camp, Nov. 26, 1915, in Camp Papers, Reel 15.

33. Weyand, *Saga of American Football,* 56; Roberts, *The Big Nine,* 139; A. A. Stagg to George Woodruff, Feb. 18, 1898, Box 42, folder 6, Stagg Papers.

34. Nelson, *Anatomy of a Game,* 49, 128, 159; Danzig, *History of American Football,* 25–28, 45–46; Presbrey and Moffatt, *Athletics at Princeton,* 398–399; Roberts, *The Big Nine,* 141; Box 24, folder 1, Stagg Papers, on contrasting styles.

35. *Chicago Tribune,* Nov. 29, 1901, 5; Lester, *Stagg's University,* 201; Roberts, *The Big Nine,* 41–42; Jim Koger, *National Champions* (Columbus, GA: Atlantic Pub. Co., 1970), 10.

36. Nelson, *Anatomy of a Game,* 87–88.

37. Danzig, *History of American Football,* 33–39, 67; *Chicago Tribune,* Dec. 2, 1902, 9; Dec. 7, 1902, 9; *New York Times,* Dec. 7, 1902, 17; *Chicago Tribune,* Nov. 29, 1903, 9–10; Dec. 1, 1903, 6; *New York Times,* Nov. 21, 1903, 7; Nov. 27, 1903, 7; Nov. 29, 1903, 16; Walter Eckersall, "My Twenty-five Years in Football," *Liberty,* Oct. 23, 1926, 59–62.

38. Camp, *Foot-ball Guide for 1903,* 11; cited in Nelson, *Anatomy of a Game,* 92.

39. Lester, "Michigan–Chicago 1905."

40. Minutes of the Football Rules Committee for the Year 1906, (quote), Box 50, folder 1; see Joseph Raycroft to Stagg, Feb. 10, 1906, Box 12, folder 3; H. P Judson to Stagg, Mar. 21, 1906; Mar. 30, 1906; Box 15, folder 5, and Box 84, folder 2, Stagg Papers, on the near ban at Chicago.

Davis, *Football,* 495–503; Park, "Football to Rugby and Back." See James Orin Murfin Papers, Box 8, folder 2, University of Michigan Archives, on the Michigan decision and its aftermath. Wisconsin temporarily suspended football and Northwestern opted for rugby.

Camp, "Football Reform in the West;" see Edward S. Jordan, "Buying Football Victories," *Collier's,* Nov. 11, 1905, 19–20, 23, for charges against Chicago and Michigan.

41. Nelson, *Anatomy of a Game,* 129, 131, 139, 160; Danzig, *History of American Football,* 37–38.

42. Nelson, *Anatomy of a Game,* 140; "What Reform?," *College Football Historical Society,* 8:3 (May 1995), 4; see Camp Papers, Box 40, folder 127, for 1910 rule revisions.

43. Danzig, *History of American Football,* 38; Lester, *Stagg's University,* 102; University of Chicago, *President's Report, 1906–07,* 102–103; University of Chicago Archives.

Chicago Tribune, Dec. 24, 1902, 4; Joseph Raycroft to Amos Alonzo Stagg, Nov. 21, 1913, Box 12, folder 6, Stagg Papers (quote).

44. Numerous works address the Midwestern role in the Progressive reform movement. See Allen F. Davis, *American Heroine: The Life and Legend of Jane Addams* (New York: Oxford University Press, 1973); Allen F. Davis, *Spearheads for Reform: The Social*

Settlements and the Progressive Movement, 1890–1914 (New York: Oxford University Press, 1967); Charles MacArthur Destler, *Henry Demarest Lloyd and the Empire of Reform* (Philadelphia: University of Pennsylvania Press, 1963); David John Hogan, *Class and Reform: School and Society in Chicago, 1880–1930* (Philadelphia: University of Pennsylvania Press, 1985); Robert M. Crunden, *Ministers of Reform: The Progressive Achievement in American Civilization, 1889–1920* (New York: Basic Books, 1982); Heise and Frazel, *Hands On Chicago,* 28–29, 109–110, 122.

Peterson, *Pigskin,* 52: *College Football Historical Society,* 10:1 (Nov. 1996), 17 (quote).

45. Davis, *Football,* 117; Fielding H. Yost, "Western Football Against Eastern," *Collier's* (Jan. 10, 1914), 9, 26.

46. Rockne quote from College Football Hall of Fame exhibit, South Bend, IN, June 27, 1996.

47. *Chicago Tribune,* Nov. 2, 1913, pt. 3:1, *Chicago Evening Post,* Nov. 1, 1913, n.p. ; Nov. 2, 1913, 4; *Chicago Daily News,* Nov. 2, 1913 (tenth ed.), 2.

48. *Chicago Inter Ocean,* Nov. 2, 1913, n.p.

49. *Chicago Evening Post,* Nov. 2, 1913, 4.

50. *Chicago Evening Post,* Nov. 2, 1913, 4; *Chicago Daily News,* Nov. 3, 1913 (tenth ed.), 2.

51. Edward Wakin, *The Catholic Campus,* 1963, 60, cited in Sperber, *Shake Down the Thunder,* 41.

52. Sperber, *Shake Down the Thunder,* 45–46.

53. Weyand, *Saga of American Football,* 92–93, 104–107; Sperber, *Shake Down the Thunder,* 24–42, 98–113; University of Notre Dame Archives, UADR, Box 6, files 58, 61, 62, 80 (quote), 97.

See Myron J. Smith, ed., *The College Football Bibliography* (Westport, CT: Greenwood Press, 1994) on the Catholic coaching network; as well as Gerald R. Gems, "The Prep Bowl" on the phenomenon of Catholic football. See Jeffrey P. Moran, "Modernism Gone Mad; Sex Education Comes to Chicago, 1913," *Journal of American History* (Sept. 1996), 481–513, on Catholic opposition to the modernizing secular world.

54. NCAA memo, Nov. 25, 1913; 1916 NCAA convention announcement, both on Reel 13, Camp Papers.

55. Weyand, *Saga of American Football,* 124–125 (quote); Walter Camp, ed., *Spalding's Official Football Guide for 1906* (New York: American Sports Pub. Co., 1906), 53; Box 24, folder 3, Stagg Papers.

56. Russell R. Whitman to Football Manager, Nov. 8, 1897; Joseph J. Emery to Ward Hughes, Nov. 8, 1897; Jesse C. Dann to Football Manager, Dec. 14, 1900; Board in Control of Intercollegiate Athletics, Box 1; Ezra Decote and James Wayne correspondence with Charles Baird, Michigan Athletic Director, 1901, Box 1, University of Michigan, Bentley Historical Library.

Carroll, *Fritz Pollard,* 77–90; Seward A. Simons to Walter Camp, Dec. 20, 1916; Jan. 2, 1917; Jan. 8, 1917 (quote), Walter Camp Papers, Reel 16. R. C. Sackett to Camp, Nov. 26, 1915, Reel 15, had predicted a western win.

57. Joe Marvin, "The Old P.C.C.," *College Football Historical Society,* 9:2 (Feb. 1996), 1–3; John C. Hibner, "Brick Muller," *College Football Historical Society,* 9:3 (May 1996), 15–18; Hibner, *Rose Bowl,* 69–83.

58. "The American South," Mind Extension University, Aug. 12, 1994; Foster, *Ghosts of the Confederacy;* Charles Reagan Wilson, *Baptized in Blood: The Religion of the Lost Cause, 1865–1920* (Athens: University of Georgia Press, 1983); John T. Graves, *The Fighting South* (Birmingham: University of Alabama Press, 1985, reprint of 1943 ed.); Bertram Wyatt-Brown, *Honor and Violence in the Old South* (New York: Oxford University Press, 1986); Grantham, *The South in Modern America,* 322 (quote).

59. Brian S. Butler, "'Gain Ground and Glory': Metropolitan Athletic Clubs and the Promoting of American Football—the Case of the Louisville Athletic Club," *International Journal of the History of Sport,* 9:3 (Dec. 1992), 378–396; Andrew Doyle, "'Causes Won, Not Lost': College Football and the Modernization of the American South," *International Journal of the History of Sport,* 11:2 (Aug. 1994), 231–251; Sugar, *The SEC,* 118 (quote).

60. Miles, "Football in the South."

61. Fountain, *Sportswriter,* 43.

62. Presbrey and Moffatt, *Athletics at Princeton,* 389; Board in Control of Intercollegiate Athletics, Box 48; account book, Apr. 13, 1899, University of Michigan Archives; Sugar, *The SEC,* 327; *Chicago Tribune,* Nov. 25, 1900, 19; Weyand, *Saga of American Football,* 114.

63. Fountain, *Sportswriter,* 87; Weyand, *Saga of American Football,* 115 (quote). Prominent sportswriters ranked teams, but there was no official consensus.

64. Sugar, *The SEC,* 209, 250, 258, 268, 274; Danzig, *History of American Football,* 168–169 (quote).

65. Nelson, *Anatomy of a Game,* 148; Danzig, *History of American Football,* 43–44; Umphlett, *Creating the Big Game,* 133.

66. Bolton, *War Eagle,* 121–122.

67. Bob Royce, "Unsung Heroes of the South," *College Football Historical Society,* 4:3 (May 1991), 1–3; *College Football Historical Society,* 8:2 (Feb. 1995), 11, offers an alternative spelling, as Leach.

68. Jim Naughton, "Centre College Remembers the Day When It Was King of the Gridiron," *Chronicle of Higher Education,* Oct. 4, 1996, A46.

69. Stagg to Rockne, Nov. 7, 1921, UADR, Box 6, file 62, Notre Dame Archives.

70. Sugar, *The SEC,* 2; 207 (quote).

71. Smith, *Big-Time Football at Harvard,* 268, fn. 67; 286, fn. 78; "Football As Our Greatest Popular Spectacle," *Literary Digest,* 75 (Dec. 2, 1922), 52–57; Elmore C. Patterson, "Football as the West Played It," *Outing,* Jan. 22, 1922, 162–164; *The Story of the Stadium,* Zuppke Papers, Box 1, Series 28/3/20, University of Illinois Archives.

72. Patrick Clark, *Sports Firsts* (New York: Facts on File, 1981), 42; *Aurora Beacon-News,* Nov. 25, 1995, n.p.; Lester, *Stagg's University,* 101, 188–120.

73. Hibner, *Rose Bowl,* 141–148.

74. Ibid., 152–162; "Yes, Suh, The Old South is Lookin' Up," *Literary Digest,* 57 (Nov. 19, 1930), 36–39 (quotes).
Umphlett, *Creating the Big Game,* 141–146; McCallum and Pearson, *College Football,* 177; Andy Doyle, "Paying Homage to the Brilliant Sons of Alabama: The Southern Response to University of Alabama Football, 1920–1931," North American Society for Sport History Convention, Albuquerque, New Mexico, May 29, 1993; Doyle, "Causes Won, Not Lost," on southern revelry.

75. Sugar, *The SEC,* 123–124, 192; Andrew J. Kozar, "And the Big Orange Caissons Went Rolling Along," and Wendell Givens, "1934 Alabama," both in *College Football Historical Society,* 8:1 (Nov. 1994), 17–18; and 1–3, respectively. Amy Scott, "Hold That Tiger: Huey

Long and Louisiana State University Football, 1928–1935," North American Society for Sport History Convention, Auburn, Alabama, May 25, 1996.

76. Sperber, *Shake Down the Thunder,* 442–443; Graves, *The Fighting South,* 101; Andrew Doyle, "Bear Bryant: Symbol of an Embattled South," *Colby Quarterly,* 32:1 (Mar. 1996), 72–86; Charles Martin, "Integrating New Year's Day: The Racial Politics of College Bowl Games in the American South," North American Society for Sport History Convention, Auburn, Alabama, May 25, 1996; Stephen T. Foster, "The Bonnie Blue Flag," (Columbus: Newfield, 1993); CBS, "60 Minutes," June 8, 1997.

77. Ray Schmidt, "The Dixie Classic," *College Football Historical Society,* 1:2 (Nov. 1987), 1–2; John C. Hibner, "The First Palm Bowl," *College Football Historical Society,* 5:3 (May 1992), 8–10, indicates that the Palm Bowl evolved into the Orange Bowl.
See Doyle, "Causes Won, Not Lost," on football and modernization in the South.

78. Butler, "Confederate Flags, Class Conflicts, a Golden Egg, and Castrated Bulls;" see Bertram Wyatt-Brown, *Honor and Violence in the Old South* (New York: Oxford University Press, 1986), 131–146, on the tradition of dueling and sport to rectify wrongs.

79. Butler, "Confederate Flags, Class Conflicts, a Golden Egg, and Castrated Bulls," 132–133.

80. Charles H. Martin, "Racial Change and 'Big-Time' College Football in Georgia: The Age of Segregation, 1892–1957," *Georgia Historical Quarterly,* 80:3 (Fall 1996), 532–562; Thomas G. Smith, "Outside the Pale: The Exclusion of Blacks from the National Football League, 1934–1946," *Coffin Corner,* 11:4 (Summer 1989), 4–14.

81. Ashe, *A Hard Road to Glory,* 36–37; Martin, "Integrating New Year's Day"; Martin, "Racial Change and 'Big-Time' College Football in Georgia."

82. Ronald E. Marcello, "The Integration of Intercollegiate Athletics in Texas: North Texas State College as a Test Case, 1956," *Journal of Sport History,* 14:3 (Winter 1987), 286–316; Doyle, "Bear Bryant."

Chapter 6

Epilogue: Keeping the Score

By the mid-twentieth century football had helped to resolve the cultural tensions that beset the United States in the aftermath of the Civil War. The nation had moved from its agrarian roots to an urban, commercial lifestyle, and taken its place of leadership among the countries of the world. Football fostered that transition by reinforcing and promoting particular values essential to the American character and spirit.

The nature of the game required aggressiveness, courage, and physical prowess, decidedly masculine qualities that addressed the nineteenth century fear of the feminization of culture. Football remains the lone bastion of masculinity, as women now engage in auto racing, ice hockey, basketball, baseball, horseracing, and boxing.

The American need to win proved evident by the 1870s as the rivalries of Harvard, Princeton, and Yale led to strategic innovations and rules violations in the attempt to gain victory. In the first Army-Navy game in 1890, Army protested its opponents' use of fakes as ungentlemanly and dishonorable. Nevertheless, Navy claimed a 24–0 win at West Point. The following year Army outposts around the country sent financial support to the West Point team, who avenged themselves, 32–16, at Annapolis. Within two years the rivalry drew 10,000 fans and numerous altercations, including an alleged gunfight between a general and a rear admiral that resulted in a six-year hiatus. The 1909 contest was also canceled when both teams had players killed in previous games that season, perhaps a prelude to the ultimate sacrifice faced by all soldiers and sailors who served their country in real wars. Army soon began using older, more experienced players who had completed their eligibility elsewhere, and enjoyed the number one ranking by 1914.[1]

In an effort to win, coaches often employed "tramp" athletes, who offered their services to the highest bidder. In a 1910 scrimmage against Notre Dame, Amos Alonzo Stagg, Chicago's coach, rationalized such a violation of the amateur code as "only a practice game," when he enlisted such a player.[2] Such employment only encouraged assistance by team managers and loyal alumni in gaining the best players for their schools. In 1913–1914 Percy Graves, a multisport athlete at the University of Illinois, held the rights to the concession stands for its football and baseball games. At Notre Dame star athletes got $200, a charge account, and alumni support; and by 1920 a midwestern sportswriter claimed that "practically all schools are guilty of using "traveling athletes."[3] The Savage Report, a national investigation for the Carnegie Foundation in 1929, confirmed widespread recruiting violations, subsidization of athletes, and the commercialization of college sports. The exposé revealed at least one in seven athletes and almost half of the starting football players receiving some form of aggrandizement. Such abuses continue today as the entrenched emphasis on winning and the influence of free market capitalism encourages players and coaches to seek the most lucrative offers and results in the annual merry-go-round of personnel changes at all levels.[4]

The assault on amateurism began with the need to win among the Big 3 (Harvard, Princeton, Yale) in the nineteenth century. Inducements offered to athletes for their services reached national proportions by 1900. As principle gave way to practicality, "scholarships" were officially endorsed as a necessary part of the system in the NCAA's "sanity code" of 1948. It soon gave way to full athletic scholarships in 1952.[5]

The incorporation of football in the commercial culture and the alignment of higher education with capitalism became readily apparent by the 1880s. In 1881 the championship game between Yale and Princeton drew 10,000 spectators to New York's Polo Grounds. Teams chose such urban sites to maximize fans and profits, and by 1887 the 23,000 viewers paid up to $2 for the privilege. College presidents soon realized that winning teams generated capital and alumni support, and even losing teams won free promotion in media accounts of their games. Such exposure produced tuition-paying students, and even small schools embarked on national schedules and highly visible contests in the major urban centers thereafter. In 1920 the University of Chicago endured a losing season; but still earned more than a quarter million dollars in receipts by scheduling all but one game at home. Today bowl games produce even greater recognition and profit for colleges, and corporate sponsors line up for promotional opportunities. The Super Bowl for the professional championship provides the ultimate marriage between football and American capitalism.[6]

Businessmen and civic boosters promoted football games for pride and profit as the sport became a means to publicize goods, people, and places. In 1892 the J. P. Stevens Company offered a silver trophy to the winner of the Georgia-Auburn game, and the *Atlanta Journal* awarded a victory banner for the contest, which it billed as the championship of the South. The A. G. Spalding Company even canvassed high school leagues in an attempt to sell its sporting goods. Such opportunities as well as commercial and civic rivalries proliferated by the turn of the century. A 1905 study of 555 cities found that 432 fielded football teams. The *American Physical Education Review* conducted another survey from 1905–1907 that determined that 78 percent of high schools had football teams, practically insuring that the game's values would be transmitted to future generations.[7] The symbiotic relationship of football and business has grown with each new decade.

The 1902–1903 high school series between New York and Chicago has become a national enterprise over the course of the century. High school teams continue to travel cross country in search of laurels and national rankings. High school coaches have their own radio shows; teams play in multimillion dollar stadiums and travel on chartered airplanes. Football serves as a secular religion throughout the South. Each weekend 4 million Texans attend high school games. In the Midwest, the Massillon, Ohio Tigers had won twenty-two state championships by 1996, and Coach Jack Rose remarked that "Nine-and-one's not a good year here." Massillon drew more than 120,000 fans in 1995, demonstrating that even high school football is big business.[8]

Neighborhood teams, athletic clubs, and small towns operated outside the jurisdiction of college regulating agencies and offered the working class lucrative opportunities as well, as some evolved into semipro or fully professional contingents. Such outlaw teams fostered gambling and produced a leveling effect as the incorporation of noncollegiate players diminished the game's elitist image starting in the 1890s, and enhanced the perception of sport as a meritocracy and a means to social mobility thereafter. Professionalism appeared in Pennsylvania as early as 1892, but spread as far as Butte, Montana by 1896. The Columbus, Ohio Panhandles, a team of players who worked on a division of the Pennsylvania Railroad, organized in 1901. A machinist, Joe Carr, served as manager; but the team featured the six Nesser brothers, the sons of German immigrants. All brawny boilermakers, they supplemented their paychecks into the 1920s by battering their opponents. The Columbus roster showed twenty players by 1921; but only three had attended college. All but one of the original fourteen teams in the new professional league employed noncollegians. Despite a fifth grade education, Joe Carr became president of the National Football League from 1921–1939, earning a salary of $1,000 per year.[9] Such men fueled the aspirations of working class boys and sustained their perception of sport as a meritocracy.

The renegade form of football thus brought a popular element to the game; and college authorities disdained its concomitant and overt gambling as well as the blatant rejection of the amateur ideology. Major John L. Griffith, Big Ten Commissioner, declared "pro football as decadent," and W. G. Manly, the faculty representative at Missouri, stated that "We wish to deal a death blow to professional football." Stagg revoked the varsity letters won by Chicago athletes who turned pro, and the Missouri Valley Conference banned all association with professional players, managers, and officials. The Big Ten also outlawed any officials who consented to referee pro contests.[10]

The draconian measures failed to deter players. Six Notre Dame players won $400 each for their services in the 1919 city championship in Rockford, Illinois. A 1921 game, supposedly between two small Illinois towns, featured ten University of Illinois players on the Taylorville side, opposed by at least nine Notre Damers, who had been recruited by Carlinville. An informant soon wrote Knute Rockne that two of his star players had spent their Sundays with pro teams in Wisconsin. The revelation was hardly news to Rockne, who had himself been a participant in such games a few years before. Notre Dame eventually expelled George Trafton and Curly Lambeau for such transgressions; but both proceeded to Hall of Fame careers in the pro ranks. Nor was Notre Dame unique. In its initial season of 1920 the American Professional Football Association featured players from over ninety different colleges. Illinois's biggest star, Red Grange, signed a pro contract immediately after his last college game in 1925, despite the incriminations against professionalism. That same year the Milwaukee Badgers even drafted four high school boys for an impromptu game with the Chicago Cardinals. Their consequent loss of eligibility seemingly paled relative to the celebrity earned.[11]

Football had clearly attracted the working class, immigrant offspring, and African-Americans by the 1920s; but the professional version of the game had yet to win full acceptance in the mainstream culture. The transition to middle class values and urban commercial culture became more apparent in the 1930s, as evidenced by the Portsmouth Spartans' history. Situated in southern Ohio, near the Kentucky and West Virginia state lines, Portsmouth had a number of semipro and pro teams throughout the 1920s. The desire to beat nearby rival Ironton caused local businessmen to organize the Portsmouth Football Association in 1928. Both teams recruited college players, and by 1930 all but one of Portsmouth's thirty-one men had played at that level. In 1930 Portsmouth joined the NFL. Despite a post-season playoff berth in 1932 that resulted in a famous indoor game against the Bears in Chicago Stadium, the Depression devastated the small town team. In 1934 George Richards, a wealthy radio station owner, bought the franchise and transfered it to Detroit.[12]

Other teams sought college players as well, and the NFL officially instituted its draft in 1936. The draft was spurred by George Preston Marshall, a showman, promoter, and entrepreneur, who entered the league as owner of the Boston franchise in 1933 and brought business acumen and a more modern reorganization structure to the league. Marshall soon moved his team to Washington, D.C. in search of greater profits.

A similar process played out throughout the United States as small town rivalries engendered professionalism and civic pride fostered attempts to compete on a national level. Between 1920 and 1939 the renamed National Football League had granted more than fifty different franchises; but only Green Bay remained among the small town teams by the onset of World War II.[13] Vestiges of the past, the small town team and working class ideals of physicality, survive in the spirit and competition of the game.

As teams sought larger audiences, technology, too, brought the game to millions. Radio greatly expanded football markets in the 1920s, and television assured the sustenance of the NFL in the 1950s. The first televised game occurred in the fall of 1939 when Fordham hosted Waynesburg. Frank Wolf, the Waynesburg coach, sacrificed his Pennsylvania team to the then nationally powerful Rams, 34–7, for the profit gained by a New York game. Mo Scarry, the Waynesburg center, stated that "It was a terrific thrill for a group of country boys like us to get to New York." Bill Meighen, another Waynesburg player, claimed that the 9,000 fans "was the biggest (crowd) we had ever seen." Of greater importance, however, were the unseen spectators, for RCA had chosen the game to make its first television broadcast for an NBC station. It used two primitive on-field cameras that relayed pictures by cable to the top of the Empire State Building, where they were then transmitted to the few who could afford the new technology that allowed home viewing. A few weeks later, on October 22, 1939, RCA first televised a pro game at the New York World's Fair, a 24–13 win for the Brooklyn Dodgers over the Philadelphia Eagles. Four more college telecasts ensued and the new medium gradually transformed both football and American culture.[14]

Pro football, the renegade version of the sport, clearly sought a mainstream audience by World War II. In 1941 team owners selected Elmer Layden, who had been one of Notre Dame's famed Four Horsemen and a well-known coach, as the first commissioner of the NFL. The commissioner system, though dictatorial, had brought stability and profit to baseball. The NFL began to portray a more respectable image by instituting regulations more congruent with middle class values. Neither coaches nor players could endorse liquor or cigarettes, and all players had to be properly dressed, with clean uniforms and mandatory stockings for any photos. By that time, all teams had gone through the modernization process that earlier affected baseball, and represented major urban centers that promised the greatest profit.[15]

The popularity of the game insured such profit. Collegiate football continued apace throughout the century, and the success of the professional game spawned several new leagues. As early as 1926 an alternative American Football League fielded nine teams; but lasted only a year. Some regional professional leagues enjoyed a measure of success; but the All-American Football Conference (1946–1949) spanned the country, and, once again, desegregated professional football, a year before Jackie Robinson appeared for the Dodgers. Another American Football League began play in 1960, opening additional new markets and an infusion of television money that benefited both leagues, which merged at the end of the 1969 season. By the 1970s football had surpassed baseball in game attendance and television viewers to become the new "national game," spawning the World Football League (1974–1975), the United States Football League (1983–1985), and an indoor version of the game, known as "arena" football.[16]

During that period football also addressed severe social divisions as the civil rights movement and the Vietnam War split the country. In response, football produced heroes for all constituencies, from the youthful, rebellious, hedonistic Joe Namath to the conservative George Allen, or old-fashioned, disciplined Vince Lombardi. African-American stars proliferated on college gridirons and in the professional ranks. Some, like Jim Brown, became outspoken activists for social change.[17]

Football continued to reinforce its link with leadership as well. Former players Dwight Eisenhower, John Kennedy, and Gerald Ford held the highest office in the nation; while Richard Nixon, an avid fan, even sent plays to coaches and relished his interactions with players.[18]

In more recent years football has become a global enterprise. The NCAA Rules Committee Advisory Group includes representatives from Canada, Great Britain, Australia, Japan, and Italy. Mexican and European players exhibited their skills as part of the 1997 Sugar Bowl festivities. American professional and college teams now appear in stadiums in Mexico, Japan, England, and Ireland, and the Dallas Cowboys' fan base clearly crosses national boundaries. The World League of American Football, a joint venture of the NFL and corporate sponsors, is an attempt to bring an American sport, American products, and American values to an international public.[19]

While that process has now reached global proportions it first required the establishment of a unified American identity and commonly shared values. Ideology had to be defined and accepted before it could be exported. The explosive growth of football reached nationwide proportions by the 1890s, and colleges faced national opposition when, after 1905, violence and mortality issues caused some schools to opt for rugby. In 1908 Bill Reid, the former Harvard coach, wrote to Walter Camp about two of the recalcitrants,

> ...if California and Stanford were playing the game played by other colleges and schools of the country there would be a binding together of the athletic interests of the country... (a) Stanford alumnus in New York...could get no one to discuss the game with him and where everyone else was interested in another game. In this sense certainly California and Stanford are isolated.[20]

College football united fans for reasons of regional pride or religion as well. Even those who had not gone to college claimed allegiance to particular schools. One claimed Boston College as his "alma mater"; because it was "a little college

with so much spunk." Another followed his "native" West
Virginia; while a Yale supporter stated that it "represented
home and all it stood for." Others admitted to being "grouchy,
out of sorts, downhearted and touchy" whenever Notre Dame
lost.[21] In October 1910 Illinois moved to solidify such support
by instituting a homecoming weekend for its game against
rival Chicago. Illinois won 3–0 en route to a Western Conference championship and other college presidents soon realized
the remunerative value of establishing such institutional
loyalty.[22] Over the next two decades the increased incorporation of ethnic immigrant offspring and African-Americans as
players generated support among marginalized groups and
fostered the perception of football as a meritocracy, and a field
of opportunity for all. Whereas the "national game" of baseball
still excluded blacks, football represented a truer democracy.

Ethnic beliefs and black hopes in democracy spurred some
to patriotism. The alliance of football and patriotism had
already been established. The Thanksgiving Day rituals tied
the game to a particular American tradition, and the All-
America teams created national sports heroes to be emulated
by youth. Both had become annual features by the 1890s,
reinforced by boys' literature and media spectacles thereafter.
Even southern states that failed to celebrate Lincoln's birth-
day and still constructed Confederate memorials were drawn
into the football craze. The territorial nature of the game,
which required both teamwork and individual brilliance to
mount an offense that penetrated the opponents' territory, as
well as the defense of one's own territory, replicated the
American frontier experience. Football followed America
westward, reinforcing in the game a progress marked by gain,
domination, conquest, and profit. It demanded and promoted
the aggressive martial spirit that culminated in America's
Manifest Destiny and produced world leadership.[23]

For more than a century football stadiums have marked the
close association of the game with that martial spirit by
memorializing fallen heroes. When Henry L. Higginson presented an athletic space to Harvard in 1890 he stated that

> The only wish on my part is that the ground shall be called
> "The Soldier's Field," and marked with a stone bearing the

names of some dear friends—alumni of the University and
noble gentlemen—who gave freely and eagerly to all that
they had hoped for, to their country and to their fellowmen
in the hour of great need—the War of 1861–1865 in defense
of the Republic.[24]

Following World War I both Chicago's Soldier Field and the
University of Illinois's Memorial Stadium commemorated the
dead of that conflict, with the 183 columns of the latter site
each honoring one of its own killed in action. Philadelphia's
Veterans Stadium and numerous other memorial playing
sites throughout the country continue the tradition linking
football to patriotism.[25]

That pantheon of heroes expanded shortly after the turn of
the century when the prestigious All-America team selections
began including ethnics, Catholics, and eventually Jewish
and African-Americans in a symbolic portrayal of American
pluralism. Professional football fostered even greater cohesiveness with more overt ties to the working classes. Team
designations, such as the Packers or Steelers, continue to
extol their working class origins, while the Patriots, 49ers,
and Cowboys present nationalistic icons and promote a particular cultural heritage. The latter invoke the frontier im-
agery and the rugged masculinity required to tame the
West.[26]

Just as football assuaged concerns over declining masculinity in the late nineteenth century, the game continues to
provide psychic release today. As a form of popular culture it
provides immediate gratification with relatively little need for
education; in contrast to the more exclusive pursuit of high
culture, which requires cultivation and knowledge to elicit
satisfaction. Moreover, as a cyclical ritual, it reoccurs each fall
season, and provides a sense of stability and order to increasingly harried lives. Such shared experiences reinforce common interests, common values, and a sense of tradition in a
sometimes fragmented pluralistic society. The pageantry and
spectacle of football games celebrate American life and symbolically portray its characteristics in a pervasive manner.
More than half of the United States citizenry tuned in to the

1996 Super Bowl and the broadcast reached 175 countries around the globe.[27]

The 1998 Super Bowl drew more than 13 million viewers in the United States, and more than 800 million worldwide. The game was broadcast in 17 languages to 144 countries. The 1999 game accentuated football's ties to commercialized capitalist culture as sponsors paid $1.6 million for a 30-second advertising spot. Airplanes with company banners contributed to the 300 aircraft hovering over the stadium, saturation that required the installation of federal air traffic controllers within the ballpark. Football thus claims the fascination and allegiance of fans, as Super Bowls have produced ten of the top twenty television shows of the all-time ratings.[28]

Such binding rituals portray traditional values, the belief in the work ethic, self-sacrifice, and success, and produce a collective identity that unifies schools, communities, and generations in a cultural tradition. The shared practices bring subordinate groups into the process of culture formation, and reinforce dominant group norms. Whereas African-American athletes have changed the nature of basketball by introducing their own cultural style to the game, football reinforces white, middle class value systems by restricting black expression. The NCAA rules committee forbid celebratory acts, such as decorated goalposts and spiking the ball as early as 1971, as increasing numbers of black players began to appear on college teams. Despite the preponderance of African-Americans in the NFL the professional league has reinforced such arbitrary, racial, and class-based restrictions by prohibiting alternative celebrations after touchdowns.[29]

Despite such ongoing differences football has managed to fuse disparate values by combining rugged, rural, and frontier characteristics within an urban, commercial, and corporate structure. The game symbolizes both the physicality and prowess cherished by the working class, and the commercialism central to middle class lives. As early as 1931 post-season games raised money for the unemployed and other charitable causes to demonstrate the practical, and social value of the game. Such humanitarian causes transcend religious differences; but the nature of the game brought greater cohesion even in that regard. Teamwork and the communal huddle might symbolize the group orientations of Catholics, Mormons, and Jews, while individual play allowed room for Protestant beliefs. The Chicago Prep Bowl series, which pitted the Catholic champion against its public school counterpart, celebrated such differences with its inauguration in 1927. Yet by 1937 a combined team of all-stars from both leagues culminated their season by upholding city pride in games against Phoenix and Los Angeles.[30]

Such visible symbols of inclusion continued to reinforce beliefs in a multicultural democracy, and were not lost on immigrant offspring. In succeeding years a survey of Catholic participants in the Prep Bowl attested to its meaning and the ideology that it portrayed. For some it provided greater opportunities in the form of college scholarships or professional careers. Others claimed to be haunted by a loss even 50 years later; but even in defeat they felt that they had gained respect. Almost all considered their involvement to have been a character building experience.[31]

Even seemingly contradictory philosophies found common cause in football. Idealists extolled the character building qualities of the game, personified by the All-America team. They proclaimed it a training ground for critical thinking, sportsmanship, and ethical behavior; while realists counted wins and profits, and lauded the violent, aggressive qualities necessary for world leadership. A recent analysis of world dominance asserted that "The West won the world not by the superiority of its ideas or values or religion (to which few members of other civilizations were converted) but rather by its superiority in applying organized violence."[32]

By 1920 the western nations controlled more than 84 percent of the world and the United States had taken its place as foremost in the hierarchy of nations. To achieve that position it first had to coalesce in a common identity and a common value system. Football helped Americans do so by distinguishing itself as a nationalistic game, distinct from its British forebears, and one that promoted a martial spirit. The sport served as a rite of passage for young males eager to assert their masculinity in the face of a growing feminism. It produced aggressive, competitive, disciplined, and self-sacrificing workers and leaders for a capitalist economy as it merged commercial values with the ideals of higher education on college campuses. Football marked the American coming of age with the closing of the frontier, the transition to an urban society, and the amalgamation of regional differences.[33]

Football allowed such cultural tensions to be contested and resolved through play rather than the more overt hostility of civil war, resulting in a regeneration of southern pride and western recognition. As the game spread to include other racial, ethnic, religious, and working class groups it fostered the perception of a meritocracy and the principles of democracy, opportunity, and equality that immigrants and migrants had desired. Labor unrest expressed itself within the system rather than overturning it, as subordinate groups found solace and the means to more immediate gratification congruent with their own values. Victories by underdogs, regional aspirants, or the socially dispossessed reinforced perceptions of equality by providing temporary assertions of dominance. The negotiation of regional and class differences eventually produced a leveling effect and a popular culture that distanced itself from the original elitism. Professional and semipro football revolved around gambling and the physicality of industrial life. The perseverance, success, and eventual acceptance of that alternative and residual form brought greater cohesiveness to American society and its shared values. Both the collegiate and professional versions assumed corporate bureaucratic structures that replicated workplace attitudes and specialized roles to produce wins and profits. In the postmodern world such values are symbolically and literally portrayed in weekly rituals and flashy media spectacles that package and commercialize an entertainment product for a consumer society.[34]

The process of negotiating both the nature of the game and the nature of the society produced a homogenization of culture which defined its intrinsic characteristics. During the twentieth century the United States took its place on the world stage as an aggressive, commercial, white, Protestant, male society that allowed for the expression of pluralistic values and the limited inclusion of others. Football helped Americans achieve that definition of themselves as a weekly anthropological play,

a cultural performance of symbols, rituals, and ceremonies
that enabled us to tell ourselves who we were.

Notes

1. John Dizikes, *Sportsmen and Gamesmen* (Boston; Houghton
Mifflin, 1981), shows an emphasis on winning during the antebellum
era. Gene Schoor, *100 Years of Army–Navy Football* (New York:
Henry Holt & Co., 1989), 1–19, 37, 51; states that the top ranking
came from the All-America coaches committee. Dan Jenkins, *Saturday's America* (Boston: Little, Brown & Co., 1970), appendix, lists
both Illinois and Army as No. 1 that year. Donald J. Mrozek, "The
Habit of Victory: the American Military and the Cult of Manliness,"
in J. A. Mangan and James Walvin, eds., *Manliness and Morality:
Middle-class Masculinity in Britain and America, 1800–1940* (New
York: St. Martin's Press, 1987), 220–239.

2. Chet Grant, *Before Rockne at Notre Dame* (Notre Dame, IN:
Dujarie Press, 1968), 38.

3. Lon Eubanks, *The Fighting Illini: A Story of Illinois Football*
(Huntsville, AL: Strode Pub., 1976), 60–61; Patrick Chelland, *One for
the Gipper: George Gipp, Knute Rockne and Notre Dame* (Chicago:
Henry Regnery Co., 1973), 45; Harry J. Costello to Walter Camp, Nov.
4, 1920, Reel 6, Camp Papers, (quote).

4. Sperber, *Shake Down the Thunder,* 306.

5. Rader, *American Sports,* 268.

6. Steven A. Riess, *City Games: The Evolution of American Urban
Society and the Rise of Sports* (Urbana: University of Illinois Press,
1989), 56, 271, fn. 8; Umphlett, *Creating the Big Game,* 183–187;
Chicago Tribune, Nov. 22, 1920, 19.

7. Bolton, *War Eagle,* 30; W. E. Mellinger, ed., *High School Journal,* 4:5 (Feb. 1886), 5; 1:1 (May 1886), 1,3; Minutes of the Cook
County Indoor Baseball League, Jan. 2, 1896: Dec. 18, 1896; Dec. 3,
1897; Dec. 7, 13, 19, 1898; Pope, *Patriotic Games,* 91, 128, on surveys.

8. Pruter, "Intersectional Football Contests, 1900–1995;"
Naperville Sun, Oct. 11, 1996, 61 (quote); Aug. 22, 1997, 61–62; Sept.
2, 1998, 67; Sept. 4, 1998, 44; Barber and Didinger, *Football America,*
87–92.

9. Peterson, *Pigskin,* 43, 76; Stephen Fox, *Big Leagues: Professional Baseball, Football, and Basketball in National Memory* (New
York: William Morrow & Co., 1994), 242, 244–245; Keith McClellan,

The Sunday Game: At the Dawn of Professional Football (Akron: University of Akron Press, 1998), 49–63; Bob Carroll, *The Ohio League, 1910–1919* (Pro Football Researchers Assn., 1991), 7; Pro Football Researchers Assn., *Bulldogs on Sunday, 1920,* 133–171; *1921:* 100, 111; *1922:* 138.

10. Maltby, *Origins and Early Development of Professional Football,* 92, 97–100, records bets ranging from $3,000-$50,000 per game during 1905–1906. Peterson, *Pigskin,* 92 (quotes); *Chicago Tribune,* Dec. 5, 1920, pt. 2:1.

11. Emil Klosinski, "When Notre Dame Won the Rockford City Championship," *Coffin Corner,* 7:11–12 (Nov.-Dec. 1985), 3–5; Eubanks, *The Fighting Illini,* 82–83; O. F. Long to Knute Rockne, Feb. 14, 1922, UADR, Box 6, file 80, Notre Dame Archives. *Bulldogs On Sunday, 1920,* 133–171, for 1920 rosters.

On the professional high school players, see Al F. Gorman, Resolution of the Chicago City Council, Jan. 16, 1926; E. C. Delaporte to Gorman, Jan. 21, 1926; Report of the Committee on Relation of Professional Athletics as it Concerns High School Athletics, Coaches, and Officials, Jan. 20, 1926, all in the football file, Chicago Public Schools Athletic League Archives; Bob Carroll, "Bulldogs on Sunday," *Coffin Corner,* 11:1 (Winter 1989), 56–57.

12. Carl M. Becker, "The 'Tom Thumb' Game: Bears vs. Spartans, 1932," *Journal of Sport History,* 22:3 (Fall 1995), 216–227.

13. Tod Maher, "In the Beginning," *Coffin Corner,* 15:3 (June 1993), 7–10, 15–16.

See Scott Parker, *http://www.angelfire.com/ks/parker/index. html,* on Kansas town teams; and Brian S. Butler, "Independent Football Organizes, 1923–1935," manuscript in author's possession, for the situation in Louisville.

14. Stan Grosshandler, "TV's First Game," *College Football Historical Society,* 6:4 (August 1993), 4–5 (quotes), indicates that television sets cost as much as $600.

Peterson, *Pigskin,* 124–125.

15. Peterson, *Pigskin,* 136–137; Barber and Didinger, *Football America,* 210–223. Previously the top league executive held the title of president.

16. Carroll, *Fritz Pollard,* 177; see Rader, *American Sports,* 255–258, on the AFL-NFL merger; 259, on attendance and television.

17. Ibid., 259–260.

18. Ibid., 262–263.

19. Nelson, *Anatomy of a Game,* 432; "American Football Around the Globe," *American Football Quarterly,* 2:3 (July-Sept. 1996), 89.

20. William T. Reid to Walter Camp, Feb. 28, 1908, Reel 14, Camp Papers.

21. Manuscript, Box 38, folder 7, Camp Papers.

22. Linda Young, *Hail to the Orange and Blue: 100 Years of Illinois Football Tradition* (Champaign, IL: Sagamore Pub., 1990), 20.

23. Wilbur Zelinsky, *Nation Into State: The Shifting Symbolic Foundations of American Nationalism* (Chapel Hill: University of North Carolina Press, 1988), is instructive of the nationalistic process.

24. Bealle, *History of Football at Harvard,* 6.

25. *The Story of the Stadium,* Box 1, Zuppke Papers.

26. Bernie McCarty, *All America: The Complete Roster of Football's Heroes* (privately published, 1991).

27. Lawrence Levine, *Highbrow/Lowbrow: The Emergence of Cultural Hierarchy in America* (Cambridge, MA: Harvard University Press, 1988); John Marshall Carter and Arnd Kruger, eds., *Ritual and Record: Sports Records and Quantification in Pre-Modern Societies* (Westport, CT: Greenwood Press, 1990), 144; Connerton, *How Societies Remember;* Barber and Didinger, *Football America,* 245, lists 134,488,000 television viewers.

28. ABC Nightly News, Jan. 28, 1999; Jan. 30, 1999; *http://superbowl.lycos.com; http://www.nfl.com/international*

29. Andrew W. Miracle and C. Roger Rees, *Lessons of the Locker Room: The Myth of School Sports* (Amherst, NY: Prometheus Books, 1994), 11–14. For a particular example of such a process, see H. G. Bissinger, *Friday Night Lights: A Team, a Town, and a Dream.* Nelson, *Anatomy of a Game,* 345.

30. *NCAA News,* Sept. 20, 1993, 3; All-Star Game Program, Dec. 30, 1938, in Chicago Public Schools Athletic League Archives.

31. Author's survey of Weber High School teams of 1940s–1950s; Ron Chernick to author, Oct. 29, 1994; Valerie Kullick to author, Oct. 29, 1994; Richard Zaleski to author, undated; Richard A. Sieracki to author, undated; E. J. Spera to author, undated; Michael J. Haas to author, undated; Gerald L. Wallenberg to author, Jan. 12, 1995.

32. Samuel P. Huntington, *The Clash of Civilizations and the Remaking of the World Order* (New York: Simon & Schuster, 1996), 51.

33. Ibid., 43–44, 51; Janice Elich Monroe, "Developing Cultural Awareness Through Play," *Journal of Physical Education, Recreation and Dance* (Oct. 1995), 24–27.

34. Douglas Kellner, "Sports, Media Culture, and Race—Some Reflections on Michael Jordan," *Sociology of Sport Journal,* 13 (1996), 458–467.

Bibliography

Allen, Philip S. "Football in Ninety-five." *Monthly Maroon,* 2:1 (November 1903), 1–8.

Alpars, Benjamin L. "This Is the Army: Imagining a Democratic Military in World War II." *Journal of American History,* 85:1 (June 1998):129–163.

"American Football Around the Globe." *American Football Quarterly,* 2:30 (July-September 1996):89.

Armstrong, Tim, ed. *American Bodies: Cultural Histories of the Physique.* New York: New York University Press, 1996.

Ashe, Arthur R., Jr. *A Hard Road to Glory: Football.* New York: Amistad, 1993.

A Yale Player. "The Development of Football." *Outing* (November 1889),144–150.

Bailey, C. Ian, and George H. Sage. "Values Communicated by a Sports Event: The Case of the Super Bowl." *Journal of Sport Behavior,* 11:3 (September 1988):126–143.

Barber, Phil, and Ray Didinger. *Football America: Celebrating Our National Passion.* Atlanta: Turner Pub., 1996.

Battle, Kemp O. *History of the University of North Carolina.* Spartanburg, SC: Reprint Co., 1974.

Beale, Morris A. *The History of Football at Harvard, 1874–1948.* Washington, DC: Columbia Pub. Co., 1948.

Becker, Carl M. "The 'Tom Thumb' Game: Bears vs. Spartans, 1932." *Journal of Sport History,* 22:3 (Fall 1995):216–227.

Bergin, Thomas H. *The Game: The Harvard-Yale Football Rivalry, 1875–1983.* New Haven: Yale University Press, 1984.

Berryman, Jack W. "Early Black Leadership in Collegiate Football." *Historical Journal of Massachusetts,* 9 (June 1981):17–28, 85fn.51.

Betts, John Richard. *American's Sporting Heritage, 1850–1950.* Reading, MA:Addison-Wesley Pub. Co., 1974.

Bissell, Mary Taylor. "Athletics of City Girls." *Popular Science Monthly* (December 1894),145–153.

Bissinger, H. G. *Friday Night Lights: A Town, A Team, and a Dream.* New York: Harper Collins, 1991.

Blanchard, John A., ed. *The H Book of Harvard Athletics, 1852–1922.* Harvard Varsity Club, 1923.

Bolton, Clyde. *War Eagle: A Story of Auburn Football.* Huntsville, AL: Strode Publishers, 1973.

Boyer, Paul. *Urban Masses and Moral Order in America, 1820–1920.* Cambridge, MA: Harvard University Press, 1978.

Brands, H. W. *Bound to Empire: The United States and the Philip-*

pines. New York: Oxford University Press, 1992.

_____. *The Reckless Decade: America in the 1890s*. New York: St. Martin's Press, 1995.

Braunwart, Bob, and Bob Carroll. *The Alphabet Wars: The Birth of Professional Football, 1890–1892*. Professional Football Researchers Assn., 1981.

Britz, Kevin. "Of Football and Frontiers." *Journal of Sport History*, 20:2 (Summer 1993).

Bruce, H. Addington. "The Psychology of Football." *Outlook*, 96 (November 5, 1910), 541–545.

Bryson, Lois. "Sport and the Maintenance of Masculine Hegemony." *Women's Studies International Forum*, 10:4 (1987):349–360.

Buder, Stanley. *Pullman: An Experiment in Industrial Order and Community Planning, 1880–1930*. New York: Oxford University Press, 1968.

Buhle, Mary Jo. *Women and American Socialism, 1807–1920*. Urbana: University of Illinois Press, 1981.

Butler, Brian S. " 'Gain Ground and Glory': Metropolitan Athletic Clubs and the Promoting of American Football—The Case of the Louisville Athletic Club." *International Journal of the History of Sport*, 9:3 (December 1992): 378–396.

Butler, Mike. "Confederate Flags, Class Conflict, a Golden Egg, and Castrated Bulls: A Historical Examination of the Ole Miss-Mississippi State Football Rivalry." *Journal of Mississippi History*, 59 (Summer 1997):123–139.

Cahn, Susan. *Coming on Strong: Gender and Sexuality in Twentieth-Century Women's Sport*. New York: Free Press, 1994.

Calhoun, Donald W. *Sport, Culture, and Personality*. Champaign: Human Kinetics, 1987.

Camp, Walter. "The American Game of Football." *Harper's Weekly* (November 10, 1888), 858–859.

_____. *The Book of Football*. New York: The Century Co., 1910.

_____. "The Current Criticism of Football." *Century*, 47 (February 1894), 633–634.

_____. "Football." *Outing* (February 1891), 102–104.

_____. "Football—Detail of a Defensive Play." *Outing* (December 1892), 210.

_____. *Football Facts and Figures: A Symposium of Expert Opinions on the Game's Place in American Athletics*. New York: Harper and Bros., 1894.

_____. "Football in the Hands of Players." *Spalding's Official Foot Ball Guide*, 1895.

_____. "Football of 1893: Its Lessons and Results." *Harper's Weekly* (February 3, 1894), 117–118.

_____. "Football Reform in the West." *The Outlook* (February 3, 1906), 248–249.

_____. "Football Studies for Captain and Coach." *Outing* (November 1892), 104–107.

_____. "The Game and Laws of American Football." *Outing* (October 1887), 68.

_____. "Interference in Football." *Harper's Weekly* (November 19, 1892), 11–15.

_____. "Personality in Foot-Ball: A Consideration of the Contributions to the Progress of the Game by Certain Players and Coaches." *Century*, 57 (January 1910), 442–457.

_____. "A Plea for the Wedge in Football." *Harper's Weekly* (January 21, 1893),67.

_____. "Team Play in Foot-Ball." *Harper's Weekly* (October 31, 1891).

_____. "Winning a Football Goal." *The Outlook* (May 30, 1896), 980.

Camp, Walter, ed. *Spalding's Official Football Guide for 1906*. New York: American Sports Pub. Co., 1906.

Carnes, Mark C., and Clyde Griffen, eds. *Meanings For Manhood: Constructions of Masculinity in Victorian America*. Chicago: University of Chicago Press, 1990.

Carroll, Bob, ed., Coffin Corner (1985–1991).

_____. *The Ohio League: 1910–1919*. N. Huntingdon, PA: Pro Football Researchers Assn., 1997.

Carroll, John M. *Fritz Pollard: Pioneer in Racial Advancement*. Urbana: University of Illinois Press, 1992.

Carson, Mina. *Settlement Folk: Social Thought and the American Settlement Movement, 1885–1930*. Chicago: University of Chicago Press, 1990.

Cavallo, Dominick. *Muscles and Morals: Organized Playgrounds and Urban Reform, 1880–1920*. Philadelphia: University of Pennsylvania Press, 1981.

Chaffin, Nora Campbell. *Trinity College, 1839-1892: The Beginnings of Duke University*. Durham, NC: Duke University Press, 1950.

Chalk, Ocania. *Pioneers of Black Sport*. New York: Dodd, Mead & Co., 1975.

Chapman, David L. *Sandow the Magnificent: Eugen Sandow and the Beginnings of Bodybuilding*. Urbana: University of Illinois Press, 1994.

Chelland, Patrick. *One for the Gipper: George Gipp, Knute Rockne and Notre Dame*. Chicago: Henry Regnery Co., 1973.

Clark, Patrick. *Sports Firsts*. New York: Facts on File, 1981.

Coben, Stanley. *Rebellion Against Victorianism: The Impetus for Cultural Change in 1920s America*. New York: Oxford University Press, 1990.

Collier, Price. "Sport's Place in the Nation's Well-Being." *Outing* (July 1898), 382–388.

Colton, Rev. A. E. "What Football Does." *Independent*, 57 (September 15, 1904).

Connerton, Paul. *How Societies Remember*. Cambridge: Cambridge University Press, 1991.

Cooper, Helen A. *Thomas Eakins: The Rowing Pictures*. New Haven: Yale University Press, 1996.

Corbin, John. "The Modern Chivalry." *Atlantic Monthly*, 89 (May 1902), 601–611.

Craig, John. "Football on the Pacific Slope." *Outing* (September 1893), 448–456.

Crawford, Albert B., ed. *Football Y Men, 1872-1919*. New Haven: Yale University Press, 1962.

Crowl, R. S. "A Justification for the Grudge of the West Against Walter Camp." *The Wisconsin Athletic Bulletin* (December 14, 1912), 23–24.

Crunden, Robert M. *Ministers of Reform: The Progressive Achievement in American Civilization, 1889–1920*. New York: Basic Books, 1982.

Cutler, John Levi. *Gilbert Patten and His Frank Merriwell Saga: A Study in Sub-Literary Fiction, 1896–1913*. Orono, ME: University Press, 1934.

Danzig, Allison. *The History of American Football*. Englewood Cliffs, NJ: Prentice-Hall, 1956.

Davis, Allen F. *American Heroine: The Life and Legend of Jane Addams*. New York: Oxford University Press, 1973.

_____. *Spearheads for Reform: The Social Settlements and the Progressive Movement, 1890–1914*.

New York: Oxford University Press, 1967.

Davis, Parke H. *Football: The American Intercollegiate Game.* New York: Scribner's, 1911.

Davis, Richard Harding. "The Thanksgiving Day Game." *Harper's Weekly* (December 9, 1893), 1170.

DiNunzia, Mario R., ed. *Theodore Roosevelt: An American Mind.* New York: St. Martin Press, 1994.

Dizikes, John. *Sportsmen and Gamesmen.* Boston: Houghton Mifflin, 1981.

Doezema, Marianne. *George Bellows and Urban America.* New Haven: Yale University Press, 1992.

Douglas, Ann. *The Feminization of American Culture.* New York: Anchor Books, 1977.

Doyle, Andrew. "Bear Bryant: Symbol of an Embattled South." *Colby Quarterly,* 32:1 (March 1996):72–86.

———. "'Causes Won, Not Lost': College Football and the Modernization of the American South." *International Journal of the History of Sport,* 11:2 (August 1994):231–251.

Duberman, Martin Bauml. *Paul Robeson.* New York: Alfred A. Knopf, 1988.

Duis, Perry. *The Saloon: Public Drinking in Chicago and Boston, 1880–1920.* Urbana: University of Illinois Press, 1983.

Eckersall, Walter. "My Twenty-five Years in Football." *Liberty* (October 23, 1926), 59–62.

Ernst, Robert. *Weakness is a Crime: The Life of Bernarr MacFadden.* Syracuse, NY: Syracuse University Press, 1991.

Eubanks, Lon. *The Fighting Illini: A Story of Illinois Football.* Huntsville, AL: Strode Pub., 1976.

Evans, Arthur L. *Fifty Years of Football at Syracuse University, 1889–1930.* Syracuse University: Football History Committee, 1939.

"Football As Our Greatest Popular Spectacle." *Literary Digest,* 75 (December 2, 1922), 52–57.

Foster, Gaines M. *Ghosts of the Confederacy: Defeat, The Lost Cause, and The Emergence of the New South.* New York: Oxford University Press, 1987.

Fountain, Charles. *Sportswriter: The Life and Times of Grantland Rice.* New York: Oxford University Press, 1993.

Fox, Stephen. *Big Leagues: Professional Baseball, Football, and Basketball in National Memory.* New York: William Morrow & Co., 1994.

Fry, Richard. *The Crimson and the Grey.* Pullman, WA: Washington State University, 1989.

Garrison, Lloyd M. *Echoes of the Harvard-Yale Football Game of 1890.* Cambridge, MA: Charles H. Thurston, 1890.

Gems, Gerald R. "The Construction, Negotiation, and Transformation of Racial Identity in American Football." *American Indian Culture and Research Journal,* 22:2 (July 1998):131–150.

———. "The Neighborhood Athletic Club: An Ethnographic Study of a Working Class Athletic Fraternity in Chicago, 1917–1984." *Colby Quarterly,* 32:1 (March 1996):36–44.

———. "The Prep Bowl: Football and Religious Acculturation in Chicago." *Journal of Sport History* (Fall 1996):74–92.

———. *Windy City Wars: Labor, Leisure, and Sport in the Making of*

Chicago. Lanham, MD: Scarecrow Press, 1997.

Gems, Gerald R., ed. *Sports in North America: A Documentary History.* Vol. 5: *Sports Organized, 1880–1900.* Gulf Breeze, FL: Academic International Press, 1996.

Givens, Wendell. *Ninety-Nine Iron: The Season Sewanee Won 5 Games in 6 Days.* Birmingham, AL: Seacoast Pub., 1992.

Glassberg, David. *American Historical Pageantry: The Uses of Tradition in the Early Twentieth Century.* Chapel Hill: University of North Carolina Press, 1990.

Goodman, Cary. *Choosing Sides: Playgrounds and Street Life on the Lower East Side.* New York: Schocken Books, 1979.

Gordon, Lynn D. *Gender and Higher Education in the Progressive Era.* New Haven: Yale University Press, 1990.

Gorn, Elliott, and Warren Goldstein. *A Brief History of American Sports.* New York: Hill and Wang, 1993.

Grant, Chet. *Before Rockne at Notre Dame.* Notre Dame, IN: Dujarie Press, 1968.

Grantham, Dewey W. *The South in Modern America: A Region at Odds.* New York: Harper Collins, 1994.

Graves, John T. *The Fighting South.* Birmingham: University of Alabama Press, 1985.

The Greatest of Expositions. St. Louis: Louisiana Purchase Exposition, 1904.

Guttmann, Allen. *From Ritual to Record: The Nature of Modern Sports.* New York: Columbia University Press, 1978.

Halas, George, with Gwen Morgan and Arthur Veysey. *Halas by Halas.* New York: McGraw-Hill Co., 1979.

Hammel, George Milton. "Brawl and Brawn or Brain?" *The Union Signal* (December 19, 1895),3.

Hanson, Mary Ellen. *Go! Fight! Win! Cheerleading in American Culture.* Bowling Green, OH: Bowling Green University Popular Press, 1995.

Hardy, Stephen H. "Entrepreneurs, Organizations and the Sports Marketplace." In S. W. Pope, ed. *The New American Sport History.* Urbana: University of Illinois Press, 1997, 341–365.

_____. *How Boston Played: Sport, Recreation and Community, 1865–1915.* Boston: Northeastern University Press, 1982.

Harmond, Richard. "Progress and Flight: An Interpretation of the American Cycle Craze of the 1890s." *Journal of Social History,* 5 (Winter 1971):235–257.

Harris, Janet C. *Athletics and the American Hero Dilemma.* Champaign: Human Kinetics, 1994.

Harvard College Report Upon Athletics. Cambridge, MA: John Wilson & Son, 1888.

Heisman, John. "Signals." *Collier's* (October 6, 1928), 32.

Helen, Sister M. "The Power Behind the Team." *Notre Dame Alumnus* (March 1936), 156, 160.

Hennesey, James. *American Catholics: A History of the Roman Catholic Community in the United States.* New York: Oxford University Press, 1981.

Hibner, John C. *The Rose Bowl, 1902–1929.* Jefferson, NC: McFarland & Co., 1993.

Hicks, William E. "The Military Worthlessness of Football." *Independent,* 67 (November 25, 1909), 1201–1204.

Higgs, Robert J. *God in the Stadium: Sports and Religion in America.* Lexington: University Press of Kentucky, 1995.

Higham, John. "The Reorientation of American Culture in the 1890s." In John Higham, ed. *Writing American History: Essays on Modern Scholarship.* Bloomington: Indiana University Press, 1972, 73–102.

Hoberman, John. *Darwin's Athletes: How Sport Has Damaged Black America and Preserved the Myth of Race.* Boston: Houghton Mifflin, 1997.

Hobsbawm, Eric, and Terence Ranger, eds. *The Invention of Tradition.* Cambridge: Cambridge University Press, 1983.

Hodge, Lt. Richard Morse. "American College Football." *Outing,* 40:6 (March 1888), 483–498.

Hoxie, Frederick E. *A Final Promise: The Campaign to Assimilate the Indians, 1880–1920.* New York: Cambridge University Press, 1989.

Hult, Joan S. "The Story of Women's Athletics: Manipulating a Dream, 1890–1985." In D. Margaret Costa and Sharon R. Guthrie, eds. *Women and Sport,* 84.

Hult, Joan S., and Marianna Trekell, eds. *A Century of Women's Basketball: From Frailty to Final Four.* Reston, VA: American Alliance for Health, Physical Education, Recreation and Dance, 1991.

Hurd, Michael. *Black College Football: 1892-1922: One Hundred Years of History, Education, and Pride.* Virginia Beach, VA: Donning Co., 1993.

Ingham, Alan G., and Stephen Hardy. "Introduction: Sport Studies Through the Lens of Raymond Williams." In Alan G. Ingham and John Loy, eds. *Sport in Social Development.* Champaign, IL: Human Kinetics, 1993, 1–19.

Isenberg, Michael R. *John L. Sullivan and His America.* Urbana: University of Illinois Press, 1988.

Jable, J. Thomas. "The Birth of Professional Football: Pittsburgh Athletic Clubs Ring in Professionals in 1892." *The Western Pennsylvania Historical Magazine,* 62:2 (April 1979), 131–147.

_____. "The Public Schools Athletic League of New York City: Organized Athletics for City School Children, 1903–1914." In Steven A. Riess, ed. *The American Sporting Experience: An Historical Anthology.* West Point, NY: Leisure Press, 1984, 219–238.

Jaher, Frederic Cople. *The Urban Establishment: Upper Strata in Boston, New York, Charleston, Chicago, and Los Angeles.* Urbana: University of Illinois Press, 1982.

Jenkins, Dan. *Saturday's America.* Boston: Little, Brown & Co., 1970.

Johnson, Alexander. "The American Game of Football." *Century,* 12 (1887), 898.

Jordan, Edward S. "Buying Football Victories." *Collier's* (November 11, 1905), 19–20, 23.

Kammen, Michael. *Mystic Chords of Memory: The Transformation of Tradition in American Culture.* New York: Alfred A. Knopf, 1991.

Kearney, Pat. *Butte's Big Game: Butte Central vs. Butte High.* Butte, MT: Artcraft, 1989.

Keeth, Kent. "Looking Back at Baylor." *The Baylor Line* (October 1975).

Kellner, Douglas. "Sports, Media Culture, and Race—Some Reflections on Michael Jordan." *Sociology of Sport Journal,* 13 (1996):458–467.

Kennedy, Susan Estabrook. *If All We Did Was to Weep at Home: A History of White Working Class Women in America*. Bloomington: Indiana University Press, 1979.

Kimmel, Michael S. "Men's Response to Feminism at the Turn of the Century." *Gender and Society*, 1:3 (September 1987):261–283.

Kingsdale, Jon M. " 'The Poor Man's Club': Social Functions of the Urban Working-Class Saloon." *American Quarterly*, 25 (October 1973):472–489.

Kirsch, George B. *Sports in North America: A Documentary History*. Vol. 3: *The Rise of Modern Sports, 1840–1860*. Gulf Breeze, FL: Academic International Press, 1992.

Klosinski, Emil. "Inflation of 1920: A Tale of Two Cities." *Coffin Corner,* 14:3 (July 1992),15–19.

_____. *Pro Football in the Days of Rockne*. New York: Carlton Press, 1970.

Krzywonos, D. M., ed. *The Poles of Chicago, 1837–1937*. Chicago: Polish Pageant, Inc., 1937.

Lears, T. J. Jackson. *No Place of Grace: Antimodernism and the Transformation of American Culture, 1880–1920*. New York: Pantheon Books, 1981.

Lee, Mabel. *Memories of a Bloomer Girl*. Washington, DC: American Alliance for Health, Physical Education, and Recreation, 1977.

Lester, Robin. "Michigan-Chicago, 1905: The First Greatest Game of the Century." *Journal of Sport History*, 18:2 (Summer 1991):267–273.

_____. *Stagg's University: The Rise, Decline, and Fall of Big-Time Football at Chicago*. Urbana: University of Illinois Press, 1995.

Levine, Lawrence W. *Highbrow/Lowbrow: The Emergence of Cultural Hierarchy in America*. Cambridge, MA: Harvard University Press, 1988.

Levine, Peter. *Ellis Island to Ebbets Field: Sport and the American Jewish Experience*. New York: Oxford University Press, 1992.

Longoria, Mario. *Athletes Remembered: Mexicano/Latino Professional Football Players, 1929–1970*. Tempe, AZ: Bilingual Press, 1970.

Maltby, Marc S. *The Origins and Early Development of Professional Football*. New York: Garland Pub., 1997.

Mangione, Jerre, and Ben Morreale. *La Storia: Five Centuries of the Italian-American Experience*. New York: Harper Collins, 1992.

Mann, Arthur. *The One and the Many: Reflections on the American Identity*. Chicago: University of Chicago Press, 1979.

Marcello, Ronald E. "The Integration of Intercollegiate Athletics in Texas: North Texas State College as a Test Case, 1956."*Journal of Sport History*, 14:3 (Winter 1987):286–316.

Marks, Patricia. *Bicycles, Bangs, and Bloomers: The New Woman in the Popular Press*. Lexington: University Press of Kentucky, 1990.

Martin, Charles H. "Racial Change and 'Big-Time' College Football in Georgia: The Age of Segregation, 1892–1957." *Georgia Historical Quarterly*, 80:30 (Fall 1996):532–562.

Maysel, Lou. *Here Come the Texas Longhorns, 1893–1970*. Fort Worth: Stadium Pub. Co., 1970.

McCallum, John D. *Big Eight Football*. New York: Charles Scribner's Sons, 1979.

McCarty, Bernie. *All America: The Complete Roster of Football's Heroes*. Privately published, 1991.

McClellan, Keith. *The Sunday Game: At the Dawn of Professional Football.* Akron, OH: University of Akron Press, 1998.

McGreevy, John T. "Thinking On One's Own: Catholicism in the American Intellectual Imagination, 1928–1960." *Journal of American History,* 84:1 (June 1997):97.

Mennell, James. "The Service Football Program of World War I: Its Impact on the Popularity of the Game." *Journal of Sport History,* 16:3 (Winter 1989):248–260.

Messenger, Christian K. *Sport and the Spirit of Play in American Fiction: Hawthorne to Faulkner.* New York: Columbia University Press, 1981.

Messner, Michael A. *Power At Play: Sport and the Problem of Masculinity.* Boston: Beacon Press, 1992.

_____. "When Bodies Are Weapons: Masculinity and Violence in Sport." *International Review of the Sociology of Sport,* 25:3 (1990):203–218.

Miles, Lovick Pierce. "Football in the South." *Outing* (December 1894), 257–264.

Miller, Patrick B. "The Manly, the Moral, and the Proficient: College Sport in the New South." *Journal of Sport History,* 24:3 (Fall 1997):285–316.

Millis, Walter. *The Martial Spirit.* Chicago: Elephant Paperbacks, 1989.

Miracle, Andrew W., Jr., and G. Roger Rees. *Lessons of the Locker Room: The Myth of School Sports.* Amherst, NY: Prometheus Books, 1994.

Mirel, Jeffrey. "From State Control to Institutional Control of High School Athletics: Three Michigan Cities, 1883–1905." *Journal of Social History,* 6 (1982):82–99,136.

Monroe, Janice Elich. "Developing Cultural Awareness Through Play." *Journal of Physical Education, Recreation and Dance* (October 1995):24–27.

Moore, John Hammond. "Football's Ugly Decades, 1893–1913." *Smithsonian Journal of History,* 11 (Fall 1967):49–68.

Mouffe, Chantal. "Hegemony and New Political Subjects: Toward a New Concept of Democracy." In Cary Nelson and Lawrence Grossberg, eds. *Marxism and the Interpretation of Culture.* Urbana: University of Illinois Press, 1988, 89–104.

"Mr. Hooley on Debrutalized Football." *University of Chicago Magazine,* 3 (December 1910), 108–111.

Mrozek, Donald J. "The Habit of Victory: The American Military and the Cult of Manliness." In J. A. Mangan and James Walvin, eds. *Manliness and Morality: Middle-class Masculinity in Britain and America, 1800–1940.* New York: St. Martin's Press, 1987), 220–239.

_____. *Sport and American Mentality, 1880–1910.* Knoxville: University of Tennessee Press, 1983.

Nasaw, David. *Going Out: The Rise and Fall of Public Amusements.* New York: Basic Books, 1993.

Naughton, Jim. "Centre College Remembers the Day when It Was King of the Gridiron." *Chronicle of Higher Education* (October 4, 1996), A46.

Nauright, John. "Writing and Reading American Football: Culture, Identities and Sport Studies." *Sporting Traditions,* 13:1 (November 1996), 109–127.

Nelson, David M. *Anatomy of a Game: Football, The Rules, and the Men Who Made the Game.* Newark: University of Delaware Press, 1994.

Newcomb, Jack. *The Best of the Athletic Boys: The White Man's Impact on Jim Thorpe.* Garden City, NY: Doubleday, 1975.

Oriard, Michael. *Reading Football: How the Popular Press Created an American Spectacle.* Chapel Hill: University of North Carolina Press, 1993.

_____. *Sporting with the Gods: The Rhetoric of Play and Games in American Culture.* New York: Cambridge University Press, 1991.

Overman, Steven J. *The Influence of the Protestant Ethic on Sport and Recreation.* Brookfield, VT: Avebury, 1997.

Park, Roberta J. "Football to Rugby and Back." *Journal of Sport History,* 11 (1984):15–40.

_____. "Physiologists, Physicians, and Physical Educators: Nineteenth Century Biology and Exercise, Hygienic and Educative." *Journal of Sport History,* 14 (Spring 1987):28–60.

_____. "Physiology and Anatomy are Destiny!?: Brains, Bodies and Exercise in Nineteenth Century American Thought." *Journal of Sport History* 18:1 (Spring 1991):31–63.

Parratt, Catriona M. "From the History of Women in Sport to Women's Sport History: A Research Agenda." In D. Margaret Costa and Sharon R. Guthrie, eds. *Women in Sport: Inter-Disciplinary Perspectives.* Champaign, IL: Human Kinetics, 1994.

Patrick, G. L. W. "The Psychology of Football." *American Journal of Psychology,* 14 (July-October, 1903):104–117.

Patterson, Elmore C. "Football as the West Played It." *Outing* (January 22, 1922), 162–164.

Paxon, Frederick L. "The Rise of Sport." *Mississippi Valley Historical Review,* 4 (1917):143–168.

Perrin, Tom. *Football: A College History.* Jefferson, NC: McFarland & Co., 1987.

Peterson, Robert W. *Pigskin: The Early Years of Pro Football.* New York: Oxford University Press, 1997.

Pollock, Ed. "Pennsylvania Football History." *Franklin Field Illustrated,* 1951.

Pope, Steven W. "An Army of Athletes: Playing Fields, Battlefields, and the American Military Sporting Experience, 1890–1920." *Journal of Military History,* 59 (July 1995):435–456.

_____. "God, Games, and National Glory: Thanksgiving and the Ritual of Sport in American Culture, 1876–1926," *International Journal of the History of Sport,* 10 (August 1993):242–249.

_____. *Patriotic Games: Sporting Tradition in the American Imagination, 1876–1926.* New York: Oxford University Press, 1997.

Porter, David L., ed. *Biographical Dictionary of American Sports: 1989-1992 Supplement for Baseball, Football, Basketball and Other Sports.* Westport, CT: Greenwood Press, 1992.

Presbrey, Frank, and James H. Moffatt, eds. *Athletics at Princeton: A History.* New York: Frank Presbrey Co., 1901.

Pruter, Robert. "The Birth of High School Football in Illinois." *http/www.HSA.org*

_____. "The Greatest High School Football Rivalry in Illinois." *http/www.HSA.org*

Rader, Benjamin G. *American Sports: From the Age of Folk Games to the Age of Spectators.* Englewood Cliffs, NJ: Prentice-Hall, 1983.

Richards, Eugene L., Jr. "Football in America." *Outing* (April 1885), 62–66.

Riesman, David, and Reuel Denney. "Football in America: A Study in Cultural Diffusion." *American Quarterly,* 3 (1951):309–325.

Riess, Steven A. *City Games: The Evolution of American Society and the Rise of Sports.* Urbana: University of Illinois Press, 1989.

_____. "A Social Profile of the Professional Football Player, 1920–1982." In Paul A. Staudohar and James A. Mangan, eds. *The Business of Professional Sports.* Urbana: University of Illinois Press, 1991, 222–246.

_____. "Sport and the American Jew: A Second Look." *American Jewish History,* 83:1 (March 1995):6.

_____. "Sport and the Redefinition of American Middle-Class Masculinity." *International Journal of the History of Sport,* 8:1 (1991):5–27.

Reiss, Steven A., ed. *Major Problems in American Sport History.* Boston: Houghton Mifflin, 1997.

Roberts, Howard. *The Big Nine: The Story of Football in the Western Conference.* New York: G. P. Putnam's Sons, 1948.

Rockne, Bernie Skiles, ed. *The Autobiography of Knute K. Rockne.* Indianapolis, IN: Bobbs-Merrill, 1930.

"Rockne's Wonder Teams Built on Notre Dame's Virility." *The Notre Dame Scholastic* (November 21, 1924), 222, 224.

Roosevelt, Theodore. "The Value of Athletic Training." *Harper's Weekly* (December 23, 1893), 1236.

Rotundo, E. Anthony. *American Manhood: Transformations in Masculinity from the Revolution to the Modern Era.* New York: Basic Books, 1993.

Ruck, Rob. *Sandlot Seasons: Sport in Black Pittsburgh.* Urbana: University of Illinois Press, 1987.

Rust, Edna, and Art Rust, Jr. *Art Rust's Illustrated History of the Black Athlete.* Garden City,NY: Doubleday & Co., 1985.

Sabo, Don. "Sport Patriarchy, and Male Identity: New Questions About Men and Sport." *Arena Review,* 9:3 (1985):1–15.

Sack, Alan. "Yale 29-Harvard 4: The Professionalization of College Football." *Quest,* 19 (January 1973), 24–34.

Sack, Allen L., and Robert Thiel. "College Football and Social Mobility: A Case Study of Notre Dame Football Players." *Sociology of Education,* 52 (January 1979):60–66.

Schmidt, Ray, ed. *College Football Historical Society* (1987–1996).

Schoor, Gene. *100 Years of Army-Navy Football.* New York: Henry Holt, 1989.

Sears, Hal D. "The Moral Threat of Intercollegiate Sports: An 1893 Poll of Ten College Presidents, and the End of 'the Champion Football Team of the Great West'." *Journal of Sport History,* 19:3 (Winter 1992):211–226.

Sears, Joseph. "Foot-Ball: Sport and Training." *North American Review,* 53 (1891,750–753.

Sharp, Grace Hastings. "Mothers and the Game." *Outlook* (November 12, 1910), 589–591.

Sheard, K. G. "The Webb Ellis Myth." In David Levinson and Karen Christensen, eds. *Encyclopedia of World Sport: From Ancient Times* to the Present. Vol. 2. Santa Barbara, CA: ABC-Clio, 1996, 842.

Smith, Michael D. "A Topology of Sports Violence." In Stanley Eitzen, ed. Sport in Contemporary Society. New York: St. Martin's Press, 1993, 87–88.

Smith, Myron J., ed. The College Football Bibliography. Westport, CT: Greenwood Press, 1994.

Smith, Ronald A. "Harvard and Columbia and a Reconsideration of the 1905-06 Football Crisis." Journal of Sport History, 8 (Winter 1981):5–19.

_____. "The Historic Amateur-Professional Dilemma in American College Sport." British Journal of Sport History, 2:3 (December 1985):221–231.

_____. "Prelude to the NCAA: Early Failures of Faculty Intercollegiate Athletic Contol." In David K. Wiggins, ed. Sport in America: From Wicked Amusement to National Obsession. Champaign, IL: Human Kinetics, 1995:151–162.

_____. Sports and Freedom: The Rise of Big-Time College Athletics. New York: Oxford University Press, 1988.

Smith, Ronald A., ed. Big-Time Football at Harvard, 1905: The Diary of Coach Bill Reid. Urbana: University of Illinois Press, 1994.

Somers, Dale. The Rise of Sport in New Orleans, 1850-1900. Baton Rouge: Louisiana State University Press, 1972.

Sperber, Murray. Shake Down the Thunder: The Creation of Notre Dame Football. New York: Henry Holt, 1993.

Stanley, Gregory Kent. Before Big Blue: Sports at the University of Kentucky, 1880–1940. Lexington: University of Kentucky Press, 1996.

Steckbeck, John S. Fabulous Redmen: The Carlisle Indians and Their Famous Football Teams. Harrisburg, PA: J. Horace McFarland Co., 1951.

Steinberg, Stephen. The Ethnic Myth: Race, Ethnicity, and Class in America. Boston: Beacon Press, 1989.

Studwell, William E. "American College Fight Songs: History and Historiography." Journal of American History, 19 (Fall 1995):125–130.

Sugar, Bert Randolph. The SEC: A Pictorial History of Southeastern Conference Football. Indianapolis: Bobbs-Merrill Co., 1979.

Sumner, Jim L. "John Franklin Cowell, Methodism, and the Football Controversy at Trinity College, 1887-1894." Journal of Sport History, 17 (Spring 1990):5–20.

Talbot, Marion. The Education of Women. Chicago: University of Chicago Press, 1910.

_____. More Than Lore: Reminiscences of Marion Talbot. Chicago: University of Chicago Press, 1936.

Townsend, Kim. Manhood at Harvard: William James and Others. New York: W.W. Norton, 1996.

Trachtenberg, Alan. The Incorporation of America: Culture and Society in the Gilded Age. New York: Hill and Wang, 1982.

Umphlett, Wiley Lee. Creating the Big Game: John W. Heisman and the Invention of American Football. Westport, CT: Greenwood Press, 1992.

Vertinsky, Patricia. The Eternally Wounded Woman: Women, Exercise and Doctors in the Late Nineteenth Century. Manchester, England: Manchester University Press, 1990.

Wakefield, Wanda Ellen. *Playing to Win: Sports and the American Military, 1898–1945.* Albany: State University of New York Press, 1997.

Walker, Francis A. "College Athletics." *Harvard Graduates Magazine* 2:5 (September 1893), 1–18.

Warner, Glenn S. "Heap Big Run—Most—Fast." *Collier's* (October 24, 1931).

_____. "The Indian Massacres." *Collier's* (October 17, 1931), 8, 63.

Watterson, John S. "The Death of Archer Christian: College Presidents and the Reform of College Football." *Journal of Sport History,* 22:2 (Summer 1993):149–167.

_____. "The Football Crisis of 1909–1910: The Response of the Eastern 'Big Three'." *Journal of Sport History,* 8 (Spring 1981):33–49.

Wenner, Lawrence A. "The Super Bowl Pregame Show: Cultural Fantasies and Political Subtext." In Lawrence A. Wenner, ed. *Media, Sports and Society.* Newbury Park, CA: Sage Pub., 1989, 157–179.

Westby, David, and Allen Sack. "The Commercialization and Functional Rationalization of College Football." *Journal of Higher Education,* 47 (November/December 1976):625–647.

Weyand, Alexander M. *The Saga of American Football.* New York: Macmillan, 1955.

Whitney, Caspar. "The Athletic Development at West Point and Annapolis." *Harper's Weekly,* 36 (May 21, 1892).

_____. "Is Football Worthwhile?" *Collier's* (December 18, 1909), 13, 24–25.

Wiebe, Robert H. *The Search for Order, 1877–1920.* New York: Hill and Wang, 1967.

Williams, Henry L. "Middle Western Football." *Outing,* 39 (November 1901), 206–208.

Wilson, Charles Reagan. *Baptized in Blood: The Religion of the Lost Cause, 1865–1920.* Athens: University of Georgia Press, 1983.

Wilson, Louis R. *The University of North Carolina, 1900–1930.* Chapel Hill: University of North Carolina Press, 1957.

Wyatt-Brown, Bertram. *Honor and Violence in the Old South.* New York: Oxford University Press, 1986.

"Yes, Suh, The Old South is Lookin' Up." *Literary Digest,* 57 (November 19, 1930).

Yost, Fielding H. "Western Football Against Eastern." *Collier's* (January 10, 1914), 9, 26.

Young, Linda. *Hail to the Orange and Blue: 100 Years of Illinois Football Tradition.* Champaign, IL: Sagamore Pub., 1990.

Zelinsky, Wilbur. *Nation Into State: The Shifting Symbolic Foundations of American Nationalism.* Chapel Hill: University of North Carolina Press, 1988.

Ziff, Larzer. *The American 1890's: Life and Times of a Lost Generation.* New York: Viking Press, 1973.

Index

About the Author

Gerald R. Gems was born and raised in Chicago. He earned his degree from Northeastern Illinois University (B.A., 1977) and taught at the universities of Arizona (M.S., 1980) and Maryland (Ph.D., 1989). He is co-editor of book reviews for the *Journal of Sport History* and edited volume five of *Sports in North America: A Documentary History*. He is Professor of Health and Physical Education at North Central College (Naperville, IL) and currently serves as chairperson of that department. Dr. Gems is the author of *Windy City Wars* (No. 8 in the American Sports History Series, Scarecrow Press). He has two children and now lives in Oswego, Illinois.